T0301669

NONLINEAR MODELS, LABOUR MARKETS AND EXCHANGE

Nonlinear Models, Labour Markets and Exchange

Introductory Surveys in Economics, Volume II

John Creedy

New Zealand Treasury

Edward Elgar

Cheltenham, UK • Northampton, MA, USA

Published by
Edward Elgar Publishing Limited
Glensanda House
Montpellier Parade
Cheltenham
Glos GL50 1UA
UK

Edward Elgar Publishing, Inc.
136 West Street
Suite 202
Northampton
Massachusetts 01060
USA

A catalogue record for this book
is available from the British Library

ISBN 1 84376 019 3

Printed on FSC approved paper
Printed and bound in Great Britain by Marston Book Services Ltd, Oxfordshire

Contents

Acknowledgements

I am grateful to the publishers of the journals in which these articles first appeared for permission to include them in the present volume.

PART I

NONLINEAR MODELS

[1]

The strange attraction of chaos in economics
John Creedy and Vance L. Martin

2.1 Introduction

Mathematical economists have traditionally shown a preference for the use of linear models, or at least the linearization of models in the region of a solution. The use of models which have only one solution or equilibrium position, which can be solved explicitly rather than by using iterative numerical procedures, and which have reasonably simple comparative static properties is perhaps understandable in the early stages of development. Models can be analysed using a limited range of techniques and fairly clear-cut results can often be obtained. The early non-linear models containing multiple solutions, such as those produced by economists as important as Marshall and Walras, were ignored for many years.

In the analyses of dynamic processes, the emphasis has been on the use of simple linear differential equations which produce regular types of cycle. It seemed that a clear distinction could be drawn between deterministic systems which produce regular, and therefore predictable, behaviour and series which reflect stochastic or random behaviour which cannot be predicted. Apparently chaotic behaviour was seen simply as stochastic. In estimating linear models, inconvenient observations were labelled as 'outliers' and then ignored.

More recent years have, however, seen a huge growth in the analysis of non-linear systems. This work, started by researchers in mathematics and the natural sciences, has led to the development of new and exciting concepts and methods of analysis. The application of these methods in economics is still in its early stages, but has already produced results of much interest. There appear to be many contexts in which non-linear methods may prove to be very useful. These include stock market and foreign exchange market behaviour, external debt problems, depressions, hyperinflations and bank runs, to name just a few examples.

There is no doubt that the development of non-linear concepts and methods has been a product of the computer age. Much of the early work began with the numerical analysis, often using what now seem to be very basic calculators and computers, of extremely 'simple' non-linear models. It was found that even the simplest of non-linear models were capable of displaying what initially appeared to be a vast range of properties. Very small changes in parameters, for example, were found to produce startling results such that models displaying simple types of cyclical and easily predictable behaviour suddenly showed

8   Chaos and non-linear models in economics

patterns that bore more relation to those which would formerly have been described as stochastic or chaotic. This led naturally to the idea of 'deterministic chaos'.

This type of numerical exercise can be replicated by anyone with a programmable calculator or personal computer. The numerical results using specific models led, perhaps not surprisingly, to the search for more general results, involving the development of entirely new concepts, often at a high level of abstraction. In particular, concepts of equilibrium, stability and dimension had to be revised. The aim of this chapter is to discuss models exhibiting chaotic behaviour and emphasize their relevance to economics. Section 2.2 examines the logistic equation as an introduction to the basic ideas of chaos. Properties of one-dimensional discrete maps are discussed more formally in section 2.3. Higher order discrete maps are discussed in section 2.4 and the properties of continuous time models are investigated in section 2.5. Some brief conclusions are given in section 2.6.

2.2   The logistic equation

The logistic equation has played an important role in the development of the mathematics of chaos and, combined with the fact that it has been used extensively in applied economics, it provides a useful starting point in presenting some of the basic ideas. Consider the variable Y_t where $0 \leq Y_t \leq 1$ and $t = 1,2,3 \ldots$ The discrete time dynamic system:

$$Y_{t+1} = f(Y_t)$$
$$= \mu Y_t (1 - Y_t) \tag{2.1}$$

is known as a logistic equation. An example is provided by the following simple dynamic model of advertising. Assume that as advertising expenditure, Y_t, rises, profits, X_t, first rise, then level off and finally decline. Next period's advertising is proportional to current profits. Therefore

$$X_t = \lambda Y_t (1 - Y_t), \quad \lambda > 0 \tag{2.2}$$
$$Y_{t+1} = \gamma X_t, \quad \gamma > 0 \tag{2.3}$$

Combining these and lagging one period gives the logistic equation in (2.1) where $\mu = \lambda \gamma$.

Other types of logistic equations are examined in Chapter 4. The function (2.1) is symmetrical about $Y_t = 0.5$, so that values of Y_t between 0 and 0.5 imply values of Y_{t+1} between 0 and $\mu/4$, while values of Y_t between 0.5 and 1 generate values of Y_{t+1} from $\mu/4$ to 0. The logistic equation may thus be viewed in terms of a mapping involving stretching or compressing combined with folding. If $\mu <$

The strange attraction of chaos in economics   9

2 the Y_t values are compressed. Values of $\mu > 4$ imply a stretching outside the interval $0 \le Y_t \le 1$, so these are excluded and attention is restricted to the range:

$$0 \le \mu \le 4 \tag{2.4}$$

Equation (2.1) appears to be extremely simple, and this is enhanced by the fact that it depends on only one parameter, μ. It is a simple matter to use (2.1) to produce as many iterations as required, starting from some initial value of Y_t for $t = 1$. The question arises of what sort of sequence of values might be expected. In particular, would the values of Y_t converge to some fixed value, such that $Y_{t+1} = Y_t = Y^*$, say. Geometrically, a fixed point is represented in a graph of Y_{t+1} plotted against Y_t by the intersection of an upward sloping 45-degree line through the origin with the quadratic logistic curve given by (2.1).

In order to examine fixed points, substitute $Y_{t+1} = Y_t = Y^*$ into (2.1) and rearrange to give:

$$Y^* \, [Y^* - (1 - 1/\mu)] = 0 \tag{2.5}$$

Hence if $0 \le \mu \le 1$, the only feasible root of (2.5) is the origin where $Y^* = 0$, since the restriction $0 \le Y_t \le 1$ has been imposed. But for $1 \le \mu \le 4$, there are two roots, 0 and $1 - 1/\mu$.

It is necessary to consider the stability of these roots. Economists, familiar with the standard cobweb analysis of stability in the partial equilibrium supply and demand analysis, will have no difficulty in drawing a similar cobweb path in this case. For $Y^* > 0$, stability requires that in the region of the fixed point, the logistic curve must intersect the 45-degree line through the origin from above, but must not be falling steeper than a downward-sloping 45-degree line. When the logistic is upward sloping at the point where it cuts the 45-degree line through the origin, the path to the fixed point, irrespective of the starting value, is found to be monotonic (see Figures 2.1(a) and 2.1(b)). However, where the logistic curve is downward sloping at the fixed point, the path spirals, or the value of Y oscillates, towards the fixed point. Examples are given in Figure 2.1(c) and 2.1(d).

More formally, the condition on the slope of the logistic at the fixed point can be examined by differentiating (2.1) as follows:

$$\left.\frac{df}{dY}\right|_{Y = Y^*} = \mu(1 - 2Y^*) \tag{2.6}$$

Hence the origin is stable only if $\mu < 1$. For $1 < \mu < 4$ substitution of the fixed value $Y^* = 1 - 1/\mu$ into (2.6) gives the slope of $2 - \mu$, so for this to be less than

10   Chaos and non-linear models in economics

a downward-sloping 45-degree line, it is required to have $|2 - \mu| < 1$. This means that the process will only converge to the fixed point when $\mu < 3$. For values of μ of around 2, convergence is extremely rapid, irrespective of the starting value of Y. When μ is closer to 3, however, convergence is extremely slow and several thousand iterations may be required.

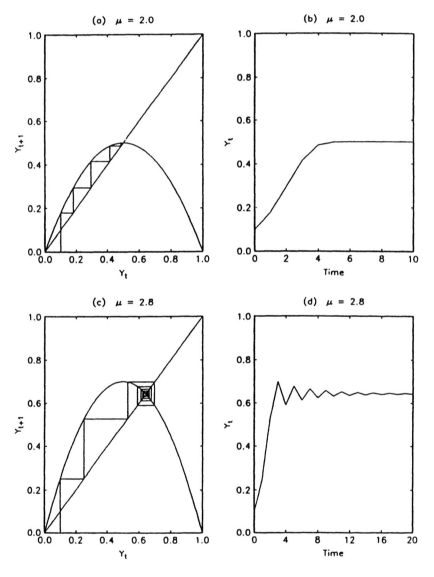

Figure 2.1   Fixed point properties of the logistic model

The strange attraction of chaos in economics   *11*

It is this type of stable fixed point which has received most attention in economic models, in terms of stable equilibria. The implications for such equilibria of changes in specified parameters of a model, the traditional type of comparative static analysis, can be carried out using standard calculus techniques. Where models also have only one stable equilibrium position,

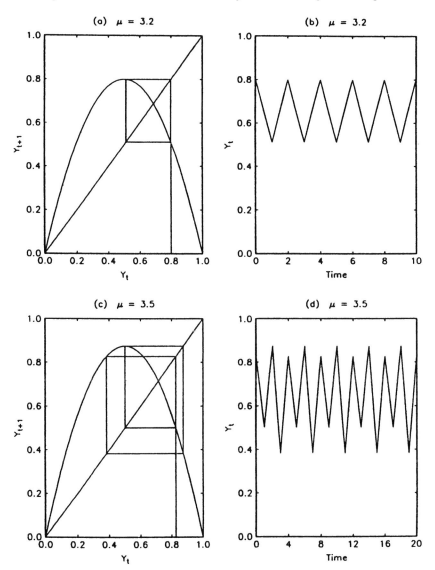

Figure 2.2   Period doubling in the logistic model

12   Chaos and non-linear models in economics

which is the usual case, any problems of the possibility of the system jumping from one equilibrium to another, as a stable equilibrium suddenly becomes unstable, are also avoided. This phenomenon is discussed in Chapter 6 in the context of an exchange model.

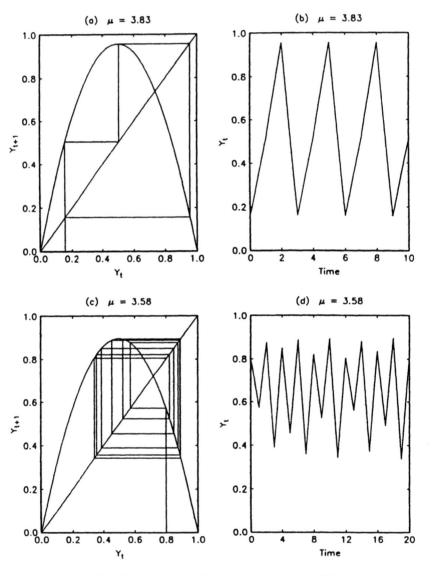

Figure 2.3   Odd order cycles and chaos in the logistic model

The strange attraction of chaos in economics   13

Instead of ignoring the range of values which are known to be associated with unstable fixed points, fascinating results have been discovered by concentrating attention precisely on that region. If μ is increased beyond 3 it is found that, irrespective of the starting value of Y_t, the cobweb cycles eventually settle into a loop around a fixed square. This means that the values alternate between two values; that is, it reaches a stable cycle of two periods. For example if μ is 3.1, Y_t alternates between 0.764566520 and 0.558014125. This two-period cycle is shown in Figures 2.2(a) and 2.2(b). When μ reaches 3.449 it is found that the system settles down to a four-period cycle. Thus if μ is 3.51 the values of Y_t eventually alternate between 0.877341821, 0.377722156, 0.825018932 and 0.506713055. This four-period cycle is shown in Figure 2.2(c) and 2.2(d).When μ reaches 3.544, eight-period cycles appear, and for $\mu = 3.564$, 16-period cycles are observed. Beyond this value, the doubling of the periods occurs at rapid intervals, until μ reaches 3.57, when the system never settles down to any fixed cycle. At this point it is said to be chaotic. An example, for $\mu = 3.58$, is shown in Figure 2.3(c) and 2.3(d).

An even more remarkable feature is that the system is not simply chaotic for all values of μ above 3.57. At some point three-period cycles suddenly appear. For example, with μ equal to 3.836 the iterations settle down to the values 0.151479312, 0.493053855, and 0.958814917, whatever the starting point, as shown in Figures 2.3(c) and 2.3(d). Very small increases in μ again produce a doubling of the periods from 6, 12, 24 and so on, ending again in chaos. When μ reaches 3.7390, five-period cycles appear with Y_t taking values of 0.934749476, 0.228052428, 0.658230452, 0.841137120 and 0.499625614. For further increases in μ there is a rapid period-doubling sequence until again chaos is observed. These values can, as mentioned earlier, easily be produced with a very small computer program, but it should be stressed that the precise results obtained will depend on the particular computer used.

The information about the behaviour of the logistic model for variations in μ can be displayed in a diagram such as Figure 2.4 where μ is measured on the horizontal axis and the values of Y on the vertical axis. If the iterations settle down to a regular cycle, the corresponding values of Y are plotted. However, for those values of μ which generate chaotic behaviour, a solid vertical line results. Figure 2.4(a) illustrates the properties of Y for μ ranging from 2.0 to 4.0. This is referred to as a bifurcation diagram where each point corresponding to period doubling gives rise to branching of the diagram. For values of μ between 3.57 and 4.0, the bifurcation diagram exhibits black bands which correspond to chaos separated by windows. It is in these windows that the odd-order cycles, discussed above, arise. This is generally referred to as order within chaos.

A further remarkable feature of the logistic, when plotted as a bifurcation diagram, is that if any window is magnified, the diagram displays an exact copy

14   Chaos and non-linear models in economics

of the complete diagram. This is known as self-similarity and is illustrated in Figure 2.4(b).

The discussion has illustrated the rich properties of an apparently simple model where the standard idea of a static equilibrium generally used in linear economic models, describes only a very limited range of possibilities such as monotonic

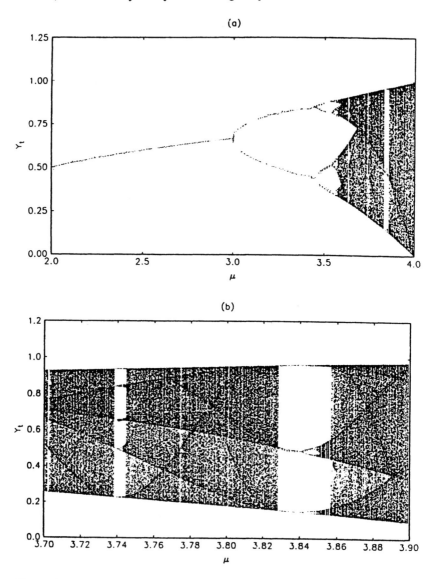

Figure 2.4   Bifurcation properties of the logistic model

The strange attraction of chaos in economics 15

or even-order oscillatory behaviour. The type of behaviour displayed by the logistic model with $0 < \mu < 3.57$, can be replicated by standard linear models. The analysis of non-linear models focuses attention on a broader concept of equilibrium, in particular one that allows for odd-order cycles. Furthermore, the analysis of the logistic model in the region of chaos, $3.57 < \mu < 4$, shows that even though behaviour is neither monotonic nor oscillatory, variations in Y are confined to a well-defined region. This region is referred to as an attractor. In the case of the logistic model, the attractor contains a single fixed point and the width of the attractor is governed by μ (see Figure 2.4). Different types of attractor are discussed below. The importance of the analysis of attractors in non-linear models in economics explains the title of the present chapter.

Sensitive dependence on initial conditions

It has been seen that, when the value of μ is such that regular cycles appear, the system will converge on the same cycle irrespective of the starting value of Y. When μ is in a region of chaos, no regular cycles appear however many iterations are performed. A feature of a region of chaos is that the path taken by Y_t is extremely sensitive to the starting value. An example is shown in Figure 2.5 where starting values of Y of 0.2 and 0.201 are used to generate subsequent time paths. For early iterations the time paths are indistinguishable, but soon diverge widely.

This property is known as sensitive dependence on initial conditions. It means that two trajectories which start very close to each other will eventually

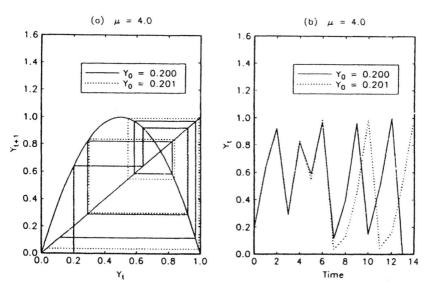

Figure 2.5   Sensitive dependence on initial conditions

16 Chaos and non-linear models in economics

diverge. It has important consequences for forecasting and simulating models since reliable predictions now depend on the accuracy of information on the initial conditions.

Suppose that the government is attempting to gauge the effect on output of a policy shock. To obtain accurate estimates of the dynamic path followed by output, it is necessary to have reliable information on the initial values of such variables as output, fiscal policy and capital. Figure 2.5(b) demonstrates the problems of simulating economic models and shows what can happen to the simulated trajectory paths for different initial values. One solution to this problem which has been suggested is to perform a sensitivity analysis by looking at the trajectory paths for a range of initial conditions. Another impli- cation suggested by the sensitive dependence on initial conditions problem is that long-term forecasts are unreliable.

2.3 One dimensional discrete maps

The logistic equation is just one example of a one-dimensional discrete time process. Other examples are the following:

$$Y_{t+1} = Y_t \exp(\mu(1 - Y_t)), \quad \mu > 0 \tag{2.7}$$

$$Y_{t+1} = 1 - 2|Y_t - 0.5| \tag{2.8}$$

$$Y_{t+1} = Y_t + \mu Y_t (Y_t^2 - 1) \tag{2.9}$$

$$Y_{t+1} = \mu \sin(Y_t) \tag{2.10}$$

These are respectively the exponential logistic, triangular, cubic and trigono- metric.

The properties of the logistic take on additional significance when it is realised that they apply to all such one-dimensional mappings. The results from such initially simple numerical exercises stimulated the search for much more general results, some of which are discussed in this section.

Feigenbaum's universal constant

Section 2.2 concentrated on the properties of the logistic equation as its parameter, μ, is gradually increased. It was found analytically that for $0 < \mu < 1$ the origin is the stable fixed point, for $1 < \mu < 3$ there is a stable fixed point equal to $1 - 1/\mu$. Numerical calculations were used to discover that as μ is increased beyond 3 the process goes through a period-doubling phase before reaching deter- ministic chaos. As μ is increased yet further, additional 'windows' of period-doubling leading to chaos were found to appear. The identification of all the values of μ which give rise to period-doubling can obviously be quite tedious if one does not have a powerful computer. It was precisely this feature which led Feigenbaum (1978) to discover a property which turned out to have much more generality than initially envisaged.

To demonstrate Feigenbaum's universal constant, define μ_n as a period doubling point. Consider the following ratio

$$\delta = \frac{\mu_n - \mu_{n-1}}{\mu_{n+1} - \mu_n} \qquad (2.11)$$

which gives the ratio of the previous change in the parameter to achieve period doubling, to the current change to achieve period doubling. Feigenbaum found that whatever the value of n, the ratio took the same value of approximately 4.6692.

Feigenbaum found that this constant arose in many one-dimensional maps. As a result, the number $\delta = 4.6692$ is known as the Feigenbaum number and is a universal constant, standing along side the other universal constants such as π.

An implication of the Feigenbaum number is that if μ_{n-1} and μ_n are known, it is then possible to determine μ_{n+1}. For example, it was seen earlier that two-period doubling points are given by $\mu_{n-1} = 3$ and $\mu_n = 3.449$. Substituting gives:

$$\mu_{n+1} = \mu_n + (\mu_n - \mu_{n-1})/\delta$$

$$\cong 3.56 \qquad (2.12)$$

It was seen in section 2.2 that values of μ in the chaotic region, $3.57 < \mu < 4$, produce cycles of odd order. The identification of a three-period cycle is particularly significant for understanding the properties of economic models since Sarkovskii has shown that if a model can be shown to exhibit a three-period cycle, it can generate cycles of all orders (see Guckenheimer and Holmes, 1983). This result was demonstrated for the logistic model in section 2.2 where this model was shown to have a three-period cycle as well as higher-order odd cycles and even order cycles.

The Li–Yorke Theorem
Li and Yorke (1975) used Sarkovskii's result to prove that if a map has a three-period cycle, then it can exhibit periodic and aperiodic behaviour. Mappings which satisfy these properties generate chaos in the Li–Yorke sense. This result can be summed up by the maxim, 'Period three implies chaos'.

Consider a time series given by Y_t. If one of the following conditions is satisfied

18   *Chaos and non-linear models in economics*

$$Y_{t+3} < Y_t < Y_{t+1} < Y_{t+2} \qquad (2.13)$$

$$Y_{t+3} > Y_t > Y_{t+1} > Y_{t+2} \qquad (2.14)$$

then two distinct time paths of Y_t can come very close to each other, but must eventually move away from each other. The time path of Y_t can exhibit k period cycles, with $k > 1$. Thus, when combined with the first proposition, a time path which exhibits a k period cycle must move away from this cycle after a while.

An implication of the results of Sarkovskii and Li and Yorke is that there can be order in a zone of chaos. Referring back to Figure 2.4, for values of μ in the chaotic region, namely $3.57 < \mu < 4.0$, there exist windows, within which stable cycles exist.

The above result suggests that an economy operating in a zone of order will experience stable and smooth cycles in prices. Within this zone the market fundamentals determine the price. However, if the key parameters of the model change, the economy can be pushed into a zone of chaos which can result in large and sudden movements in the price. These results are exploited in a model of exchange rates in Chapter 12.

2.4   Higher order discrete maps

A property of one-dimensional discrete maps is that they tend to lead to a saw-tooth trajectory. This is unrealistic for most, if not all, economic variables since it suggests that an increase in a particular economic aggregate is immediately followed by a decrease. Furthermore, one-dimensional models represent a special case of more general equilibrium economic systems. Thus it is of interest to explore the implications of non-linearities in higher dimensional systems. It should be noted at the outset that although there exist a number of theorems to help identify the structure of attractors for one-dimensional discrete maps, there is less help for n-dimensional systems (see Lauwerier, 1986, for a discussion of some theoretical results for two-dimensional maps).

The Henon map

One of the most widely known multivariate discrete maps is that of Henon (1976). This map is based on the following bivariate non-linear discrete set of equations:

$$X_{t+1} = 1 - \gamma X_t^2 + Y_t \qquad (2.15)$$

$$Y_{t+1} = \beta X_t \qquad (2.16)$$

where γ and β are positive parameters. In Figure 2.6, the properties of the Henon map are shown with $\gamma = 1.4$ and $\beta = 0.3$.

The strange attraction of chaos in economics 19

A time series plot of X_t in Figure 2.6(a) shows that the series tends to behave in an aperiodic manner. The phase diagram in Figure 2.6(b) shows that a 'banana-shaped' object appears. This is the Henon attractor since, for given starting values of X_t and Y_t, the processes converge to this region very quickly. The observed chaos in the map arises from the property that the distance between

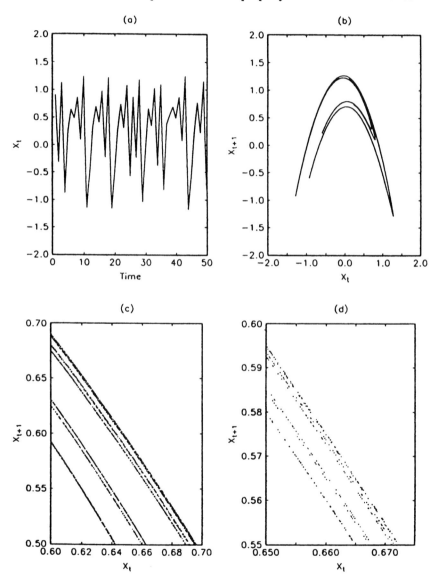

Figure 2.6 The Henon attractor

20   Chaos and non-linear models in economics

any two successive points is uncertain. This attractor also displays a self-similarity characteristic that was evident in Figure 2.4 for the logistic map. This self-similarity feature is highlighted in Figure 2.6(c) where part of the Henon attractor is magnified. The figure displays three bands consisting of a single line, a double line and a quadruple line. By zooming in on the quadruple line band in Figure 2.6(d), the same picture is repeated but at a finer scale. This is the order in the Henon map.

A Kaldor business-cycle model

As an example of a multivariate discrete non-linear model in economics, consider the following discrete time version of the Kaldor business-cycle model (see Lorenz, 1989, p. 130):

$$Y_{t+1} - Y_t = \alpha[I_t(Y_t,K_t) - S_t(Y_t)] \tag{2.17}$$

$$K_{t+1} - K_t = I_t(Y_t, K_t) - \delta K_t \tag{2.18}$$

$$I_t(Y_t, K_t) = c2^{-1/\left[(dY_t + \varepsilon)^2\right]} + eY_t + a(f / K_t)^g \tag{2.19}$$

$$S_t = sY_t \tag{2.20}$$

where Y_t is output, K_t is the stock of capital, I_t is gross investment, S_t is savings, and $\alpha = 20.0$, $\delta = 0.05$ is the depreciation rate on capital, $c = 20.0$, $d = 0.01$, $\varepsilon = 0.00001$, $e = 0.05$, $a = 5.0$, $f = 280.0$, $g = 4.5$ and $s = 0.21$, are parameters. Equation (2.17) shows that changes in output occur when there is a gap between savings and investment, whilst equation (2.18) shows that net additions to the stock of capital occur when gross investment exceeds replacement investment, δK_t. The non-linearities are introduced into the model by the sigmoidal investment function given by (2.19). Equation (2.20) represents a simple linear savings function.

The dynamics of the model are governed primarily by the parameter α. The model displays a unique stationary point for small values of α, whereas for larger values there is a closed orbit. For very large values of α, there appears to be no relationship between Y and K. This supposed chaotic pattern is highlighted in Figure 2.7(a) which gives a time series plot of Y_t. This figure also shows that the model is sensitive to initial conditions with the initial values being changed from 65 to 65.1 for Y_t, and from 265 to 265.1 for K_t. The shape of the attractor is demonstrated in Figures 2.7(b), 2.7(c) and 2.7(d) for the Y_t,K_t plane, the Y_{t+1},Y_t plane and the K_{t+1},K_t plane respectively.

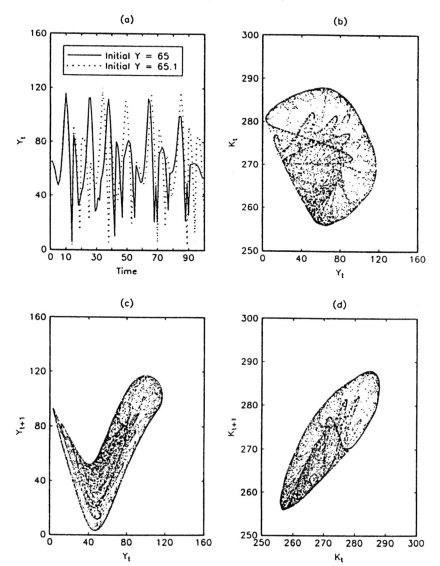

Figure 2.7   The Kaldor business cycle model

Snap-back repellers

A multivariate analogue of the Li–Yorke Theorem is given by Marotto (1978). Marotto introduces the concept of a snap-back repeller and proves that if a process has a snap-back repeller then it is chaotic. A snap-back repeller arises when for

22   *Chaos and non-linear models in economics*

'small' deviations from a fixed point the trajectory is repelled, while for 'large' deviations the process jumps on to the fixed point.

To identify a snap-back repeller, the procedure is to derive the eigenvalues of the system and show that for values of the state variables close to the fixed point the eigenvalues lie outside the unit circle, whereas for values of the state variables that are not close to the fixed point the eigenvalues lie within the unit circle.

As a practical matter however, snap-back repellers in general can only be identified using simulation procedures. For example, in a non-linear business-cycle model, a model not too dissimilar to the model given by equations (2.17) to (2.20), Hermann (1985) found that for a certain set of parameters a snap-back repeller exists.

2.5   Continuous time maps

The analysis so far has concentrated on showing how non-linearities in one-dimensional or higher-order discrete economic models can generate chaotic behaviour. In particular, chaotic motion has been identified when the process or processes jump irregularly over the attractor. Since economic models are also constructed in continuous time, it is of interest to investigate the conditions which generate chaos in this class of models. By virtue of the properties of continuous time models, chaos cannot be defined in terms of discrete jumps over an attractor as is the case in discrete models. Rather, the trajectory path over the attractor needs to be smooth. This has led to the definition of 'strange' attractors by Ruelle and Takens (1971).

Strange attractors

The concept of a strange attractor was originally couched in terms of continuous time systems by Ruelle and Takens (1971), although the definition now tends to be applied to discrete time systems as well. For an attractor to be 'strange' the following properties need to be satisfied (see Ruelle, 1979):

1.   all trajectories remain within a region;
2.   sensitive dependence on initial conditions;
3.   the attractor cannot be split into two or more pieces.

The relationship between strange attractors and chaos is that if a system has a strange attractor, then the system is chaotic.

For an attractor to be identified as strange, the dimension of a continuous time system needs to be at least equal to three. The reasons for this are as follows. In a one-dimensional continuous time model the trajectory of the state variable is smooth and thus the irregular jumps identified in the one-dimensional discrete maps are precluded in the one-dimensional continuous time maps. Two-dimensional continuous time systems also cannot exhibit chaotic behaviour since the trajectory cannot intersect itself. It is only for three-dimensional or higher-order

The strange attraction of chaos in economics 23

continuous time systems that a smooth trajectory can behave in a supposedly irregular pattern over the attractor without intersecting another trajectory. Some examples of continuous time systems which exhibit strange attractors are now given.

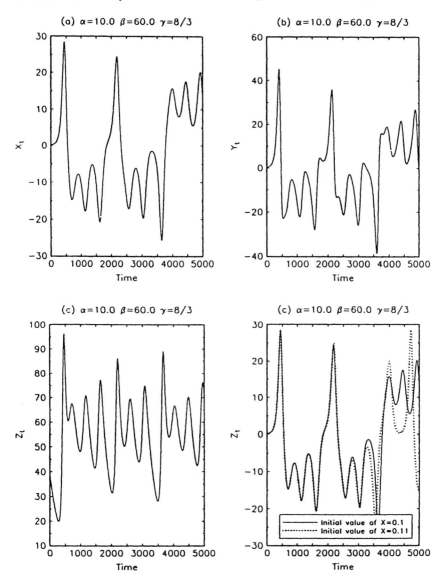

Figure 2.8 The Lorenz attractor in the time domain

24   *Chaos and non-linear models in economics*

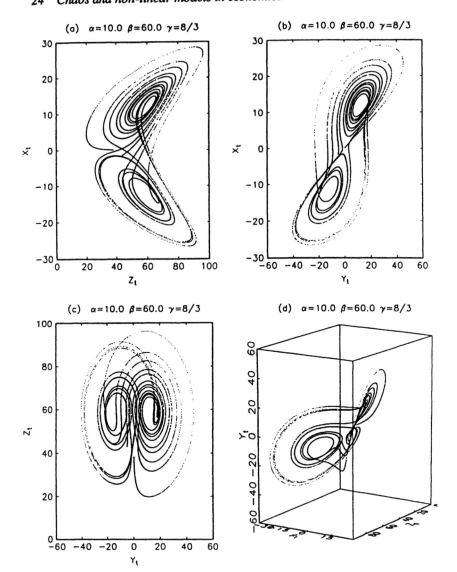

Figure 2.9   The Lorenz attractor in the space domain

The Lorenz attractor

The Lorenz attractor is based on a continuous time non-linear trivariate system of equations (see Lorenz, 1963). The equations are:

The strange attraction of chaos in economics 25

$$dX/dt = -\alpha(X - Y) \tag{2.21}$$
$$dY/dt = \beta X - Y - XZ \tag{2.22}$$
$$dZ/dt = -\gamma Z + XY \qquad \alpha, \beta, \gamma > 0 \tag{2.23}$$

The properties of the Lorenz attractor are highlighted in Figures 2.8 and 2.9 for the parameter values $\alpha = 10.0$, $\beta = 60.0$, $\gamma = 8/3$. It can be shown that although the system is summarized by three parameters, the key parameter is β (see Gilmore, 1981). The random behaviour of all series is highlighted in Figures 2.8(a), 2.8(b) and 2.8(c). In Figure 2.8(d) the sensitive dependence to initial condition property is demonstrated. The structure of the Lorenz attractor is shown in Figure 2.9. The key feature of the attractor is the 'butterfly' shape. Associated with each wing of the attractor is an unstable fixed point. The trajectory over the attractor is as follows. If the trajectory starts on the left wing in Figure 2.9(a), there is an outward clockwise spiralling motion away from the fixed point. The trajectory eventually traverses to a position near the centre of the right wing where it begins spiralling outwards in an anticlockwise direction. When the trajectory approaches the outer boundary of the wing it traverses back to a point near the centre of the left wing and the process is repeated.

The Rossler attractor
An attractor which is also strange was given by Rossler (1976). The Rossler attractor is based on the following continuous time trivariate system of equations:

$$dX/dt = -(Y + Z) \tag{2.24}$$
$$dY/dt = X + \alpha Y \tag{2.25}$$
$$dZ/dt = \beta - \gamma Z + XZ \qquad \alpha, \beta, \gamma > 0 \tag{2.26}$$

The amazing feature of this model is that chaotic behaviour is generated from a model with an even simpler non-linear structure than the Lorenz system of equations.

The key parameter in determining the characteristics of the trajectory paths of the variables in (2.24) to (2.26), is γ. This parameter performs the same role as the parameter μ in the logistic model since it determines the critical points where period doubling occur as well as the point where chaos emerges. The period doubling effect is depicted in Figure 2.10 for alternative values of γ with $\alpha = \beta = 0.2$. A two-period cycle is shown in Figures 2.10(a) and 2.10(b) for $\gamma = 2.4$, which changes to a four-period cycle for $\gamma = 3.5$ in Figures 2.10(c) and 2.10(d), and an eight-period cycle for $\gamma = 4.0$ in Figures 2.10(c) and 2.10(d). The period doubling sequence continues until the trajectory is chaotic; that is, the attractor becomes strange. The structure of the Rossler strange attractor is shown in Figure 2.11. Two-dimensional plots of the attractor in Figures 2.11(a) and 2.11(b) show that the attractor looks like a funnel with the width increasing as γ increases.

26   Chaos and non-linear models in economics

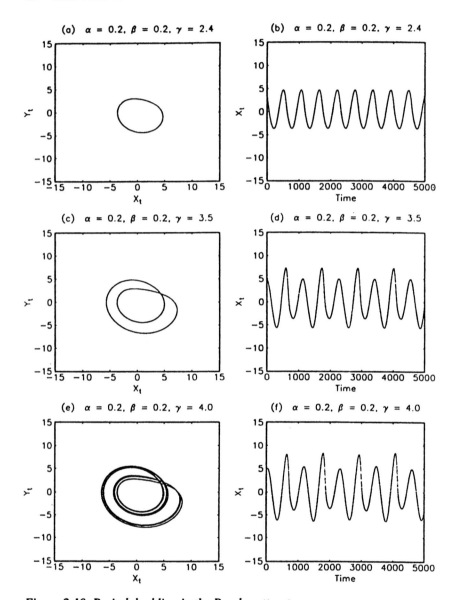

Figure 2.10 Period doubling in the Rossler attractor

Three-dimensional views of the attractor are given in Figures 2.11(c) and 2.11(d). A feature of the attractor is that there is just one fixed point, which contrasts with the Lorenz attractor where there were two fixed points. In fact,

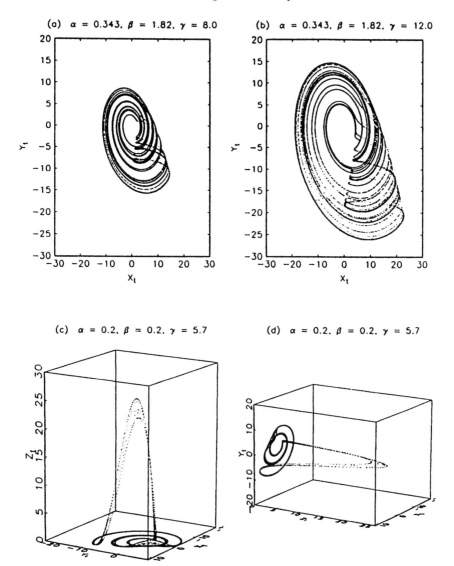

Figure 2.11 The Rossler attractor

the Rossler attractor can be considered as a special case of the Lorenz attractor
where the trajectory is restricted to just one of the wings of the Lorenz attractor.

28   Chaos and non-linear models in economics

Forced oscillators

The class of models considered in this section has consisted of systems of non-linear first-order differential equations. Higher-order differential equations have also been investigated. For example, consider the following univariate second-order non-linear differential equation:

$$d^2Y/dt^2 + f(Y)dY/dt + g(Y) = 0 \qquad (2.27)$$

where $f(Y)$ and $g(Y)$ represent functions. Even though equation (2.27) is a univariate model when viewed in terms of Y, it is actually a two-dimensional system since its properties can be investigated in terms of Y and dY/dt. This can be seen by writing this equation as a system of two non-linear first-order differential equations as follows:

$$dX/dt + f(Y)X + g(Y) = 0 \qquad (2.28)$$

$$dY/dt = X \qquad (2.29)$$

Although the class of models given by (2.28) and (2.29) can generate a wide range of dynamic behaviour, it cannot generate chaotic behaviour since it is a continuous time system with dimension less than three. One way of raising the dimension of this system is to include time explicitly as follows:

$$dY^2/dt^2 + f(Y)dY/dt + g(Y) = h(t) \qquad (2.30)$$

where $h(t)$ is a general function. This equation is known as a forced oscillator where the forcing term is given by the function $h(t)$. It is a three-dimensional system and it can generate chaotic trajectories. (For a discussion of the theory of forced oscillators, see Guckenheimer and Holmes, 1983.) Some economic examples of these models are given by Lorenz (1989).

2.6   Conclusions

This chapter has discussed the properties of both discrete and continuous time non-linear models. An important property of these models is that, unlike standard linear models in economics, they can exhibit not only monotonic and even-order cycles, but also cycles which are of odd order. Furthermore, these models can display random behaviour even though they are deterministic. An important concept which arises in these models is that of an attractor which is a much richer equilibrium concept than that used in describing standard linear economic models. The situations in which chaos arises in single and multi-dimensional discrete models were presented. It was shown for continuous time models that chaos can arise if either the dimension is at least three, or for at least two-dimensional systems with a forcing term.

This chapter has concentrated on the basic concept of chaos and the associated idea of an attractor. In the next chapter, the characteristics of particular attractors will be explored in more detail. In this analysis the concept of a fractal dimension is introduced, extending the standard concept of an integer dimension.

[2]

Bulletin of Economic Research 50:3, 1998, 0307-3378

NONLINEAR MODELLING USING THE GENERALIZED EXPONENTIAL FAMILY OF DISTRIBUTIONS*

John Creedy and Vance L. Martin

ABSTRACT

This paper introduces an approach to nonlinear modelling which is based on the use of the generalized exponential family of distributions. The flexibility of the approach is illustrated using hypothetical data based on an economic model which exhibits multiple equilibria for certain periods of time and a unique equilibrium for other periods. The distributional analogue of multiple equilibria is multimodality. An advantage of this framework is that discrete jumps can be modelled without the need for identifying the timing of jumps *ex post*. The framework also has the advantage of explaining how smooth changes in market fundamentals can give rise to large and sudden changes in prices. The introduction of economic assumptions into nonlinear models is explained, and it is shown how an explicit form for the distribution of the dependent variable can be derived. It is suggested that the approach has considerable potential in a wide variety of economic contexts.

I. INTRODUCTION

The purpose of this paper is to provide an introduction to nonlinear economic modelling using the generalized exponential family of distributions. The approach is very flexible and extremely powerful, but it is not yet widely used by economists. The development of this type of nonlinear modelling is enhanced by advances in computers which have made possible the use of computationally intensive numerical iterative procedures. However, the paper does not emphasize the technical

* We are grateful to two referees and the Editors for helpful comments on an earlier version of this paper.

details involved, particularly concerning methods of estimation, but instead provides appropriate references to the growing literature. The aim of the paper is rather to illustrate the power of the approach and show how it can be used in a variety of economic contexts. The method is illustrated by examining a time series of hypothetical data and comparing nonlinear and linear approaches. It is suggested that there are contexts in which the assumptions of linear models are not appropriate, even though they may sometimes appear to produce quite good results.

An economic model to be estimated is characterized by a specification in which an endogenous variable is related in some way to a set of exogenous variables. In linear models it is possible to express the model, using a transformation of variables if necessary, so that the conditional value of the endogenous variable is expressed as a linear function of the exogenous variables. The conditional distribution of the endogenous variable is usually regarded as following the normal distribution or one of the other standard unimodal distributions. This paper discusses the advantages of using, instead of a given form of unimodal distribution, the family of distributions known as the generalized exponential family; examples of the application of this family can be found in Cobb *et al.* (1983), Cobb and Zachs (1985), Creedy and Martin (1994), Creedy *et al.* (1996a, b), Fischer and Jammernegg (1986), Lye and Martin (1993a), and Martin (1990).

Nonlinear modelling using the generalized exponential family is particularly useful because it can handle phenomena such as large discrete 'jumps' in the endogenous variable that cannot easily be modelled using modifications of the linear model, such as the addition of dummy variables which require the investigator to specify precisely when the jump takes place. An important feature is that the approach is able to provide a link between simple economic models and the distributional forms of economic variables. This link can be derived directly from the structural form of the model rather than involving the more or less arbitrary imposition of a form of distribution at the estimation stage. The flexibility of the approach means that a wide range of models can be 'nested' and therefore more easily compared. Importantly, it also allows for the possibility that the form of the conditional distributions may themselves change over time, and indeed may sometimes be multimodal.

In order to illustrate alternative approaches, a hypothetical time series of prices is used. The prices are regarded as being influenced by two fundamental variables that are treated as exogenous. Results using a standard linear approach are obtained in Section II. This section also presents an alternative way of specifying the linear model, which facilitates an immediate comparison with the nonlinear approach. The extension of the linear model is presented in Section III, where the

NONLINEAR MODELLING 231

generalized exponential family of distributions is introduced. The results of estimating a nonlinear model are contrasted with the use of the linear model. A further valuable feature of the approach is that, starting from a simple economic model, it is possible explicitly to generate the distributional implications of a stochastic process imposed on the model. The way in which the distributions can be generated is described in Section IV. Some examples showing how the general result can easily be applied in special cases are provided in Section V. Brief conclusions are given in Section VI. As mentioned above, the emphasis of this paper is on illustrating the great potential of the approach, not on presenting the technical details in full. However, references are made to more technical studies.

II. LINEAR MODELS

Basic courses in econometrics stress the idea that in a standard regression analysis each observed value of an endogenous or dependent variable is usually regarded as being an observation selected at random from a conditional distribution, for a given set of values of exogenous or independent variables. The estimation and testing of models proceeds by specifying an assumed form for the conditional distributions, and this is combined with the idea of random independent selection. In practice, only one observation from each conditional distribution is available, so the form of the conditional distribution cannot be observed directly. The assumptions that the conditional means are given by a linear combination of the exogenous variables while the conditional variances are homoskedastic are therefore very convenient. With the additional assumption of normality of the conditional distributions, it is easy to show that maximum likelihood estimation reduces to ordinary least squares and has other desirable properties such as efficiency.

Within the context of this type of linear model, it is of course possible to allow for additional complexities, arising for example if the selection process is not random, so that the probability of observing a value from one conditional distribution depends in some way on the values drawn from other conditional distributions, or if the conditional variances are not all the same. When such modifications to the basic model are made, such as assuming that the data generation process involves some serial correlation or introducing heteroskedasticity, the assumption is retained that all the conditional distributions take the same fundamental form, that is the unimodal normal distribution. Even where nonnormal distributions are specified, it is typically assumed that they are unimodal.

This assumption of unimodality often appears to be supported by the available evidence. For example, in the context of the analysis of a stationary time series of relative prices, it is possible to produce an unconditional distribution by a simple process of temporal aggregation, whereby all the relative prices are treated as coming from the same distribution. Such empirical distributions obtained in this way are typically unimodal, although they tend to exhibit sharper peaks and fatter tails than a normal distribution with the same mean and variance. For example in the context of exchange rate returns, see Boothe and Glassman (1987), Friedman and Vandersteel (1982), Hsieh (1989), Mandelbrot (1963), and Tucker and Pond (1988).

II.1. Estimation and prediction

Suppose that an economist has a set of data consisting of a time series of 200 observations on a variable, p_t, that will for convenience be called a price. The price is thought to be influenced by two exogenous variables, x_t and y_t. The price series and the two exogenous variables are shown in Figure 1 · The precise model used to generate these hypothetical time series is described in the Appendix; in practice the 'true' model must of course remain unknown.

Linear regression analysis proceeds by specifying an equation in which the price, or a simple transformation such as its logarithm, is a linear function of the exogenous variables, x_t and y_t, or transformed values, and an additive stochastic term, u_t. Faced with the data in Figure 1, alternative specifications or functional forms within the context of linear regression analysis would be estimated and a range of tests applied, starting with the simplest assumptions about the stochastic term, u_t.

Suppose that the linear model is specified as

$$p_t = \alpha_0 + \alpha_1 x_t + \alpha_2 y_t + u_t \tag{1}$$

with the u_ts assumed to be independently distributed as $N(0, \sigma_u^2)$. Each value of u_t is regarded as being independently drawn from a distribution which is assumed to have the same form, $N(0, \sigma_u^2)$, irrespective of the values of x_t and y_t. This implies that prices are also normally distributed, although around a time-varying conditional mean which is a function of both x_t and y_t. Estimation by ordinary least squares produces the following results, where absolute values of t-statistics are given in brackets:

$$\hat{p}_t = -1.746 + 0.185x_t - 0.020y_t \tag{2}$$
$$(5.068)\ (59.166)\quad (0.663)$$

with $\hat{\sigma}_u = 0.462$; $\bar{R}^2 = 0.947$; $DW = 1.327$; $BP(2) = 69.142$; $ARCH(1) = 45.018$; $RESET(1) = 68.213$.[1]

Using conventional criteria of goodness of fit, the linear model

---

[1] The reported diagnostics are: $\hat{\sigma}_u$, the standard error of estimate; $\bar{R}^2$, the degrees of freedom adjusted coefficient of determination; DW, the Durbin–Watson statistic for first-order autocorrelation; $BP(2)$, the Breusch–Pagan statistic for heteroskedasticity which is distributed as χ_2^2; $ARCH(1)$, Engle's statistic for testing for first-order autoregressive conditinal heteroskedasticity which is distributed as χ_1^2; $RESET(1)$, statistic to test for nonlinearities which is distributed as χ_1^2.

performs well. The value for $\bar{R}^2$ shows that a high proportion of variation in p_t is explained by a linear relationship between the dependent
variable and the independent variables x_t and y_t, as well as the intercept
term. A comparison of the actual and the predicted price series, $\hat{p}_t$, that
is the conditional mean in each period, is shown in Figure 2. This shows
that the linear model is able to predict very well the general swings in p_t
over most of the sample. However, closer inspection of Figure 2 reveals
some evidence of misspecification as the linear model fails to capture
the large swings in prices at the start, middle and end of the sample
period. Evidence of misspecification is also highlighted by the *DW* and
BP statistics which both suggest significant serial correlation and heteroskedasticity respectively. These results suggest that there is some underlying characteristic which is not being captured by this linear model. This

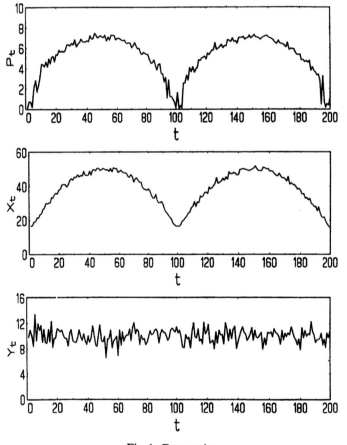

Fig. 1. Data series

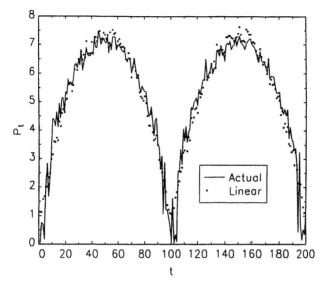

Fig. 2. Actual and predicted p_t based on the linear model

is supported by the *ARCH* and *RESET* test statistics which suggest that there is strong evidence of nonlinearities in the residuals.

One way to test the normality assumption of u_t, and hence p_t, is to construct a histogram of the ordinary least squares residuals. This is presented in Figure 3 and shows that there is no evidence to reject the hypothesis that the distribution of u_t is unimodal. A more formal test of

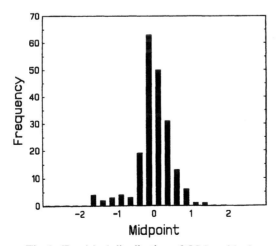

Fig. 3. Empirical distribution of OLS residuals

normality is given by the Jarque–Bera test. The computed value of the test statistic is 114.071. Comparing this value with a χ_2^2 critical value shows that the null hypothesis that the disturbance term u_t is normally distributed is rejected at standard significance levels.

A standard approach to solve the problems of autocorrelation, hetero-skedasticity and *ARCH*, are to re-estimate (1) by generalized least squares. It is important to stress at this stage that these solutions are based, implicitly at least, on the assumption that the underlying distribution of p_t is unimodal. There is no sign of multimodality. In fact, as is highlighted by the nonlinear modelling framework developed in Section III below, the rejection of normality using the Jarque–Bera test potentially provides the most illuminating information of all of the diagnostics reported so far, concerning the presence of multimodality.

II.2. A structural form

The linear approach described above began, as do many empirical studies, by writing a linear regression model relating the relevant variables; it was not derived directly from an economic theory of price determination. The specification in (1) may, however, be regarded as the reduced form of a model which is based on a structural form consisting of linear demand and supply functions. The price changes are assumed to be generated by shifts over time in these structural equations. Thus, suppose the demand, q_t^d, and supply, q_t^s, of the good in question can be written respectively as

$$q_t^d = a_t - bp_t \tag{3}$$

$$q_t^s = c_t + dp_t. \tag{4}$$

The intercepts, a_t and c_t, are assumed to be linear functions of the 'fundamental' exogenous variables x_t and y_t respectively, while the slope coefficients, b and d, are assumed to be constant, reflecting the idea that the price changes are produced by shifts in the curves rather than changes in their slopes, although this assumption can be easily relaxed. In equilibrium, $q_t^d = q_t^s$, so the equilibrium price in period t is given by the root of the equation:

$$p_t - \frac{a_t - c_t}{d + b} = 0. \tag{5}$$

II.3. A distributional specification

One way to introduce stochastics into the structural model in (3) and (4) is to include additive shocks in the intercept terms in the supply and demand functions. This has the effect of forcing p_t to deviate from its equilibrium price h_t. Assuming that the shock, v_t, is distributed as $N(0, 1)$, equation (5) generalizes to

$$p_t = h_t + \sigma_u v_t \qquad (6)$$

where h_t is given by

$$h_t = \frac{a_t - c_t}{d + b} \qquad (7)$$

and is the equilibrium price. A comparison between (1) and (6) shows that the equilibrium price, h_t, is also the conditional mean $\alpha_0 + \alpha_1 x_t + \alpha_2 y_t$. It also shows that the linear equation given in (1) can be interpreted as the reduced form of this model.

The conditional price distribution, $f(p_t)$, which follows immediately from (6) and by use of the additive property of the normal distribution, is given by

$$f(p_t) = N(h_t, \sigma_u^2). \qquad (8)$$

The observed prices are treated as being random drawings from a conditional normal distribution whose mean in period t is given by the root of equation (5), which is of course $h_t = (a_t - c_t)/(d + b)$.

The form of the density function for the normal distribution is given by

$$f(p_t) = \frac{1}{\sqrt{2\pi\sigma_u^2}} \exp\left[-\frac{1}{2\sigma_u^2}(p_t - h_t)^2\right]. \qquad (9)$$

It is useful to consider an alternative way of specifying this density which helps to make the contrast between linear models and the class of nonlinear models developed below more clearly. First, noting that $1/\sqrt{(2\pi\sigma^2)}$ can be expressed as $\exp\left[-\frac{1}{2}\log(2\pi\sigma^2)\right]$, $f(p_t)$ can be rearranged in the form of a second-order polynomial in p_t given by

$$f(p_t) = \exp(\theta_{1,t} p_t + \theta_{2,t} p_t^2/2 - \eta_t^*) \qquad (10)$$

where the coefficients on p_t and $p_t^2/2$ are respectively given by

$$\theta_{1,t} = \frac{h_t}{\sigma_u^2} \qquad (11)$$

$$\theta_{2,t} = -\frac{1}{\sigma_u^2} \qquad (12)$$

and η_t^* is

$$\eta_t^* = \frac{1}{2}\left[\frac{h_t^2}{\sigma_u^2} + \log(2\pi\sigma_u^2)\right].\tag{13}$$

This term varies with t because h_t contains x_t and y_t. Essentially its role is to ensure that $f(p_t)$ qualifies as a density function; that is, it is required to have $\int_{-\infty}^{+\infty} f(p_t)\,dp_t = 1$. For this reason η_t^* is known as the 'normalizing constant'. The term $\theta_{2,t}$ in (10) involves only the variance σ_u^2, which in the present model is assumed to be constant over time. The first term $\theta_{1,t}$ is a function of the exogenous variables and the variance term. This approach to the linear model, involving rewriting the standard expression for the normal distribution as a second-order polynomial, may at first sight appear cumbersome, but it provides the clearest way to see how it can be extended.

III. A NONLINEAR APPROACH

III.1. The generalized exponential family

A nonlinear approach can be developed as a natural extension of the above linear model by the simple addition of terms in the expression for the price distribution in equation (10). These terms may be powers of prices or transformations of prices such as reciprocals or logarithms. This is all that is required to produce the generalized exponential family of distributions. In the case where only additional powers are used, the price distribution, $f(p_t)$, takes the form

$$f(p_t) = \exp\left(\theta_{1,t}p_t + \theta_{2,t}p_t^2/2 + \theta_{3,t}p_t^3/3 + \ldots + \theta_{k,t}p_t^k/k - \eta_t\right)\tag{14}$$

where η_t is a normalizing constant defined as

$$\eta_t = \log\int \exp\left(\theta_{1,t}p_t + \theta_{2,y}p_t^2/2 + \theta_{3,t}p_t^3/3 + \ldots \theta_{k,t}p_t^k/k\right)\,dp_t.\tag{15}$$

This corresponds to η_t^* above for the normal distribution and ensures that $f(p_t)$ qualifies as a density function. There is thus a direct comparison between equations (14) and (10).

The term in brackets in (14) may contain any number of terms in the polynomial, and as noted above may also contain terms involving transformed values of p, such as its logarithm. If only terms in p_t and p_t^2 appear in (14), then the price distribution reduces to the normal distribution by comparison with (10). If only terms in $\log(p_t)$, where p_t is strictly positive, and p_t appear, the distribution follows the unimodal gamma distribution; whereas if only p_t appears in (14), then it is a simple exponential distribution. Other forms contained within the generalized exponential family include the generalized gamma and generalized Student's t distributions; see Cobb *et al.* (1983), and Lye and Martin (1993a).

The terms $\theta_{j,t}$ in equation (14) are in general assumed to be functions of the fundamental or exogenous variables, x_t and y_t. For example, they could be written as linear functions such as

$$\theta_{j,t} = \alpha_{j,0} + \alpha_{j,1}x_t + \alpha_{j,2}y_t \tag{16}$$

for $j = 1, 2, \ldots, k$. This means that over time the θs can change. This has the far-reaching implication that the form of the conditional price distribution can change over time. This occurs not necessarily as a result of a changing conditional mean, as in the case of the linear model, or a changing conditional variance, as in the case where there is heteroskedasticity, but as a result of changes in higher-order conditional moments such as skewness and kurtosis. More interestingly, there is also a possibility that the distribution can change over time from being unimodal to being multimodal. In practice, the precise relationship between the θs and the exogenous variables is not known. However, a significant advantage of the approach is that a form of (14) can be derived from an economic model, as described in the following section. First, the remainder of this section examines the condition under which the distribution has more than one mode and then considers the performance of the nonlinear approach when faced with the hypothetical data used earlier.

III.2. Bimodality and the generalized exponential

It is important to be able to identify whether or not the generalized exponential distribution displays multimodality in any time period. This information is particularly valuable because multimodality may be associated with large discrete jumps in the price, where a movement takes place from one mode to another. Such a jump in the price need not be associated with large changes in the fundamental, or exogenous variable, of interest. This type of phenomenon is observed during stock market crashes where smooth changes in the economic fundamentals, as represented by dividends, are associated with relatively larger movements in the share price; see for example Barskey and De Long (1993), Genotte and Leland (1990), and Lim et al. (1998). This phenomenon is also typical of foreign exchange markets where large swings in exchange rates are associated with relatively smaller movements in the economic fundamentals; see Creedy et al. (1996b).

For the purpose of identifying bimodality, it is convenient to transform the model. This alternative form exhibits the same qualitative properties as the original model. To show this, consider (14) with $k=4$, whereby

$$f(p_t) = \exp\left(\theta_{1,t}p_t + \theta_{2,t}p_t^2/2 + \theta_{3,t}p_t^3/3 + \theta_{4,t}p_t^4/4 - \eta_t\right). \tag{17}$$

This can be transformed to a distribution in the variable w_t by using

NONLINEAR MODELLING   239

$$w_t = p_t(-\theta_{4,t})^{0.25} + \theta_{3,t}(-\theta_{4,t})^{-0.75}/3. \tag{18}$$

After some tedious algebra it can be shown that

$$f(w_t) = \exp\left(\tau_{0,t}w_t + \tau_{1,t}w_t^2/2 - w_t^4/4 - \eta_t^{**}\right) \tag{19}$$

where the terms $\theta_{0,t}$ and $\tau_{1,t}$, are expressed as functions of the θs, and η_t^{**} is the normalizing constant. Notice that the coefficient on $w_t^3/3$ is zero, so that the cubed term is eliminated and the coefficient on $w_t^4/4$ is minus unity. This type of variate transformation is known as a 'diffeomorphism'; in general, in a polynomial of order k, the $(k-1)$th term can be eliminated. For further discussion of this type of transformation see Gilmore (1981).

The importance of the transformation in (18) is that the transformed distribution in (19) exhibits the same characteristics as the untransformed distribution in (17); in particular, if (17) exhibits bimodality then so will (19). The advantage of eliminating the cubic term is that it is easier to examine the conditions for multimodality. It is possible to show, as in Cobb *et al.* (1983, p. 128), that a necessary and sufficient condition for (19) to exhibit bimodality involves the term, δ_t, defined by

$$\delta_t = \frac{\tau_{0,t}^2}{4} - \frac{\tau_{1,t}^3}{27}. \tag{20}$$

This is known as Cardan's discriminant, and it needs to be negative for (19) to have two modes and one antimode. As $\tau_{0,t}$ and $\tau_{1,t}$ are functions of the exogenous variables x_t and y_t, which vary over time, then δ_t also varies over time. Hence δ_t can change sign, say from positive to negative over the sample period, which means that the conditional distribution changes from being unimodal to being multimodal. Inspection of (20) also shows that a necessary condition for bimodality is that $\tau_{1,t}$ needs to be positive; for a discussion in the context of multiple equilibria, see Creedy and Martin (1993, pp. 343–5).

III.3. Estimation and prediction

The generalized exponential family, such as the model described in equations (14) and (16), or the simplified transformed version in equation (19), can be estimated using maximum likelihood methods. For a time series consisting of observations on $t=1, 2, \ldots T$ periods, the log-likelihood is

$$L(\Psi) = \sum_{t=1}^{T} \log f(p_t; \Psi) \tag{21}$$

where Ψ represents the set of parameters that need to be estimated. The maximum likelihood point estimates, given by $\hat{\Psi}$, are those values which maximize $L(\Psi)$. Quasi maximum-likelihood standard errors can be computed in the usual way from the hessian and outer-product of the log-likelihood when evaluated at the maximum-likelihood estimates. Asymptotic t-statistics can be constructed which are asymptotically distributed as $N(0, 1)$ under the usual regularity conditions.

The log-likelihood in (21) is maximized using standard iterative gradient algorithms. This contrasts with the linear model where the first-order conditions for maximum likelihood are solved explicitly for the coefficients. While the use of an iterative algorithm to compute maximum-likelihood estimates is standard, what is not standard for the model developed in this paper is that special attention has to be given to the normalizing constant, η_t. This is because, as inspection of (15) shows, in general η_t is different for each time period, and numerical methods of integration have to be used. Further, as the normalizing constant is a function of the parameters, the first-order conditions for maximum-likelihood estimation also contain the derivatives of η_t with respect to the parameters in Ψ. However, as mentioned earlier, the aim of the present paper is to introduce the approach, so that the more technical aspects of estimation are not discussed here; see Cobb *et al.* (1983) and Lye and Martin (1993a). Computer software for alternative specifications has been developed using GAUSS routines which are available from the authors.

It has been mentioned that a standard approach to prediction with the linear model is simply to take the conditional mean of the dependent variable, for given values of x_t and y_t. With a normal distribution, this conditional mean corresponds to the single model. With the nonlinear model, however, it is necessary to devise an appropriate convention for obtaining predictions because of the possible multimodality of the distribution. One approach, called the 'global' convention, is based on choosing that value corresponding to the highest mode; see Creedy and Martin (1994) for a discussion of other conventions.

As when using the linear model, the true data-generating model cannot be known to the investigator, and it is necessary to specify a form for the distribution. If there is no *a priori* information concerning its form (for example, using the type of model discussed in the following section), one approach is to adopt a general specification whereby the θ terms in (17) are regarded as being functions of both x_t and y_t. An appropriate order for the polynomial in p_t must also be chosen.

The results of estimating one of many potential nonlinear model specifications are as follows, where absolute values of t-statistics, as based on the quasi maximum-likelihood standard errors, are given in brackets:

$$f(p_t) = \exp\left(\hat{\theta}_{1,t} p_t + \hat{\theta}_{2,t} p_t^2/2 + \hat{\theta}_{3,t} p_t^3/3 + \hat{\theta}_{4,t} p_t^4/4 - \hat{\eta}_t\right) \tag{22}$$

where

$$\hat{\theta}_{1,t} = 3.437$$
$$(3.333)$$

$$\hat{\theta}_{2,t} = -5.663 - 0.174y_t - 0.220x_t$$
$$(2.160)\,(0.803)\quad(1.805)$$

$$\hat{\theta}_{3,t} = 3.805 + 0.304x_t - 0.043y_t$$
$$(4.945)\,(6.684)\quad(1.073)$$

$$\hat{\theta}_{4,t} = -2.261$$
$$(7.343)$$

$\hat{\eta}_t$ is the normalizing constant which is written with a circumflex to signify that it is a function of the estimated parameters, and $\hat{\sigma}_u = 0.328$; $\bar{R}^2 = 0.973$; $DW = 2.051$; $BP(2) = 24.844$; $ARCH(1) = 0.946$; $RESET(1) = 6.609$, with the residuals defined as the difference between p_t and the predictions based on the global mode of (22) at each t.[2] In this specification, a fourth-order polynomial is chosen, and the terms $\theta_{1,t}$ and $\theta_{4,t}$ are treated as constant. As explained in the next section, this specification is motivated by a supply and demand model where the slopes of the respective curves are assumed to be constant. A comparison of the adjusted coefficient of determination shows some marginal improvement in goodness of fit with $\bar{R}^2$ increasing from 0.947 for the linear model to 0.973 for the nonlinear model.

Inspection of the t-statistics in (22) suggests that the coefficient on the variable y_t in the function $\theta_{3,t}$ is insignificant. However, the coefficients on both x_t and y_t in the function $\theta_{2,t}$ appear to be insignificant. Faced with these results, a sensible approach is to re-estimate the model deleting only the variable y_t in $\theta_{3,t}$. This gives the following results:

$$\hat{\theta}_{1,t} = 3.374$$
$$(3.192)$$

$$\hat{\theta}_{2,t} = -4.013 - 0.367y_t - 0.186x_t$$
$$(1.861)\,(3.812)\quad(1.357)$$

$$\hat{\theta}_{3,t} = 3.260 + 0.294x_t$$
$$(4.307)\,(6.083)$$

$$\hat{\theta}_{4,t} = -2.203$$
$$(6.746)$$

(23)

It can be seen that the coefficient on y_t in $\theta_{2,t}$ has become significant,

[2] The degrees of freedom used in computing $\bar{R}^2$ equals the total number of parameters estimated. For the estimated non-linear model in equation (22), the number of estimated parameters is 8. The diagnostics reported for the estimated non-linear model in (22), as well as subsequent estimated nonlinear models, are the same diagnostics reported for the linear model. For the present purposes, these diagnostics are used as portmanteau tests for identifying the presence of nonlinearity by identifying if there is any additional information in the residuals. On testing for $ARCH$ where the conditional distribution is from the generalized exponential family, see Lim *et al.* (1998).

while that on x_t clearly remains insignificant. Dropping this last term leads to the following estimated model, where as before absolute values of t-statistics are given in brackets:

$$\hat{\theta}_{1,t} = 2.819$$
$$(3.260)$$
$$\hat{\theta}_{2,t} = -5.563 - 0.380 y_t$$
$$(3.622)\,(3.878) \tag{24}$$
$$\hat{\theta}_{3,t} = 2.633 + 0.254 x_t$$
$$(5.251)\,(7.940)$$
$$\hat{\theta}_{4,t} = -1.982$$
$$(8.117)$$

with $\hat{\sigma}_u = 0.379$; $\bar{R}^2 = 0.965$; $DW = 2.022$; $BP(2) = 26.572$; $ARCH(1) = 0.657$; $RESET(1) = 3.744$. The coefficients are now all significantly different from zero.

In terms of standard criteria, the adjusted coefficient of determination shows that there is a marginal improvement in goodness of fit over the linear model, while the DW statistic shows no evidence of autocorrelation. The $ARCH$ and $RESET$ test statistics show no evidence of nonlinearities, and while the BP statistic still points to some evidence of heteroskedasticity the degree of significance of heteroskedasticity has been dramatically decreased from the result reported for the linear model. Comparing the predictions of this model, shown in Figure 4, with

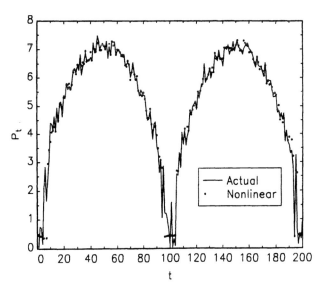

Fig. 4. Actual and predicted p_t based on the estimated nonlinear model in equation (24)

the predictions of the linear model given in Figure 2, shows that the nonlinear model performs better in predicting the price in those periods where prices are relatively low.

More importantly, by using Cardan's discriminant as given in equation (20), the nonlinear model is able to identify periods of bimodality. This is shown by the negative values of Cardan's discriminant, displayed in Figure 5. The bimodal properties of the model are further demonstrated in Figure 6, which gives snapshots of the distribution of prices conditional on specific values of x_t and y_t. Hence, it is concluded that the prices observed for the relevant periods shown in Figure 4 have been selected from an underlying distribution that is multimodal. This has been revealed by the nonlinear approach, in contrast with the linear approach which, at best, suggests only that the tails of the homoskedastic price distribution are somewhat fatter than the normal distribution and that it is a little more peaked.[3] The distribution obtained by temporal aggregation may not, as in the case here, reveal the informa-

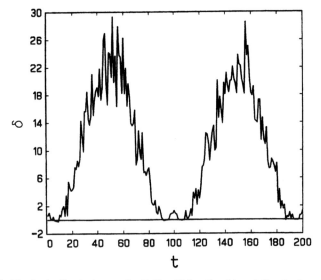

Fig. 5. Cardan's discriminant: $\delta_t < 0$ $(\delta_t > 0)$ implies bimodality (unimodality)

[3] In particular, Lye and Martin (1993b) show that a Lagrange multiplier test of the joint restrictions $\theta_3 = \theta_4 = 0$, in the density

$$f(p_t) = \exp\ (\theta_1 p_t + \theta_2 p_t^2/2 + \theta_3 p_t^3/3 + \theta_4 p_t^4/4 - \eta)$$

is equivalent to the Jarque–Bera test of normality. The implication of this result for empirical research is that when the normality assumption is rejected, this could be the result that the underlying distribution comes from the generalized exponential family which can exhibit multimodality.

tion that multimodality is present in some of the periods, particularly if there are relatively few periods of such multimodality.

It is shown later, and in the Appendix, that this is in fact the model used to generate the hypothetical data. The parameter estimates are close to those used to generate the data, and the three periods of multimodality identified in Figure 5, namely at the start, middle and end of the sample, are the correct periods. In particular, the number of

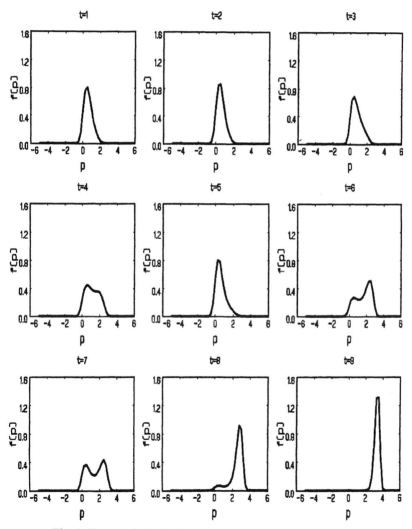

Fig. 6. Temporal distribution snapshots: periods $t = 1, 2, \ldots, 9$

points in time where the actual distribution is bimodal is 24, of which the estimated model predicts 17 correctly. The estimated model does not predict any periods of bimodality when the true distribution is unimodal. In comparison with the linear model, the nonlinear model is able to capture a great deal more of the properties of the data generation process. The investigator does not need to know *ex ante* which periods display multimodality and involve jumps from one mode to another.

IV. DATA GENERATING PROCESSES

The procedure followed in Section III is one in which the price distribution at any time is specified as a generalized exponential distribution which is conditional on the exogenous variables. Without knowing anything about the true data generation process, it was shown how an investigator might select various specifications. The purpose of this section is to show how it is possible to start from an *a priori* specification of a model and generate the implied form of the distribution. Instead of the linear structural form of the model where the equilibrium priced is the unique root of the linear equation (5), it is possible to start with a nonlinear structure whereby the equation giving the equilibrium price may have more than one root. In addition, as shown in the following subsection, the stochastics can be introduced into the structure in a more complex manner.

IV.1. *The stochastic differential equation*

Suppose an economic model of price determination generates the equilibrium price as the root, or an appropriate root, of the equation

$$\mu(p_t) = 0. \tag{25}$$

The function $\mu(p_t)$ may, for example, be a polynomial in p_t, where the coefficients on p_t are time-varying as they depend in some way on exogenous economic variables. This represents the deterministic form of the price model. For example, in the partial equilibrium supply and demand model discussed in Section II, $\mu(p_t)$ is a linear function, $p_t - h_t$, with the equilibrium price given as a linear function of the exogenous variables. In that linear context, the observed price in each period is regarded as a random drawing from a normal distribution with the equilibrium price as the arithmetic mean. Examples of alternative models which give rise to nonlinear forms of $\mu(p_t)$ are given below, but at this stage it is useful to concentrate on the stochastics of the general form of the model.

Stochastics can be introduced into the deterministic model in various ways. One approach is to assume that (25) represents the mean of a stochastic process and that deviations from the mean are regarded as arising from continuous additive stochastic shocks. The stochastic representation of the model is then given by

$$\frac{dp_t}{dt} = -\mu(p_t) + \sigma_t v_t \tag{26}$$

where the stochastic term, v_t, is assumed to follow a normal distribution with zero mean and unit variance. This differential equation can be interpreted as an 'error correction' model whereby the price adjusts continuously from its mean as a result of short-run stochastic shocks, v_t; see Creedy et al. (1996b). The negative sign means that on average the price adjusts over time back to the long-run equilibrium position, that is it 'error corrects'. Indeed, (25) can be regarded as a special case of (26) since in the absence of random shocks, $v_t = 0$, prices are in equilibrium and $dp_t/dt = 0$. The formulation in (26) may usefully be compared with the linear model as expressed in (6). The latter introduces stochastics simply by adding a normally distributed 'disturbance' term to the equilibrium price.

Since it is assumed that p_t and v_t are continuous random variables, it is convenient to express (26) in its stochastic continuous time form, which produces what is known as an Ito process (see Kamien and Schwartz, 1981, pp. 243–4). This can be written as follows:

$$dp_t = -\mu(p_t)\, dt + \sigma(p_t)\, dW_t. \tag{27}$$

In this formulation, $\mu(p_t)$ is the (instantaneous) mean given by (27) and $\sigma^2(p_t)$ is the (instantaneous) variance; the latter is in general also a function of p_t. The term dW_t is equal to $(v_t/\sigma(p_t))\, dt$, where W_t is known as a Wiener process, such that dW_t is distributed as $N(0, dt)$. This represents the continuous time analogue of the normal distribution. For a more formal discussion of the relationship between (26) and (27), see Brock and Malliaris (1982, pp. 67–8).

IV.2. Transitional and stationary distributions

For a given set of structural parameters, the imposition of the above stochastic process implies that p_t is a random variable with density function $f(p_t)$. In view of the fact that the structural parameters themselves may change as a result of changes in any exogenous variables of which the structural parameters are functions, it is necessary to distinguish two types of distribution. First, if in the deterministic form of the model, adjustment of prices towards equilibrium is instantaneous, then the continuous stochastic process described in (27) results in a stable distribution. This can be referred to as a stationary distribution. Secondly, when adjustment is not instantaneous, the process can be regarded as moving through a sequence of transitional distributions before converging to the stationary distribution. It is important to stress that the stationary distribution is in general a function of exogenous variables. By changing the values of the exogenous variables this gives rise to a sequence of transitional distributions which converges to a stationary distribution. If the values of the exogenous variables do not change thereafter, realized observations on p_t will come from this stationary distribution.

This transitional distribution can be examined by considering a shock to the system resulting from an exogenous change in the structural parameters in $\mu(p_t)$. If adjustment is not instantaneous, then over time the process moves through a sequence of temporary equilibria. Associated with each temporary equilibrium is the transitional density of p_t. The dynamics of the process given by (27) are summarized by the Kolmogorov forward equation (see, for example, Cox and Miller, 1984, p. 208):

$$\frac{\partial f_t(p_t)}{\partial t} = \frac{\partial}{\partial p_t}[\mu(p_t)f_t(p_t)] + \frac{1}{2}\frac{\partial^2}{\partial p_t^2}[\sigma^2(p_t)f_t(p_t)]. \tag{28}$$

This is a partial differential equation which defines the transitional density, $f_t(p_t)$, at each point in time. Unfortunately, except for very simple expressions for both the mean and the variance, $\mu(p_t)$ and $\sigma^2(p_t)$, no analytical solution for this partial differential equation exists. The complexity of apparently simple processes is highlighted in Soong (1973). One procedure to overcome this problem is the concept of the stationary density mentioned above, and discussed by Soong (1973, pp. 197–9).

The stationary density represents the stochastic analogue of long-run equilibrium in the deterministic model; see Brock and Malliaris (1982, pp. 106–8). It is possible to derive analytical expressions for the stationary density using general expressions for the mean and the variance. From (28), the stationary density, $f(p_t)$, is found by setting

$$\frac{\partial f(p_t)}{\partial t} = 0. \tag{29}$$

This converts the partial differential equation in (28) to an ordinary differential equation in the stationary density $f(p_t)$ which is independent of time. The general expression for the stationary density is derived as follows. First combine (28) and (29) to get

$$0 = \frac{d}{dp_t} [\mu(p_t)f(p_t)] + \frac{1}{2} \frac{d^2}{dp_t^2} [\sigma^2(p_t)f(p_t)]. \tag{30}$$

Expanding the second term using the product rule, (30) can be rewritten as

$$0 = \frac{d}{dp_t} [\mu(p_t)f(p_t)] + \frac{1}{2} \frac{d}{dp_t} \left[f(p_t) \frac{d\sigma^2(p_t)}{dp_t} + \sigma^2(p_t) \frac{df(p_t)}{dp_t} \right]. \tag{31}$$

Integrating both sides with respect to p_t gives a first-order linear differential equation

$$k = \mu(p_t)f(p_t) + \frac{1}{2} \left[f(p_t) \frac{d\sigma^2(p_t)}{dp_t} + \sigma^2(p_t) \frac{df(p_t)}{dp_t} \right] \tag{32}$$

where k is a constant of integration. Solving for $df(p_t)/dp_t$ gives

$$\frac{df(p_t)}{dp_t} = \frac{2k}{\sigma^2(p_t)} - \left[\frac{2\mu(p) + d\sigma^2(p_t)/dp_t}{\sigma^2(p_t)} \right] f(p_t). \tag{33}$$

Finally, the stationary density is given as the solution of this differential equation:

$$f(p_t) = \exp \left[-\int_0^{p_t} \left(\frac{2\mu(s) + d\sigma^2(s)/ds}{\sigma^2(s)} \right) ds - \eta_t \right] \tag{34}$$

where η_t denotes the appropriate normalizing constant to ensure that $f(p_t)$ qualifies as a density. This density represents the generalized exponential distribution discussed in Section III.

It is also possible to show that the number of modes and antimodes of the density is given by the number of roots of

$$2\mu(p_t) + d\sigma^2(p_t)/dp_t = 0. \tag{35}$$

For the case where the variance is constant, $d\sigma^2(p_t)/dp_t = 0$, the modes and antimodes equal the stable and unstable equilibrium values respectively. In the general case where the variance is not constant, the modes and antimodes are displaced from the equilibrium points by the factor $d\sigma(p_t)/dp_t$. The variance of the process, $\sigma^2(p_t)$, plays an important part in determining the form of the stationary density; see Cobb *et al.* (1983).

The result shown in equation (34) is extremely useful. It can be applied directly to a wide variety of contexts, where the forms of $\mu(p_t)$ and $\sigma^2(p_t)$ are given from basic economic arguments. The way in which it can be applied is perhaps best illustrated by considering a number of examples, and several special cases are therefore discussed in the following section.

V. EXAMPLES OF NONLINEAR MODELS

V.1. *Partial equilibrium analysis*

In order to illustrate how the above results can be used, consider again the special case where the equilibrium price in a partial equilibrium model is given by the root of equation (5). This can be written as $\mu(p_t) = p_t - h_t$, where the variable h_t is understood to be a function of the exogenous variables. Suppose also that the variance is constant, so that $\sigma^2(p_t) = \gamma$. Substituting these assumptions into (34) gives the stationary distribution

$$f(p_t) = \exp\left[-\int_0^{p_t}\left(\frac{2(s-h_t)}{\gamma}\right)ds - \eta_t\right].\tag{36}$$

Integrating and collecting terms gives the result that

$$f(p_t) = \exp\left(\theta_{1,t}p_t + \theta_{2,t}p_t^2 - \eta_t\right)\tag{37}$$

with

$$\theta_{1,t} = 2h_t/\gamma\tag{38}$$

$$\theta_{2,t} = -1/\gamma.\tag{39}$$

Comparison with (10) shows that this stationary distribution corresponds to the familiar normal distribution. Substitution of these assumptions into (35) shows, not surprisingly, that this distribution has just one mode. This example serves to illustrate the link between the linear and nonlinear models: the former is just a special case of the latter.

V.2. *Variance proportional to price*

A modification of the model of the previous subsection is obtained by allowing the variance, $\sigma^2(p_t)$, to be proportional to the price instead of being constant, so that $\sigma^2(p_t) = \gamma p_t$. Substitution into (34) gives

$$f(p_t) = \exp\left[-\int_0^{p_t}\left(\frac{2(s-h_t)+\gamma}{\gamma s}\right)ds - \eta_t\right].\tag{40}$$

The integration of the term in $1/s$ introduces $\log(p_t)$, so that the stationary distribution becomes

$$f(p_t) = \exp\left(\theta_{1,t}\log(p_t) + \theta_{2,t}p_t - \eta_t\right)\tag{41}$$

with

$$\theta_{1,t} = -(1 - 2h_t/\gamma)\tag{42}$$

$$\theta_{2,t} = -2/\gamma.\tag{43}$$

This is the unimodal gamma distribution. The term $\theta_{1,t}$ is a function of the exogenous variables which produce the shifts in the structural equations, while the term $\theta_{2,t}$ depends only on the variance term γ.

V.3. A structural model with multiple equilibria

The previous two examples have involved the linear reduced form of a partial equilibrium structural model. Consider next an exchange model involving two goods, where the demands for these goods at time t, $q_{i,t}^d$ ($i=1, 2$) are assumed to be linear functions of the relative price, where now $p_t = p_{1,t}/p_{2,t}$, such that

$$q_{1,t}^d = a_t - b_t p_t \qquad (44)$$

$$q_{2,t}^d = c_t - d_t p_t^{-1}. \qquad (45)$$

In this formulation, the intercepts and slopes of the two demand curves, $a_t, \ldots, d_t$, are given t subscripts to indicate that they can change over time. Each parameter may be specified as a function of a set of exogenous variables. The fundamental reciprocal demand and supply concept means that only the two demand curves need to be specified. This is in fact a special case of an exchange model which has a long pedigree; see Creedy (1992, 1996). If $q_{2,t}^s$ denotes the supply of good 2 in period t, then

$$p_{1,t}/p_{2,t} = q_{2,t}^s/q_{1,t}^d \qquad (46)$$

so that the supply of good 2 in period t is given by $p_t q_{1,t}^d$. Equating this with the demand for good 2, $q_{2,t}^d$ gives the equilibrium price as the root or roots of

$$b_t p_t^3 - a_t p_t^2 + c_t p_t - d_t = 0. \qquad (47)$$

The reduced form of the model in (47) is thus a cubic, which can have up to three distinct roots. Substitution into (34), with the additional assumption that the variance, $\sigma^2(p_t)$, is constant at γ, gives the result that the equilibrum distribution of the relative price is

$$f(p_t) = \exp\left[-\frac{2}{\gamma} \int_0^{p_t} (b_t s^3 - a_t s^2 + c_t s - d_t)\, ds - \eta_t \right]. \qquad (48)$$

The integration of this expression gives

$$f(p_t) = \exp\left(\theta_{1,t} p_t + \theta_{2,t} p_t^2/2 + \theta_{3,t} p_t^3/3 + \theta_{4,t} p_t^4/4 - \eta_t \right) \qquad (49)$$

where

$$\theta_{1,t} = 2d_t/\gamma \qquad (50)$$

$$\theta_{2,t} = -2c_t/\gamma \qquad (51)$$

$$\theta_{3,t} = 2a_t/\gamma \qquad (52)$$

$$\theta_{4,t} = -2b_t/\gamma. \qquad (53)$$

In this model, shifts in the two demand curves are produced solely by variations over time in the intercepts, a_t and c_t, resulting from changes in the exogenous variables which influence them. Hence the two terms $\theta_{2,t}$ and $\theta_{3,t}$ can also be expressed as the same types of function of the exogenous variables. If the slope coefficients, b_t and d_t, are constant over time, so that $b_t = b$ and $d_t = d$ for all t, then inspection of (50) and (53) shows that the terms $\theta_{1,t}$ and $\theta_{4,t}$ are also constant over time. This is indeed the basic model used to generate the hypothetical data used above, as explained in the Appendix.

It can also be seen by comparison with the previous example that the alternative assumption that the variance term is proportional to the price, so that $\sigma^2(p_t) = \gamma p_t$, leads to what is referred to as a generalized gamma distribution because of the introduction of the term in $\log(p_t)$; see Cobb *et al.* (1983). The number of modes and antimodes of the distribution of relative prices given in (49) is given by the number of roots of (35). It can be shown that the antimode corresponds to the root of (47) which is unstable: see Creedy and Martin (1993).

The fundamental result in (34) can therefore be applied to a large variety of economic models. So far, the discussion has been in terms of time series models, but the approach can also be used in a cross-sectional context; for an application to modelling the distribution of income, see Creedy *et al.* (1996a). If the economic model does not give rise to a convenient polynomial for $\mu(p_t)$, it is usually possible to convert it to a polynomial of appropriate order using an appropriate Taylor series expansion; see Creedy and Martin (1993, pp. 346–7).

VI.   CONCLUSIONS

This paper has introduced an approach to nonlinear modelling which is based on the use of the generalized exponential family of distributions. The considerable flexibility of the approach has been illustrated using hypothetical data based on an economic model which exhibits multiple equilibria for certain periods of time and a unique equilibrium for other periods. It was shown that the distributional analogue of multiple equilibria is multimodality.

An important advantage of this framework is that discrete jumps can be modelled in a natural way without the need for identifying the timing of jumps *ex post*. This is particularly valuable for policy analysis. For example, one of the fundamental exogenous variables of the model may be a policy variable that can be controlled by the government. It is possible that a very small change in such a variable can in some time periods lead to a very large jump in the dependent variable, depending on the values of other exogenous variables. The same type of change in the policy variable may at other times have only a small effect on the dependent variable. Such jumps can be predicted even if they have never been observed during the sample period.

The framework developed in the paper also has the advantage of explaining how smooth changes in market fundamentals can give rise to large and sudden changes in prices, as is characteristic of foreign exchange and stock markets. This result is important as it suggests that when standard economic models break down during stock market crashes, for example, this need not be the result of a misspecification of the variables used to model the market fundamentals, but it may represent the adoption of an incorrect functional form.

The introduction of economic assumptions into nonlinear models has been explained, and it was shown, with the addition of stochastics, how an explicit form for the distribution of the dependent variable can be derived. It is suggested that the approach has considerable potential in a wide variety of economic contexts.

Department of Economics
University of Melbourne

Received February 1995
Final version accepted October 1997

REFERENCES

Barsky, R. B. and De Long, J. B. (1993). 'Why does the stock market fluctuate?' *Quarterly Journal of Economics*, vol. CVIII, pp. 291–311.
Boothe, P. and Glassman, D. (1987). 'The statistical distribution of exchange rates: empirical evidence and economic implications', *Journal of International Economics*, vol. 22, pp. 297–319.
Brock, W. A. and Malliaris, A. G. (1982). *Stochastic Methods in Economics and Finance*. North-Holland, New York.
Cobb, L., Koppstein, P. and Chen, N. H. (1983). 'Estimation and moment recursion relations for multimodal distributions of the exponential family', *Journal of the American Statistical Association*, vol. 78, pp. 124–30.
Cobb, L. and Zacks, S. (1985). 'Applications of catastrophe theory for statistical modelling in the biosciences', *Journal of the American Statistical Association*, vol. 80, pp. 793–802.
Cox, D. R. and Miller, H. D. (1984). *The Theory of Stochastic Processes*. Chapman & Hall, London.
Creedy, J. (1992). *Demand and Exchange in Economic Analysis*. Edward Elgar, Aldershot.
Creedy, J. (1996). *General Equilibrium and Welfare*. Edward Elgar, Aldershot.
Creedy, J., Lye, J. N. and Martin, V. L. (1996a). 'A labour market equilibrium model of the personal distribution of earnings', *Journal of Income Distribution*, vol. 6, pp. 127–44.
Creedy, J., Lye, J. N. and Martin, V. L. (1996b). 'A nonlinear model of the real US/UK exchange rate', *Journal of Applied Econometrics*, vol. 11, pp. 669–89.

Creedy, J. and Martin, V. L. (1993). 'Multiple equilibria and hysteresis in simple exchange models', *Economic Modelling*, vol. 10, pp. 339–47.

Creedy, J. and Martin, V. L. (eds) (1994). *Chaos and Nonlinear Models in Economics*. Edward Elgar, Aldershot.

Fischer, E. O. and Jammernegg, W. (1986). 'Empirical investigation of a catastrophe theory extension of the Phillips curve', *Review of Economics and Statistics*, vol. 68, pp. 9–17.

Friedman, D. and Vandersteel, S. (1982). 'Short-run fluctuations in foreign exchange rates: evidence from the data 1973–79', *Journal of International Economics*, vol. 13, pp. 171–86.

Gennotte, G. and Leland, H. (1990). 'Market liquidity, hedging, and crashes', *American Economic Review*, vol. 80, pp. 999–1021.

Gilmore, R. (1981). *Catastrophe Theory for Scientists and Engineers*. John Wiley, New York.

Hsieh, D. A. (1989). 'Modeling heteroskedasticity in daily foreign-exchange rates', *Journal of Business and Economic Statistics*, vol. 7, pp. 307–17.

Kamien, M. I. and Schwartz, N. L. (1981). *Dynamic Optimization: The Calculus of Variations and Optimal Control in Economics and Management*. North-Holland, New York.

Lim, G. C., Martin, V. L. and Teo, L. (1998). 'Endogenous jumping and asset price dynamics', *Macroeconomic Dynamics*, forthcoming.

Lim, G. C., Lye, J. N., Martin, G. M. and Martin, V. L. (1998). 'The distribution of exchange rate returns and the pricing of currency options', *Journal of International Economics*, forthcoming.

Lye, J. and Martin, V. L. (1993a). 'Robust estimation, non-normalities and generalized exponential distributions', *Journal of the American Statistical Association*, vol. 88, pp. 253–9.

Lye, J. N. and Martin, V. L. (1993b). 'Non-linear time series modelling and distributional flexibility', *Journal of Time Series Analysis*, vol. 15, pp. 65–84.

Mandelbrot, B. B. (1963). 'The variation of certain speculative prices', *Journal of Business*, vol. 36, pp. 394–419.

Martin, V. L. (1990). *Properties and Applications of Distributions from the Generalized Exponential Family*, PhD thesis, Monash University.

Soong, T. T. (1973). *Random Differential Equations in Science and Engineering*. Academic Press, New York.

Tucker, A. L. and Pond, L. (1988). 'The probability distribution of foreign exchange price changes: tests of candidate processes', *Review of Economics and Statistics*, vol. LXX, pp. 638–47.

APPENDIX: GENERATING THE HYPOTHETICAL TIME SERIES

A.1. The model

The basic model used is the exchange model introduced in Section V.3, involving two goods in a general equilibrium context. The feature of the model is that the demands are linear functions of the relative price, p_t, and the reduced form is the cubic equation in (47). It is assumed that the intercepts, a_t and c_t, of the demand curves in equations (44) and

(45), are functions respectively of the exogenous variables x_t and y_t, such that

$$a(x_t) = 3 + 0.25x_t \qquad (A1)$$

$$c(y_t) = 5 + 0.5y_t. \qquad (A2)$$

The slope terms in equations (44) and (45) are, however, assumed to be constant at

$$b = 2 \qquad (A3)$$

$$d = 3. \qquad (A4)$$

It is also assumed that the variance $\sigma^2(p_t)$ in (48) is constant, where

$$\sigma^2(p_t) = \gamma = 2. \qquad (A5)$$

It is also necessary to specify the processes used to generate hypothetical values of the exogenous variables x_t and y_t. The series x_t is generated as

$$x_t = 15 + 1.4t - 0.014t^2 + u_{x,t} \qquad (A6)$$

for $1 \leq t \leq 100$. For $100 < t \leq 200$, t and t^2 on the right-hand side of (A6) are simply replaced by $t - 100$ and $(t - 100)^2$. The error term $u_{x,t}$ is distributed as $N(0, 1)$. The series y_t is generated as

$$y_t = 10 + u_{y,t} \qquad (A7)$$

where $u_{y,t}$ is $N(0, 1)$.

The choice of parameters and specifications of the exogenous variables in the simulation experiment give rise to 24 points in time where the price distribution is bimodal. This results in an unconditional distribution of p_t through temporal aggregation of the data which is unimodal. It has been seen that such an approach can give a misleading indication of the form of the appropriate conditional distributions. The simulation experiments could also be run where the number of points of time for which the conditional distribution is bimodal is increased. This, however, would raise the possibility that the unconditional distribution is also bimodal, which is not typical of actual data.

A.2. Simulation procedure

The above model can be used to provide a simulated price series using an approach known as the 'the inverse cumulative density method'. This involves constructing the cumulative density and using a uniform random number generator. The approach consists of the following steps. First, using the expressions for (A1)–(A5) in (50)–(53), the density function in (49) for the random variable p_t is

$$f(p_t) = \exp\left[3p_t - (5 + 0.5y_t)p_t^2/2 + (3 + 0.25x_t)p_t^3/3 - 2p_t^4/4 - \eta_t\right] \tag{A8}$$

where as before the normalizing constant for each period, η_t, is chosen to ensure that the condition $\int f(p_t)\,dp_t = 1$ is satisfied. Second, a cumulative density is constructed:

$$F(u) = \int_{-\infty}^{u} f(p_t)\,dp_t. \tag{A9}$$

As there is no explicit expression for the cumulative density, it is computed numerically by replacing the integral sign with a summation sign and choosing small steps for dp_t. Third, using the property that the cumulative density is monotonic and starts at zero and ends at unity, a uniform random number generator can be used to generate random numbers for u in (A9) on the interval $[0, 1]$. Associated with each random number u in (A9) is a value for p, which acts as the random price used.

To obtain a time series of p_t for the periods $t = 1, 2, \ldots, 200$, the approach consists of initially setting $t = 1$ in (A8). This amounts to substituting in the realized values of x_1 and y_1 in (A8). By using (A9) with $t = 1$, the realized price p_1 is generated. The time step is incremented to $t = 2$, and the process repeated until the last time step, $t = 200$. Hence at each t the density used to generate the realization of p_t varies as a result of the variation in the values of x_t and y_t when substituted in (A8).

PART II

LABOUR MARKETS

[3]

Bulletin of Economic Research 40:4, 1988, 0307-3378 $2.00

THE ECONOMIC ANALYSIS OF INTERNAL LABOUR MARKETS*

John Creedy and Keith Whitfield

I. INTRODUCTION

The internal labour market (ILM) has attained an established position within the economics literature since its initial development over 30 years ago. This paper reviews the analyses of the ILM which have been undertaken by economists and evaluates the progress made in this area. Limitations of space preclude the examination of non-economic research although some references will be made to work by sociologists and industrial relationists which is relevant to the main themes.

The most frequently cited definition of the ILM was made by Doeringer and Piore, who stated that it is:

> an administrative unit, such as a manufacturing plant, within which the pricing and allocation of labour is governed by a set of administrative rules and procedures. The internal labour market, governed by administrative rules, is to be distinguished from the external labour market of conventional economic theory where pricing, allocating, and training decisions are controlled directly by economic variables (1971, pp. 1-2).

The economic literature on the ILM has concentrated on a number of characteristics which make it distinctive. These are, *inter alia*, high employment stability, the restriction of entry to lower level positions, the filling of higher level positions by internal promotion, a heavy emphasis on seniority in promotion, the according of major importance to internal factors in wage determination and the attachment of wages to jobs rather than workers. Theoretical analysis has concentrated on the forces generating these characteristics and empirical analysis on measuring them.

The ILM raises a number of issues for economic analysis. First, to what extent is the pricing and allocation of labour within firms controlled by non-economic variables? Secondly, to the extent that non-economic vari-

*We would like to thank a referee of this journal for extremely constructive comments on an earlier version of this paper. Helpful suggestions were also made by Mark Casson. Keith Crocker, Richard Disney, Peter Elias, David Shapiro, George Strauss and participants at a seminar at the University of Sydney.

ables are important, what are the implications for economic theory? Thirdly, are the conventional methods of economics appropriate for empirical research on the ILM or is it necessary to develop alternative approaches? The objective of this paper is to outline how economists have responded to such questions.

Major Themes

The importance of the ILM concept is that it suggests that there are significant areas of the labour market where the processes emphasized in the model of wage competition do not operate or operate only to a very limited extent. Economists have responded to this observation in two distinct ways. One group has searched for rationales for the existence of ILMs which utilize concepts from the neoclassical paradigm on which wage competition is based. The result is the development of a model which emphasizes the departure of real world markets from wage competition while indicating that the principles underlying wage competition are sound. A second group is more critical of wage competition and suggests that the real world is so different that a new model is needed for labour market analysis. Central to the debate on whether the ILM is compatible with basic neoclassical principles is the issue of whether it can be explained by economic factors alone or whether it can only be understood by an analysis combining economic, sociological, political and psychological factors. This is a recurring theme in debates between authors from different schools within economics.

Some writers have questioned whether ILMs can be considered as markets at all. For instance, Marsden (1986) argues that ILMs have quite different transaction arrangements to the external labour market and that the use of the market analogy is misleading. An alternative position is held, however, by Blandy and Richardson (1982) who argue that a market exists where willing sellers trade with willing buyers and where there is a mechanism for allocating tasks to persons. On such a definition the ILM is a market although, '. . . labour markets are not like transposed vegetable markets' (1982, p. 1).

The early ILM literature suggested that the formation and character of ILMs reflected the influence of unions. There has, however, been increasing emphasis on the role of management in promoting ILMs as part of a policy to enhance labour productivity. This partly reflects the recognition that ILMs exist in sectors that are not unionized. Contemporaneously it has been argued that unions themselves have contributed to productivity gains at the workplace (Freeman and Medoff, 1979). This further complicates the problem of isolating factors promoting the growth of the ILM.

A major theme concerns the efficiency aspects of the ILM. Much of the early work suggested that ILMs, by introducing rigidities which constrain labour market adjustments, prevent allocative efficiency being achieved and deliberately trade efficiency for equity. However, later work has viewed the ILM as an efficient response to uncertainty in a market containing an idiosyncratic factor of production; the firm's internal market is seen to operate more efficiently than the external market. Other models introduce competitive elements and examine the implications of alternative labour contracts for Pareto efficiency. Nevertheless, some inefficiency is found to exist due, for example, to over-investment by individuals in 'signals' to employers concerning their quality.

A closely related aspect concerns the motivation of workers, although different authors use their own special vocabulary, making precise comparisons difficult. Some stress the 'negative' aspects of moral hazard and the enforcement of compliance with the firm's rules, while others stress more 'positive' aspects whereby individuals identify their own interests in terms of the performance of the enterprise. Despite these differences of emphasis, most authors agree that questions of work effort and motivation are central to the analysis of the ILM and its rationale.

The ILM approach has changed the focus of much labour market analysis. In particular, it has opened the 'black box' of the employing organization which was formerly regarded as the province of industrial sociologists, industrial relationists and organization theorists. It is no longer appropriate for the labour economist to deal with market operations while ignoring the internal workings of employing organizations.

Empirical work on the ILM by economists has been limited and is much less than that undertaken by other social scientists. A major reason for this seems to be the difficulty of applying standard econometric techniques to such a complex institution as the ILM. A related issue concerns the inappropriateness of aggregate data for ILM analysis; this imposes the need for researchers on the ILM to collect their own data. Economists have been more reluctant to undertake data collection than other social scientists and physical scientists. Empirical work has only occasionally been guided by an explicit model and has rarely moved beyond the classification stage towards the testing of the ILM approach against alternative theories.

II. THE ORIGIN AND NATURE OF THE ILM

The ILM concept was developed by economists in the institutionalist tradition. It represents the integration of a wide range of ideas on labour market structure, labour mobility, wage determination and adjustment mechanisms. A common element was a belief that the labour market is so distinctive that the use of the simple price-auction model for theory formulation and policy advice was inappropriate. Consequently institutionalists attempted to develop a more realistic model of the labour market and thought that research should study the distinctive institutions of the labour market so that its idiosyncrasies could be more fully understood. However, much of the early work was descriptive and showed little concern for theoretical issues. The development of the ILM concept was therefore seen as a major step from pure empiricism towards the formulation of a model richer in institutional detail than the wage competition model.

Labour Market Structure

The most important early work was that of Kerr (1951, 1954) who distinguished between two types of labour market — structured and structureless. Structureless markets were defined as those in which there is no attachment between the worker and the employer except the wage; such markets resemble the wage competition model. Structure was seen to occur when rules governing the pricing and allocation of labour are introduced and different treatment is accorded to the 'ins' and 'outs'. Hence a distinction is made between the internal and the external market. Kerr further distinguished between internal markets based on crafts ('guild' markets) and those based on manufacturing plants ('manorial' markets).

Kerr postulated that the admission policies of employers and unions were of key importance in introducing structure into labour markets. Such policies were seen to be more important with regard to the distribution of jobs than in wage setting. This emphasis was later to be fundamental to the theories of job competition. It marks a shift from the emphasis on supply side factors (such as the possession of various attributes by individuals) to the demand side of the market; that is, attention shifts from the market for persons to the market for jobs. It also recognizes that the investment by individuals in the acquisition of desirable characteristics, emphasized by human capital theory, will only be worthwhile to the extent that suitable jobs are available and attainable.

The direction of attention towards rigidity in the distribution of jobs promoted considerable research on the question of how labour markets adjust to changing economic conditions. This has emphasized that labour economists should no longer think in terms of a market in which the characteristics of jobs are simply the outcome of the preferences of their occupants.

Labour Mobility

A building-block of ILM research was the work on labour mobility that raised the question of whether mobility between firms was as prevalent as might be predicted from the wage competition model. Workers were found to exhibit low rates of mobility even when opportunities for advancement existed. The level of inter-firm mobility was deemed insufficient to promote the equalization of net advantages that is central to wage competition. Studies of local labour markets, such as Hunter and Reid (1968), also found workers undertaking similar jobs in different firms, but with very different earnings. Moreover, there seemed to be few processes promoting the elimination of these differences.

Such observations could be explained in a number of different ways, including measurement inaccuracies, imperfect information or worker inertia. However, those who believed that the explanation was more deep-seated directed their attention towards the nature of the employing organization. The major work was by Doeringer and Piore (1971), who explained low mobility by the efforts of employers to reduce turnover because of the presence of skill-specificity; that is, the existence of skills which are only useful in a small range of jobs. The consequence of such skills is that firms draw a distinction between incumbents and otherwise similar workers outside the firm. Rules develop to distinguish between 'ins' and 'outs' and prevent the firm from responding to economic events in the manner predicted by the basic wage competition model. The pricing and allocation of labour is determined by these rules rather than by the external market.

The most important rules are those governing entry and promotion. Skill-specificity is seen to promote the restriction of entry into ILMs to the lower job classifications. The criteria for entry to the lower jobs are con-trolled by management and are free to vary with conditions in the external market. Internal mobility is seen to represent a compromise between promotion by seniority and by ability; it is suggested that the former is more acceptable to the worker and the latter to the employer.

A major insight of Doeringer and Piore's analysis is the notion that the bulk of labour mobility (defined as changes in the nature of jobs under-taken by workers) occurs within the firm rather than as a result of changing firms. In particular, they stress the process of 'osmotic mobility' in which the nature of the tasks undertaken changes gradually. However, when viewed over a long time-span, the accumulation of such changes results in a major change in the type of work undertaken. This type of mobility has major implications for manpower planning and for policies designed to improve the level of skill formation in the labour market.

Wage Determination

The institutional work on wage determination was also important for ILM research. Dunlop (1957) concentrated on the concepts of the job cluster and the wage contour. The former was defined as a stable group of job classifications or work assignments within a firm that have common wage-making characteristics. The latter was defined as a stable group of wage-determining units that have common wage-making characteristics.

Dunlop argued that wages are not determined by suppply and demand in the external market but by processes involving comparisons, both within and between firms, among particular types of job. He suggested that rigidity was introduced into wage determination by formal rules or customs that kept wage relativities within a given job cluster (in a firm) in close alignment. Similarly, the existence of wage contours kept wage relativities between firms in close alignment. In these processes attention focused on key rates within the job clusters; these could be the highest rate in a cluster, the rate paid at the top step in a promotion ladder or the rate paid for a job at which a large number of workers are employed. Wage determination concentrated on fixing key rates and then passing on equivalent wage increases to other rates in the cluster.

Dunlop's work was developed by Doeringer and Piore (1971) who suggested that there are three principal elements of the ILM wage structure: (i) the plant wage level; (ii) the vertical differentiation and (iii) the horizontal differentiation of the wage structure. These are determined by job evaluation techniques, community wage surveys and engineering production standards. Much more emphasis is placed on getting internal relativities correct than ensuring that the plant is in line with others in the local labour market; that is, firms take job evaluation surveys much more seriously than community wage surveys.

Doeringer and Piore postulated that there are three main influences on wage determination. The first is the external labour market, but this simply sets a wide range within which wages must be set. The second influence results from the firm's need to allocate labour. Wage structures must be related to internal promotion lines, acting as a constraint to prevent wages from responding to changes in the external labour market. The third relates to the development of customary relationships within ILMs and the role of wages as an indicator of social status.

Labour Market Adjustment

A persistent theme in the institutional literature has been that the labour market does not adjust according to the wage competition model and, in particular, that the wage is not the principal adjustment mechanism. Emphasis is instead placed on the constraints which prevent the wage from responding to changing conditions and on the alternative adjustment mechanisms used.

A distinction was made by Doeringer and Piore (1971) between 'the more constrained' and 'the less highly constrained' adjustment mechanisms. The 'more constrained instruments' include wages, the job structure and the internal allocative structure — the conventional methods that are the focus of wage competition. Wages are said to be constrained by 'the exigencies of internal allocation and customary law' which cause adjustments in the entry wage to exert a leverage upon all wages in the enterprise and thereby make wage adjustment costly. Changes in the job structure are seen to be dominated by engineers, 'who seldom have direct contact with external market conditions and are only rarely attracted by the problems which such conditions cause' (1971, p. 98). Finally, the degree to which the internal allocative structure is flexible is reduced by the value which the existing structure has to the labour force and the effect of customary law.

The 'less highly constrained instruments' are job vacancies, subcontracting, overtime, recruitment procedures, hiring standards, screening procedures and training. These are regarded as the principal adjustment mechanisms used by firms to obtain a balance between the internal and external labour markets. The major factor determining the adjustment method selected is the relative cost and effectiveness of each.

Efficiency

The institutional literature tended to stress that many labour market structures prevent the attainment of allocative efficiency. To some extent, this reflected a reaction to those orthodox economists who emphasized the efficiency aspects of market processes. It also reflected a view that static Pareto efficiency is rather narrow and that other features of organizations are more important for the development of a high productivity labour market.

Kerr argued that institutional markets 'operate so imprecisely in allocating resources to their most efficient uses and in setting wages' (1951, p. 285). Doeringer and Piore (1971) were, however, less concerned than Kerr to stress the inefficiency aspects of ILMs. They stated that the ILM reflects the employer's interests in allocative efficiency, employee interest in job security and advancement and custom. The first of these is said to relate primarily to the need of employers to reduce training and turnover costs in the presence of skill-specificity. The second and third are seen to reduce the employer's ability to respond to these dictates.[1] The early literature did not examine efficiency in depth, so that direct comparisons with later views are difficult to make.

The Challenge of the ILM

The preliminary work on ILMs was solidly based on empirical research and the experience of policy formulation. However, while presenting a strong challenge to conventional modes of analysis, it failed to produce an alternative theoretical framework that could stand on its own. Doeringer and Piore's contribution brought a disparate literature together and thereby focused attention on the distinctive nature of the employing

---

[1] Doeringer and Piore were ambivalent about efficiency aspects; though stressing the *rigidity* of administrative rules used in the ILM (1971, p. 5), they suggested that rules are capable of 'gradual erosion' despite employees' resistance to change (1971, p. 32; see also 1971, p. 7). They also stated that pay and productivity 'need not be equated in any pay period or on any particular job classification' (1971, p. 89).

organization. Responses to this challenge can be divided into two main types. Neoclassical work has largely concentrated on integrating the ILM into orthodox theory and explaining its existence in terms which are compatible with the key principles of the neoclassical paradigm. This is examined in Section III. An alternative response has been to search for theories which are more broadly based and to develop a model which eschews wage competition. Analyses of this type are considered in Section IV.

III.   NEOCLASSICAL ANALYSES

A theme which clearly emerges from the neoclassical literature is an unwillingness to give up some form of the marginal productivity theory, combined with a strong desire to work in terms of models which imply efficient organizational structures, rather than using frameworks in which efficiency is traded for other characteristics. There seems to be a predominant tendency to see the search for efficient institutions as a driving force in industrial development. Furthermore, there has been an unwillingness to take seriously the concepts of 'power' and 'atmosphere' which have been of concern to sociologists.

In dealing with the ILM, neoclassical economists have concentrated on only a small number of the characteristics which distinguish it from wage competition, such as low turnover, internal promotion and seniority. There is a propensity for analyses to reduce the ILM to a number of constituent parts which are analysed in isolation. This form of reductionism contrasts with the more holistic approaches adopted by institutionalists and radicals.

In recent years the microeconomic analysis of the labour market has witnessed many changes which have involved modification of the wage competition model in an attempt to introduce greater reality. Many of these analyses have not examined internal labour markets directly but have concentrated on phenomena which have been associated with them. Prime examples are the analyses of specific human capital and implicit contract theory. The former suggests that both employers and employees favour long term employment relationships. Employers benefit because of their investment in specific training (in skills which are only useful in that firm) and employees favour it because of the premium they receive over their alternative wage. Implicit contract theory developed to explain the high level of wage rigidity in labour markets. Such rigidity was explained as a result of an understanding between employers and employees that wages would not be reduced in response to falls in the demand for labour. This reduces the riskiness of investment in human capital for employees and is said either to reduce the wage bill of employers or increase the work effort of employees (Okun, 1981).

While the bulk of the neo-classical literature has only indirectly examined the ILM, two related strands have examined it more directly. The most direct analysis is the work of Williamson (1975). This research has variously been called the transaction cost approach or the theory of idiosyncratic exchange. The second type of direct analysis is the more disparate literature on market signalling, selection models and principal/agent analyses.

Transaction Costs

The starting point of the transaction cost approach, originating from Coase (1938), is the question of when it is more efficient to replace market transacting with internal organization. Unlike the institutional approaches Williamson emphasizes the development of procedures to handle transaction costs (Williamson, 1975; Williamson, Wachter and Harris, 1975). He argues that the fundamental feature of labour markets is uncertainty, without which adaptive decision making problems would not be posed (Williamson, 1975, p. 80).

Two basic behavioural assumptions are made. First, individuals are assumed to have 'bounded rationality' (although intendedly rational, they have limited information processing capabilities), making it impossible to construct the complex contracts that would be required to cover all contingencies in the absence of some form of organizational structure. Secondly, workers are assumed to be 'opportunistic'; they would not honestly disclose all the information they have. Williamson suggests that individuals will acquire a monopoly of knowledge regarding their jobs, resulting from 'task idiosyncrasy'. Thus bargaining problems of bilateral monopoly arise. Some alternative to spot market contracting is therefore required, and the ILM is seen as the structure that simultaneously economizes on bounded rationality and weakens opportunism. Williamson (1975, p. 73) views the ILM in terms of a cooperative solution (arising from some sort of social contract) in order to avoid the problems of the individual pursuit of self interest in organizations. Hence restrictions on opportunistic bargaining are recognized to be in the interest of the system as a whole, in which all have a common interest.

One method of reducing such bargaining is to attach wages to jobs rather than individuals, so that small adaptations that are good for the system can be introduced without a great deal of haggling. There are also group pressures on individuals to accept small changes in their job duties when other members are indifferent. The use of low ports of entry into the organization provides an efficient screening device. Internal promotion to senior positions is seen to encourage 'consummate' rather than just 'perfunctory' cooperation from workers, as the interests of workers are tied to those of the system in a continuing way. Their use also means that individuals cannot mislead a number of organizations by moving among firms, and the use of internal promotion has 'experience rating' implications (similar to insurance).

These three characteristics emphasized by the transaction cost minimizing approach are therefore similar to those described in the earlier institutionalist literature. However, Williamson's approach gives the appearance of being based on a more formal economic model; he rejects the suggestion that any elements of ILMs are introduced for reasons of justice rather than efficiency. Furthermore, concepts such as 'power' and 'atmosphere' are not allowed to play any role on the grounds that, unlike transactions, they cannot be 'dimensionalized'. The possible inefficiency aspects of ILMs, mentioned by some of the earlier writers, are denied. Williamson argues that this brings the analysis of the ILM more into the mainstream of economic literature.[2]

In terms of marginal productivity, Williamson (1975, p. 78) suggests that the attachment of wages to jobs means that there is not necessarily a close relation between productivity and pay. The use of internal promotion based on seniority, and the payment of earnings above marginal productivity at higher ages in order to encourage attachment to the organization, introduces a need for compulsory retirement. This type of argument was later formalized by Lazear (1979). He argues that a rising earnings profile, with mandatory retirement, in which earnings exceed the value of the marginal product in later years is desired *ex ante* by workers. This is because the present value of the marginal product and hence pay is higher than otherwise, because of incentives that prevent dismissal and the loss of deferred pay. But workers *ex post* will not actually wish to retire; hence the need for a contract in which retirement is mandatory. Lazear argues that firms will not cheat because of the loss of reputation.

The transaction cost approach to the ILM can be criticized on several grounds. Despite appearances to the contrary, it has not rigorously demonstrated that the three ILM features necessarily result from the basic premises. It has also not clarified precisely the concept of efficiency used; indeed, this is complicated by the recognition of dynamic aspects and the potential importance of conflicts of interests between workers and managers. A further important criticism is that it neglects the problem of moral hazard on the side of employers.

Signalling and Incentives

It has been seen that Williamson placed great stress on uncertainty and the special access to information about their jobs that workers have. However,

---

[2] Williamson and his co-authors Wachter and Harris did, however, overstress the degree to which early writers mentioned inefficiency in explaining ILMs. This is indicated in Piore's response to a paper by Wachter. Piore (1974, p. 684) states, 'I am not arguing that the firm operates inefficiently and certainly not that management fails to minimize cost. However, when tastes and technology are made endogenous to the economy, the term "efficiency", as it is understood in neoclassical theory, loses its meaning'.

there is yet another branch of the literature that takes as its starting point imperfect, and especially asymmetric, information. The fact that the seller of a good has more information about its quality than potential buyers involves the use of various signals. Such signalling involves self-selection processes — whereby the course of action taken by the seller differs according to the quality of the good being sold. It must be unprofitable for low quality sellers to imitate the signals of the higher quality sellers. Despite the somewhat different focus of this literature (for example, no role is allowed for bounded rationality, opportunism and imperfect competition) many contributions have been explicitly concerned with labour markets and have described their results as producing features of ILMs.

An early analysis of signalling in the labour market, by Salop and Salop (1976), involves the self-selection of workers to firms according to their propensity to quit. If firms have a rising earnings profile then only those with low propensities to quit would wish to join, so that where firms have differential turnover costs this type of self-selection provides a better matching of workers to firms. An early example of over-investment in signals was provided by Akerlof's (1976) analysis of a 'rat race' in which workers signal their higher ability by their willingness to work at higher speeds (and ability is judged only by speed). At slower speeds a worker must share the output with workers of lower ability, whereas at higher speeds output is shared with workers of higher ability (but judged to be the same). The result is that lower ability workers select a higher than optimal speed.

One of the most comprehensive models in this tradition is that of Malcomson (1984), who examines a two period contracting system. In this model firms offer contracts in which a specified proportion of workers will be paid a higher wage in the second period. Such 'promotion' is based on a ranking of individuals according to the firm's assessment of performance in the first period. The firm has an incentive to promote those who perform relatively better than others because this provides the greatest incentive for employees to work hard in the first period. This type of contract works where asymmetric information about performance would prevent performance based contracts from being enforceable and, drawing on the literature of repeated games, Malcomson argues that firms cannot afford to lose reputations for keeping to their side of the contract.[3] It is shown that wages rise with seniority by more than productivity.

The approach is of course highly stylized and its links with ILMs are somewhat artificial. For example, the internal promotion gives rise to a horizontal hierarchy rather than one based on authority or autonomy.

---

[3] On reputations, see Carmichael (1984). On competitive ranking procedures, see Nalebuff and Stiglitz (1983) and Rosen (1986). Contractual models are also examined in Holmstrom (1981).

Furthermore, an important feature that distinguishes the model from ILM frameworks is the explicit introduction of competition among workers for a limited number of promotions based on a ranking of performance. This kind of competition was deliberately ruled out by early proponents of ILM theory on grounds that it would hinder the informal process of on-the-job training, involving the sharing of knowledge among workers and internal promotion by seniority. It does seem that neoclassical economists are generally unhappy with incentive devices which do not rely on competition.

The disparate contributions to the signalling/incentive literature have been synthesized and termed efficiency wage models (Akerlof and Yellen, 1986). Efficiency wage models explain why firms find it unprofitable to reduce wages when there is high unemployment. In brief, wage cuts are said to harm productivity and therefore, while they would reduce total labour costs, they may increase labour costs per efficiency unit. This simple hypothesis has been used to explain the rigidity of real wages, the existence of dual labour markets, the payment of differing wages to similar workers and discrimination between distinct groups. While not explicitly mentioned by Akerlof and Yellen, ILMs can be interpreted as institutions which reflect the interdependence of wages and productivity. This interdependence is seen to reflect either the incentive, signalling or turnover problems which are stressed by neoclassical theorists or sociological factors such as group norms based on social conventions and principles of appropriate behaviour (1986, p. 8). The latter have been more fully articulated by economists adhering to the institutional and radical schools of thought.

IV.   ALTERNATIVE APPROACHES

A number of differences emerge between the neoclassical models and those of the alternative schools. The rationales offered for the existence of ILMs are much broader, involving concepts drawn from a range of social sciences. Analyses are much less formal than their neo-classical counterparts, placing more importance on descriptive reality than analytical rigour. The methodology adopted is much more inductive than the deductive, neoclassical approach. Theories are more likely to be developed from observations and inferences made about the general case from specific studies than is the case in neoclassicism. Furthermore, there is an explicit attempt to develop an alternative model of the labour market to wage competition; the main examples are the job competition model and the dual labour market hypothesis. Finally, much emphasis is placed on the motivation of workers, although writers have not compared their arguments with, for example, Williamson's concern with attenuating opportunism or the need expressed by others to design contracts that minimize moral hazard problems. Each strand of the literature has tended to develop its own argot.

A basic divide can be observed between institutionalists and radicals. This mainly relates to the degree to which ILMs are explained as reflections of the dictates of technology on work organization or attempts by employers to gain greater control over the production process. The institutional explanations are firmly grounded in the pluralist tradition of social thought which conceives the employing organization as a coalition of competing interest groups which are kept in equilibrium by management. The radical explanations are linked to Marxian theory and view the structure of the labour market as reflecting the conflict between the owners of capital and the suppliers of labour power; management is seen as representing the interests of capital owners rather than simply as organizers.

Institutional Analyses of the ILM

The institutional analysis of the ILM has been most fully developed by Doeringer and Piore (1971). The main elements of their early work were summarized in Section II. They discussed several rationales for the existence and character of ILMs including employer attempts to reduce turnover in the presence of specific training, worker pressure to enhance job stability and the development of custom and practice in the workplace. In contrast with the neoclassical theorists, Doeringer and Piore accorded a role to unions in the establishment of labour market structure. However, it can be argued that they failed to establish the relative importance of the various factors.

While Doeringer and Piore's analysis has much in common with that of neoclassical theorists, a crucial difference is the rejection of the notion that the labour market works even remotely like a wage competition model. A consequence of this difference is the rejection of that model for manpower analysis and support for the dual labour market hypothesis. This hypothesis argues that the labour market can be divided into two sectors — a primary sector composed of 'good' jobs and a secondary sector composed of 'bad' jobs. Some formulations make a distinction between an upper and lower tier in the primary sector. The primary sector is seen to consist of a series of well-developed ILMs (Doeringer and Piore, 1971, p. 167). Secondary jobs are those outside ILMs, those in poorly developed ILMs (that is, possessing formal internal structures but many entry ports, short mobility clusters and unpleasant/low-paying work) and those in well-developed ILMs but not attached to formal promotion lines. It is suggested that secondary jobs occur because employers have little incentive to reduce turnover, because of the technical aspects of the job or because the labour force places little value on job security. This model is based on a great deal of rigidity in the job structure and suggests that there are few competitive processes to eradicate qualitative differences between jobs. Indeed, it has been argued that these differences are intensified; those in 'bad' jobs acquire behavioural traits such as lateness and absenteeism which make it increasingly difficult for them to move into 'good' jobs. In more recent work Piore (1979) has offered a more general explanation for the emergence of dualism which suggests that the differing characteristics of jobs primarily reflect the cognitive processes inherent in them. Jobs where a clear understanding must be made between ends and means are seen to generate employment characteristics similar to those in the upper tier of the primary sector. Those involving more routine thought processes are linked to the lower primary sector. All other jobs are located in the secondary sector.

Thurow (1975) also locates the development of the ILM in on-the-job training but, in contrast to Doeringer and Piore, the key link is the willingness of workers to transmit their knowledge to newcomers. The essence of Thurow's hypothesis is that the bulk of training occurs on the job and that it is crucial for employing organizations to maximize the acquisition of skills. It is argued that unless employers suppress wage and employment competition, workers will fear that the transmission of their knowledge will generate an increase in competition for their jobs. This will result in decreased job security and the undermining of their bargaining positions. Wage and employment competition which is postulated to promote labour market efficiency in the neoclassical model, is therefore seen by Thurow to give workers an incentive to hoard knowledge. He concludes that:

> the types of wage and employment competition that are the essence of efficiency in simple, static neoclassical models may not be the essence of efficiency in a dynamic economy where the primary function of the labour market is to allocate individuals to on-the-job training ladders and where most learning occurs in work-related contexts (1975, p. 84).

The job competition model therefore emphasizes quantity adjustment rather than wage adjustment. It not only draws on the ILM literature but also on the screening hypothesis which developed as a critique of human capital theory. Thurow contends that there are sectors of the labour market in which workers compete for jobs on the basis of background characteristics rather than relative wages. Within these sectors workers are ranked for available jobs according to their expected training costs; this ranking forms a 'labour queue'. The characteristics of applicants for entry level jobs (such as age, sex, IQ, education) are used as proxies for trainability; work experience is used to rank applicants for higher level jobs. Those at the top of the labour queue obtain the best jobs and those at the bottom obtain either the worst jobs or none at all. It should be stressed that Thurow is less dismissive of the principles of wage competition than Doeringer and Piore. First, he accepts the notion of competition in the process of labour allocation, although for jobs rather than for wages. Secondly, he suggests that those sectors not subject to job competition operate in a manner similar to wage competition.

Radical Analyses

A more far-reaching approach has been developed by radical economists. Edwards (1975), for example, has contended that firms established ILMs to prevent the development of class consciousness among workers and to allow employers to maintain control over the production process. The ILM is therefore said to maximize the amount of labour (effort expended in production) obtained from a given amount of labour power (the capacity to perform useful work). This requires bureaucratic control, involving the development of formal definitions for the direction of work tasks and the use of institutionalized power to enforce compliance. Thus work habits become consistent with the form of bureaucratic control rather than with the actual work tasks.

Edwards distinguishes three principal modes of compliance. The first is 'rules orientation' in which workers are made aware of the rules and are expected to follow them in an unambiguous manner. A more sophisticated form of control is based on the encouragement of habits of predictability and dependability; workers are expected to perform their tasks according to the spirit rather than the letter of work criteria. The most sophisticated form of control involves the internalization of the enterprise's goals and values; the worker is encouarged to be loyal, committed and thus self-directed.

The generation of these behavioural characteristics is said to involve both the firm's hiring and firing policy and the use of differential internal promotion. Potential rules orientation is an important determinant of whether or not a person is hired and career ladders are designed to foster and reward dependability and/or the internalization of the firm's goals.

This bureaucratic control hypothesis has been subject to considerable criticism by other writers in the radical tradition, who view employers as acting not as a class but as individuals in a competitive environment. Furthermore, Edwards sees labour force homogenization as a problem for employers, whereas others argue that it is most threatening to the bargaining position of workers. Some radical theorists suggest that the ILM results from the defensive reaction of organized workers to employer efforts to de-skill the workforce. Such action could take the form of union-organized apprenticeship schemes or promotion based on seniority. The theory suggests that the most effective tactic for workers is to differentiate themselves from potential competitors. This could involve the maintenance of skill status long after the original skill divisions become irrelevant. Hence Rubery (1980, p. 260) has argued that 'the existence of a structured labour force, where jobs are strictly defined, and workers are not interchangeable, provides a bargaining base for labour against management's attempts to increase productivity and introduce new technology'.

Most radical analyses have used the concept of labour market segmentation, which is a development of the dual labour market hypothesis. The distinction between the primary and secondary sectors and the upper and lower tiers of the primary sector are common to both. Major differences involve the explanation offered for the development of ILMs (as noted above) and in the precise nature of labour market segmentation. In particular, segmentation theorists emphasize that racial minorities and women are confined to the poorer jobs within any sector of the market.

V.   EMPIRICAL STUDIES

The ILM has not given rise to a large amount of empirical work by economists, particularly those working in the neoclassical tradition. A major problem is that the literature has not provided a framework for the empirical analysis of ILMs and the testing of its features against particular alternative models. In comparing models, Doeringer and Piore argued that:

> The requisite measures of neoclassical economic variables are unavailable at the microeconomic level, and the administrative rules which control internal labour markets in practice cannot be defined with sufficient precision to permit quantitative testing of their compatibility. As a result, the case for the internal labour market must rest on less satisfactory heuristic evidence (1971, p. 5).

Although Doeringer and Piore made some suggestions for a more heuristic procedure, requiring information from individual firms, research generally has not moved beyond taxonomy and general description and only on limited occasions can it be said to have gone beyond the classification stage.

It would be unfair, however, to criticize only ILM theorists for a failure to carry out appropriate data collection and empirical work. The same is true of a great deal of economic research and is particularly true of research in the same general area as ILM research. A prime example is work on the question of why the earnings profile rises with experience. Most analyses of this phenomenon have postulated a close relation between productivity and earnings, particularly the human capital approach. However, there are few direct attempts to test the theory.[4]

The ILM poses special problems for empirical analysis. First, it is a complex phenomenon which cannot be reduced to a small number of measures. Secondly, its characteristics have been shown to vary considerably across space and time in a manner that is not readily understandable. Thirdly, many of its principal dimensions are longitudinal in nature and cannot be analysed using cross-sectional data. The major consequence of these problems is that the types of data normally used by economists are

---

[4] The extent to which the firm specific human capital approach implies a wage profile that rises faster than productivity is examined by Carmichael who states that the derived wage profile 'corresponds closely to those we observe' (1983, p. 251); yet no empirical work is reported.

not useful for ILM research. In particular, ILM research requires that researchers collect their own data. However, this is not common among economists, although it is more common in sociology and industrial relations, where the bulk of the empirical work on the ILM has been undertaken.[5] Leontief (1983, p. viii) pointed out that only 0.8 and 1.4 per cent of articles published in the *American Economic Review* from 1972 to 1976 and from 1977 to 1981 respectively contained analyses based on data generated by the author's initiative.

Types of Approach

Empirical research on the ILM has generally adopted three main types of approach. The first involves the analysis of highly aggregative data; the second is based on case studies of particular firms and industries, using data collected specially by researchers; the third type concentrates on the analysis of career histories, usually of particular occupational groups.

Studies which use highly aggregative data can at most offer a broad description of the distribution of ILMs across industries, occupations or regions. They usually concentrate on one element of the ILM, typically the low turnover rate, and use it as a classification device. The prime example of this approach is by Alexander (1974), who divides industries into Kerr's trichotomy of unstructured, manorial and guild on the basis of their inter-firm mobility rates. A manorial industry is arbitrarily defined as having less than 10 per cent per year; a guild industry has a value of inter-firm minus inter-industry mobility of more than 10 per cent per year; an unstructured industry is a non-guild industry in which inter-firm mobility is more than 20 per cent per year.[6]

The major problem with such highly aggregative work is that it is so arbitrary. It largely concentrates on the turnover rate, to the exclusion of other aspects such as internal promotion, the use of non-wage adjustment mechanisms and the emphasis on internal considerations in wage-fixing. This is mainly due to the failure of aggregate data to relate to these factors. The case study approach is more appropriate and can provide detailed pictures where large-scale simplification can be misleading, suggest hypotheses which may not emerge from deductive reasoning and provide orders of magnitude for details which cannot be isolated in aggregative analysis (Blandy and Richardson, 1982). The major problem with case-studies is that their results do not necessarily have general applicability.

Case-studies have generally concentrated on examining whether employing organizations exhibit the characteristics ascribed to ILMs.

---

[5] Medoff and Abraham (1981, p. 215) note that, 'Unlike physical scientists, economists typically are not involved in the collection of the data they use, and, unlike other social scientists, economists usually avoid having contact with their unit of observation'.

[6] Osterman (1984) also stresses the ILM's low turnover rate. A recent such study is Collier and Knight (1985).

Mace (1979), for example, surveyed engineers in 12 firms and attempted to establish whether the firms had low turnover-rates, entry ports at the lower level jobs, a preference for current employees in filling vacancies, well-developed mobility clusters, and a willingness of firms to provide general training. He also examined whether salary differentials existed between firms employing similar types of labour over long periods and the relative importance of Doeringer and Piore's 'less constrained' adjustment mechanisms. Nowak and Crockett (1983) studied three large organizations in Western Australia in order to 'gain detailed information on the structure and dynamic responses in the labour market of particular firms and to investigate the interaction of this and employee career patterns' (1983, p. 448). The standard technique for undertaking such a case study has been to conduct a series of interviews of personnel managers and to supplement this with information obtained from company records and/or employee questionnaires. The information obtained provides a detailed picture of how firms organize their workforces and how they adjust to changing economic conditions.

A more direct attempt to address economic issues can be found in ILM orientated research using the career history method. It usually involves the replacement of the assumptions of human capital theory by an empirical analysis of the *process* of mobility within organizations. Nowak and Crockett (1983) sent questionnaires to staff in the three large organizations mentioned earlier. Creedy and Whitfield (1986, 1988) used retrospective surveys of professional scientists who are members of national scientific institutes. The questionnaires elicited information which could be used to measure both internal job mobility and the phenomenon which Doeringer and Piore termed osmotic mobility. The latter is essentially the result of gradual changes in the nature of the work performed and can be measured by the extent of changes in job duties taking place within the same job.

A problem with the career history approach is the difficulty involved in obtaining accurate information. First, accurate yet widely applicable classifications need to be developed for comparing jobs. Secondly, information must be collected relating to a long period of time, so that retrospective work histories are usually involved. Thirdly, some of the key concepts of ILM theory are extremely difficult to measure; for example, the measurement of osmotic mobility depends crucially on worker perceptions.

The Main Empirical Results

While the empirical research on ILMs is limited, it has produced a number of important results. Indeed, many of the features stressed in the ILM literature have been shown to exist across a wide range of occupations, industries and regions; the evidence suggests that many workers are employed under ILM conditions. It has also been shown that ILM structures are considerably more complex and wide-ranging than earlier writers suggested.

Low turnover rates have been found in many sectors and occupations.[7] Steinberg (1974) found that approximately half of US workers were with the same firm in 1970 as in 1965 and that lengthy attachment was greatest for higher income earners and older workers. The restriction of entry to lower levels of job classifications has been shown to be very common. Mace (1979) found that the average age of entry into nine of the firms surveyed was 25 or below and for the other three it was below 30. Nowak and Crockett (1983) found that the lowest job classification was the entry point for the majority of employees of the firms studied. Osterman (1984) found that the restriction of entry to the lower job classifications varied considerably between occupations. Managerial jobs were unlikely to be entered above the lower classifications but computer programming and clerical jobs were most likely to be entered at higher levels. Sales positions were situated between the two types.

The filling of upper level positions by internal promotion has been shown to be a very common practice. Mace (1979) found that every firm in his survey preferred internal to external appointments and that in 11 firms 90 per cent of promotions went to internal candidates. This pattern was explained as resulting from the need to maintain morale, provide a career pattern for new recruits and to appoint engineers with known and relevant experience. Nowak and Crockett (1983) also found a strong preference for internal promotion, although the emphasis placed on it varied considerably between firms. Internal mobility has also been shown to be important for the upward mobility and earnings of professional chemists. Almost 60 per cent of the upward changes of responsibility level reported in Creedy and Whitfield (1986) were made within the same organization and the majority were made within the same job, confirming the importance of osmotic mobility. Furthermore, it was shown that the experience of internal mobility is a key determinant of earnings.

A number of researchers have identified the existence of job clusters along the lines suggested by Doeringer and Piore. Mace (1979) found that 10 of the 12 firms surveyed had elaborate job description schemes and that all 12 had some job description scheme. Osterman (1984) found that movement between job ladders was relatively easy at the entry position but less so at higher levels, although the degree of upper level openness seems to vary between occupations, largely depending on the technical nature of the skills used.

The empirical research has also shown that wages are tied to jobs within ILMs and that they are not very responsive to changing labour market con-

---

[7] On low turnover in the US see Hall (1982); for Australia see Foster and Gregory (1983, p. 130) and Nowak and Crockett (1983); for UK engineers see Mace (1979, p. 55); for UK and Australian chemists see Whitfield (1982, p. 163) and Whitfield (1981).

ditions. Mace (1979, p. 57) found that, 'in setting salaries within firms, attention was primarily directed to fitting the hierarchy of salaries to the hierarchy of jobs. This was usually legitimized through job evaluation, and once the hierarchy was set it was not possible for firms to move outside the relevant salary band for a job'. Furthermore, Osterman (1984) and Nowak and Crockett (1983) found that firms operating ILMs exhibited rigid salary structures but showed a great deal of flexibility in moving workers between jobs at differing points on the classification: that is, the wages for workers were more flexible than the wages for jobs.

The ILM research has also complemented research on labour market adjustment and, in particular, has indicated that the wage competition model is at variance with reality. The key finding is that wages represent a highly constrained adjustment mechanism. Such a conclusion was reached by Mace (1979), Nowak and Crockett (1983) and by more general labour market analyses by Thomas and Deaton (1977) and Blandy and Richardson (1982). Moreover, a number of firms in Mace's study said that they would curtail production rather than use one of the adjustment mechanisms emphasized in competitive theory.

VI. CONCLUSIONS

As suggested in the introduction to this paper, the ILM has raised three principal questions for economic analysis. These concern the relevance of non-economic factors, their implications for economic theory and the possible need to develop alternative empirical approaches.

Economists are divided on the first question; some stress economic determinants and others a mixture of economic and non-economic determinants. However, even those stressing economic factors have utilized ideas and concepts which were formerly the province of non-economic disciplines such as sociology, organizational behaviour and industrial relations. In particular, the ILM has prompted economists to examine more closely questions of work effort and motivation and to recognize that labour is a qualitatively different factor of production from capital.

The main differences between economists in their rationales for the ILM relate to their analysis of efficiency. Neoclassical theorists tend to see the ILM as an efficiency-orientated response to the idiosyncrasies of labour as a factor of production. The ILM is the institution which equates wages and marginal productivity in a situation where market pressures would be insufficient to do so. Institutionalists question whether the neoclassical concept of efficiency is appropriate in a setting in which wages and productivity are interdependent and where social factors influence both. They emphasize a broader notion of efficiency which incorporates social, political and psychological factors as well as economic. Radicals question whether the concept of efficiency is as value-free as the other schools suggest. They suggest that efficiency is defined so as to be identical to the interests of capital and therefore it is an instrument which is used in the capital/labour conflict.

The recognition of non-economic determinants of the ILM (or, at least, a wider range of economic determinants) has evoked a mixed response from economists in terms of theory construction. Neoclassicists have suggested the ILMs slow down the basic processes which are outlined in the wage competition model but that the model when modified is still applicable. Institutionalists have searched for alternative models, such as job competition and dual labour markets, but have not been able to convince the bulk of economists of the utility of these constructs. Radicals view the ILM as confirming the superiority of an economic model grounded in Marxian rather than neoclassical concepts. The ILM has thus simply re-oriented the debate between the schools of thought.

Developing out of the institutionalist tradition, the ILM might have been expected to have had its major impact on the methods used in empirical analysis. Paradoxically, this is the area in which the least development has taken place. The ILM poses serious questions for the appropriateness of conventional economic methods based on highly aggregated data sets. These questions have, however, been ignored by most economists, who have either failed to undertake empirical work on the ILM or have adopted conventional and inappropriate methods. There is a need for economists to undertake detailed and disaggregated research on the relationship between the ILM and the traditional concerns of economics, such as wage determination, the distribution of earnings and employment change. To date, the ILM has been more thoroughly researched at the empirical level by non-economists.

University of Melbourne   *Invited paper, received January 1988*
and
Institute for Employment Research,
University of Warwick/University of Sydney

REFERENCES

Akerlof, G. (1976). 'The Economics of Caste and of the Rat-race and other Woeful Tales', *Quarterly Journal of Economics*, Vol. XC, pp. 599, 617.
Akerlof, G. and Yellen, J. (1986). *Efficiency Wage Models of the Labor Market*. Cambridge; C.U.P.
Alexander, A. J. (1974). 'Income, Experience and the Structure of Internal Labor Markets', *Quarterly Journal of Economics*, Vol. 88, pp. 63–86.

Blandy, R. J. and Richardson, S. (eds.) (1982). *How Labour Markets Work.* Melbourne; Longman Cheshire.

Carmichael, H. L. (1983). 'Firm Specific Human Capital and Promotion Ladders', *Bell Journal of Economics*, Vol. 14, pp. 251–8.

Carmichael, H. L. (1984). 'Reputations in the Labor Market', *American Economic Review*, Vol. 74, pp. 713–25.

Coase, R. H. (1937). 'The Nature of the Firm', *Economica*, Vol. 4, pp. 386–405.

Collier, P. and Knight, J. B. (1985). 'Seniority Payments, Quit Rates and Internal Labour Markets in Britain and Japan', *Oxford Bulletin of Economics and Statistics*, Vol. 47, pp. 19–32.

Creedy, J. and Whitfield, K. (1986). 'Earnings and Job Mobility: Professional Chemists in Britain', *Journal of Economic Studies*, Vol. 13, pp. 23–37.

Creedy, J. and Whitfield, K. (1988). 'Job Mobility and Earnings: An Empirical Analysis Using the Internal Labour Market Approach', *The Journal of Industrial Relations*, Vol. 30, pp. 100–17.

Doeringer, P. B. and Piore, M. (1971). *Internal Labor Markets and Manpower Analysis.* Lexington; D. C. Heath.

Dunlop, J. T. (1957). 'The Task of Contemporary Wage Theory'. in Taylor, G. W. and Pierson, G. W. (eds.), *New Concepts in Wage Determination*, New York; McGraw-Hill, pp. 117–39.

Edwards, R. C. (1975). 'Industrial Traits and Organizational Incentives: What Makes a Good Worker?' *Journal of Human Resources*, Vol. 11, pp. 51–68.

Foster, W. F. and Gregory, R. G. (1983). 'A Flow Analysis of the Labour Market in Australia', in Blandy, R. J. and Covick, O. (eds.), *Understanding Labour Markets*, Sydney; George Allen and Unwin, pp. 111–36.

Freeman, R. and Medoff, J. (1979). 'The Two Faces of Unionism', *Public Interest*, Vol. 57, pp. 69–93.

Hall, R. E. (1982). 'The Importance of Lifetime Jobs in the U.S. Economy', *American Economic Review*, Vol. 72, pp. 716–24.

Holmstrom, B. (1981). 'Contractual Models of the Labor Market', *American Economic Review*, Vol. 71, pp. 308–13.

Hunter, L. C. and Reid, G. L. (1968). *Urban Worker Mobility.* Paris; Organisation for Economic Cooperation and Development.

Kerr, C. (1951). 'Labor Markets; Their Character and Consequences', *American Economic Association. Papers and Proceedings*, Vol. 40, pp. 278–91.

Kerr, C. (1954). 'The Balkanization of Labor Markets', in Bakke, E. W. (ed.), *Labour Mobility and Economic Opportunity*, Cambridge; The MIT Press, pp. 92–110.

Lazear, E. P. (1979). 'Why is There Mandatory Retirement?' *Journal of Political Economy*, Vol. 87, pp. 1261–84.

Lazear, E. P. (1981). 'Agency, Earnings Profiles, and Productivity and Hours Restrictions', *American Economic Review*, Vol. 71, pp. 601–20.

Leontief, W. (1983). 'Foreword', in Eichner, A. S. (ed.), *Why Economics is Not Yet A Science*, London; Macmillan, pp. vii–xi.

Mace, J. (1979). 'Internal Labour Markets for Engineers in British Industry', *British Journal of Industrial Relations*, Vol. 17, pp. 50–63.

Malcomson, J. M. (1984). 'Work Incentives, Hierarchy, and Internal Labour Markets', *Journal of Political Economy*, Vol. 92, pp. 486–507.

Medoff, J. L. and Abraham, K. G. (1981) 'Are Those Paid More Really More Productive/ The Case of Experience', *Journal of Human Resources*, Vol. 16, pp. 186–216.

Nalebuff, B. J. and Stiglitz, J. E. (1983). 'Prizes and Incentives: Towards a General Theory of Compensation and Competition', *Bell Journal of Economics*, Vol. 14, pp. 21–43.

Nowak, M. J. and Crockett, G. V. (1983). 'The Operation of Internal Labour Markets: Three Case Studies', *Journal of Industrial Relations*, Vol. 25, pp. 445–64.

Okun, A. M. (1981). *Prices and Quantities: A Macroeconomic Analysis*. Oxford; Basil Blackwell.

Osterman, P. (ed.) (1984). *Internal Labour Markets*. London; The MIT Press.

Piore, M. J. (1979). *Unemployment and Inflation: Institutionalist and Structural Views*. White Plains, NY; Sharpe.

Piore, M. J. (1974). 'Comments and Discussion', *Brookings Papers in Economic Activity*, Vol. 3, pp. 684–8.

Rosen, S. (1986). 'Prizes and Incentives in Elimination Contracts', *American Economic Review*, Vol. 76, pp. 701–15.

Rubery, J. (1980). 'Structural Labour Markets, Worker Organization and Low Pay', in Amsden, A. H. (ed.), *The Economics of Women and Work*, Harmondsworth; Penguin, pp. 242–70.

Salop, J. and Salop, S. (1976). 'Self-selection and Turnover in the Labor Market', *Quarterly Journal of Economics*, Vol. XC, pp. 619–27.

Steinberg, E. (1974). 'Upward Mobility in the Internal Labour Market', *Industrial Relations*, Vol. 15, pp. 259–65.

Thomas, B. and Deaton, D. (1977). *Labour Shortage and Economic Analysis*. Oxford; Basil Blackwell.

Thurow, L. C. (1974). *Generating Inequality*. London; Macmillan.

Whitfield, K. (1981). 'The Job Mobility of Professional Chemists in Australia and Britain', *Chemistry in Australia*, Vol. 48, pp. 277–82.

Whitfield, K. (1982). *Occupational Labour Market Structures*. D. Phil. thesis (Oxford).

Williamson, O. E. (1975). *Markets and Hierarchies*. New York; Free Press.

Williamson, O. E., Wachter, M. L. and Harris, J. E. (1975). 'Understanding the Employment Relation: The Analysis of Idiosyncratic Exchange', *The Bell Journal of Economics*, Vol. 61, pp. 250–80.

[4]

Models of Trade Union Behaviour: A Synthesis*

JOHN CREEDY and IAN M. McDONALD

University of Melbourne,
Parkville, Victoria 3052

In this paper, the following four models of wage determination by trade unions, namely simple monopoly, wage-bargaining (or 'right to manage'), efficient bargains and insider-dominated, are placed within a single framework. It is shown that the pattern of wage behaviour is the same in each of the four models. It is also shown that when taxation is introduced the impact on wages of changes in marginal and average rates of tax is similar across the models.

I Introduction

In recent years the analysis of trade union behaviour has been seen as a fertile field for economic research. Surveys include Oswald (1985), Farber (1986), Ulph and Ulph (1990) and Nickell (1990). There has also been much stress on the importance of taxation in the decision-making of individuals, firms and trade unions. The aim of this paper is to offer a synthesis of several models of trade union behaviour and then to show how taxation can be fitted into the synthesis.

The literature on trade unions has emphasized the following four questions. First, do trade unions bargain with firms over wages or over wages and employment? Second, is the allocation of jobs to trade union members determined by a random process or by a seniority-based process? Third, are trade union decisions determined by majority voting or by maximizing the total welfare of all members? The fourth question, related to the third, asks whether trade union decisions are dominated by insiders (especially the employed) or whether the interests of outsiders (especially unemployed members) are taken into account? In this paper, four models of wage determination which capture alternative answers to these four questions are placed within a single framework. It will be seen that the pattern of wage behaviour, in particular the qualitative relation between wages and the exogenous variables, is the same in each of the four models. Furthermore it will be seen that when taxation is introduced the impact on wages of

changes in marginal and average rates of tax is similar across the models. Thus, for wage determination, it does not make much difference whether bargaining is over wages or wages and employment, whether jobs are allocated randomly or by seniority, whether trade union decisions are determined by a median voter or the entire membership, and whether insiders alone or insiders and outsiders determine union decisions.

While the synthesis covers a variety of assumptions made by different writers, there are omissions which should be noted. Assumptions of uncertain demand and asymmetric information about the firm's revenue function are not examined. Given the result shown below, that the position of the revenue function does not have an influence on wages independent of its curvature, the omission of uncertainty is not serious. This paper also ignores bargaining over the size of the capital stock, as for example in Grout (1984), bargaining over hours of work and bargaining situations involving several unions or several firms: see for example Ulph and Ulph (1990). However, from results based on these assumptions it seems unlikely that their inclusion would overturn the relations between wages and the exogenous variables stressed below.

The impact of taxation on trade union wage demands is frequently discussed in public debates over economic policy. However this concentration of interest has not been matched in the literature on the economic analysis of trade unions. Furthermore where the literature does address

346

issues involving the influence of taxation on union wages, a highly restrictive approach in which post-tax real wages are held constant is often adopted. See Nickell (1990), McDonald (1984), Corden and Dixon (1980), Corden (1981) and Pitchford (1981). The present paper derives the relations between union wages and average and marginal rates of tax. Because the analysis synthesizes a variety of different assumptions about union behaviour, the derived relations have a high degree of generality.

The outline of the paper is as follows. Section II presents two alternative specifications of a trade union's objective function. This is followed in Section III by an examination of four basic methods of modelling the wage determination process. The implications of the four models are then compared in Section IV. Comparisons are made for completely general functional forms and for constant elasticity revenue and utility functions. The effects of taxation within each model are examined in Section V. Conclusions are given in Section VI.

II The Union's Objective

The theory of the economic behaviour of a trade union is based on the idea that the union aims to maximize an objective function, usually based on the utility of a group of members. With some exceptions, for example Ashenfelter and Johnson (1969) and Borland (1985), a separate utility function for the leaders of the union is not included. Usually it is assumed that the members have identical utility functions and market opportunities, although in the median voter model of Booth (1984) and Grossman (1983) members are heterogeneous. In the present paper the members of the group are assumed to have identical tastes and market opportunities.

A Trade-off Between Employment and Wages

In McDonald and Solow (1981) the group for whom the union's objective function applies is a pool of labour which generally exceeds those workers currently employed; it includes both employed and unemployed individuals. To specify the union's objective it is useful to follow the proposal of Layard and Nickell (1990) which applies the concepts of bargaining theory in Bishop (1964) and Binmore, Rubinstein and Wolinsky (1986) to the trade union and firm bargain. The union consists of m members. At the time of bargaining, n_0 are employed at the firm. The remaining $(m - n_0)$ are engaged in the best

alternative to working at the firm, from which they receive a utility flow of $\bar{U}$. This alternative allows people to resume work at the firm if a job becomes available for them after a bargain is made. The alternative could be subsisting on unemployment benefits or working in a job which is considered inferior to working in the firm. After bargaining, the wage at the firm is w and the level of employment is n. In view of the partial equilibrium nature of the analysis in this paper, nominal values may be regarded as equivalent to real values. The $(m - n)$ members who fail to gain employment at the firm then turn to alternative activities from which they receive a utility flow of U. These alternative activities may involve a period on unemployment benefits and then employment in an alternative job. Layard and Nickell (1990) implicitly assume that $U = \bar{U}$. Given this framework, the union's utility is, after bargaining:

$$W = n\{U(w) - D\} + (m - n)U \quad \text{for } n \le m \quad (1)$$

and $W = m\{U(w) - D\}$ for $n > m$

where D measures the disutility of work and $U( )$ is the concave utility function of each member. If bargaining breaks down then there is no employment at the firm and if s represents strike income, the utility level to the union is $\bar{W}$, and is given by:

$$\bar{W} = n_0 U(s) + (m - n_0) \bar{U}. \quad (2)$$

It is useful to define $U(x) = U + D$, where x may be called 'layoff pay'; it refers to the income equivalent of not being employed by the firm after the completion of negotiations plus the disutility of work. By subtracting (2) from (1), the net payoff to the union is:

$$W - \bar{W} = n\{U(w) - U(x)\} + m(U - \bar{U}) - n_0[\bar{U} - U(s)]. \quad (3)$$

It simplifies the subsequent analysis to assume that $m(U - \bar{U}) - n_0(\bar{U} - U(s)) = 0$. This expression is zero under the Layard and Nickell (1990) assumption that $U = \bar{U} = U(s)$. However, it is reasonable to suppose that U, the alternative utility to that gained from union employment in the firm exceeds, after the bargain, $\bar{U}$, the alternative utility to union employment before the bargain is made. Furthermore, $\bar{U}$ probably exceeds $U(s)$, the utility enjoyed when on strike. The pattern $U > \bar{U} > U(s)$ is consistent with $m(U - \bar{U}) - n_0(\bar{U} - U(s)) = 0$, so the simplifying assumption is not unreasonable. Making this assumption the net payoff to the union becomes simply the first term on the right-hand side of (3), that is, $n\{U(w) - U(x)\}$.

With the objective function given by (1), employment is traded for wages. The marginal rate of substitution between employment and wages, $MRS_{n/w}$ is obtained by total differentiation of $n\{U(w) - U(x)\}$ and is given by:

$$MRS_{n/w} = \frac{-dw}{dn} = \frac{w}{n\epsilon} \qquad (4)$$

where ϵ is the elasticity of the excess utility from work with respect to the wage, defined by:

$$\epsilon = \frac{wU'(w)}{U(w) - U(x)}. \qquad (5)$$

The indifference curves in $\{w,n\}$ space are downward sloping, asymptotic to $w = x$ for $n \leq m$. For $n > m$, the entire labour pool is employed and the union is not prepared to bear any sacrifice in wages in return for higher levels of employment. Consequently for $n > m$ the indifference curves are horizontal. This pattern is shown in the indifference map of a trade union depicted in Figure 1.

An alternative frequently used specification also yields the same type of union trade-off between wages and employment. If a union has identical members who share an equal probability of employment because jobs are allocated at random, a natural objective is the expected utility of each member. If each member has a probability of employment of n/m then the expected utility of any member is the right-hand side of (3) divided by m. Taking m as exogenous to the union, the indifference curves that represent this definition of expected utility have exactly the same shape as the indifference curves discussed above.

Insider-Dominated Unions

A number of authors, especially Oswald (1984), Lindbeck and Snower (1988), Blanchard and Summers (1986) and Carruth and Oswald (1987), have emphasized the idea that the union's objective is based on the utility of the employed 'insiders'. If the group of insiders corresponds to those in employment then, as discussed in McDonald and Solow (1984) and McDonald (1989), there is a 'travelling' kink in the indifference curve; that is, the kink in the indifference map shown in Figure 1 is always at the current level of employment. A problem with this approach is that the travelling kink leads to somewhat irregular patterns of wage behaviour. For example, changes in the demand for labour can have large effects on wages with no effect on employment; but such a pattern is not usually observed.

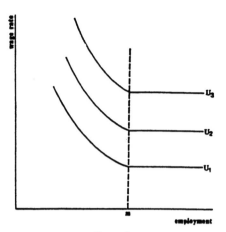

FIGURE 1
The Union's Indifference Map

An alternative objective which does not lead to this problem is based on a sub-group of the employed who face little risk of layoff, rather than all those employed by the firm. This may be called the 'insider-dominated union' in contrast with the above 'insider' model; see McDonald (1991). One situation which will lead to an insider-dominated union is where layoffs are determined by seniority and union wage decisions are made by a median voter; see Oswald (1985) and Farber (1986). The objective for an insider-dominated union is the net gain from working of each of the identical members of the dominant inside group who face no risk of unemployment, that is:

$$W = U(w) - D. \qquad (6)$$

This objective applies for all levels of employment greater than m^d, the size of the dominant inside group. It will be assumed that the bargained outcome yields employment levels greater than m^d. One case for which this assumption is guaranteed to hold is the median voter case with the franchise equal to the level of employment. If negotiations break down, each insider gets utility $U(s)$ and the objective function takes the value $\bar{W} = U(s)$. Thus the payoff to the insider-dominated union is given by:

$$W - \bar{W} = U(w) - D - U(s). \qquad (7)$$

The objective (6) does not trade-off wages against

employment, and so the indifference curves are horizontal lines in $\{w,n\}$ space over $n > m^d$. It will however be seen below that when the objective of the insider-dominated union is placed along with a firm's profit function in a bargaining model, there are strong similarities with the pattern of wage behaviour using the objective (3) in which employment is traded for wages.

In the insider-dominated model, layoff pay, x, is defined by $U(x) = D + U(s)$. This contrasts with the definition used in the first model where the payoff is given by (3), and where the layoff pay depends on market alternatives. This is a simple consequence of the assumption that the dominant insiders face no risk of unemployment. One implication of this is that, for the insider-dominated model, layoff pay may be realistically regarded as being less than the value of the outside option. As Binmore, Rubinstein and Wolinsky (1986) argue, this raises the possibility that the bargained solution will be determined by the outside option. However, it is assumed throughout this paper that the outside option is *not* a binding constraint on the wage outcome. If the outside option were a binding constraint, there would be no role for the union.

III Four Models of Wage Determination

The previous section examined two alternative specifications of the union's objective function. The next stage in the determination of the wage and the employment level requires the specification of the process by which the firm and the union reach agreement. Where the union's objective function involves an explicit trade-off between employment and wages, two basic processes may be distinguished. First, the firm may be assumed to have complete control over the level of employment, so that bargaining takes place only over the wage rate. Such bargains are constrained to be on the labour demand curve. An extreme case of this kind of process occurs when the union has the complete power to set the wage; this is considered separately below in view of its frequent use in the literature. Second, the firm and the union may be assumed to bargain over the joint determination of the wage rate and the level of employment; in the absence of transaction costs such bargains will be Pareto efficient as in the standard analysis of barter.

For the insider-dominated union, where the level of employment does not enter into the union's objective function, there is no reason to distinguish between bargaining over the wage alone and

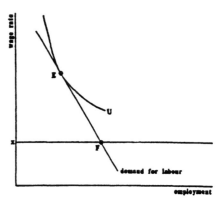

FIGURE 2

The Simple Monopoly Union Model and Wage Bargaining

bargaining over wages and employment. That is because these two bargaining processes yield the same wage and employment outcomes. Control over employment by the employer does not lead to sub-optimal outcomes.

Combining the various assumptions about the union's objective function and the bargaining process yields four models of trade union behaviour. In the *simple monopoly union* model the union has complete control over the wage. In the *wage bargaining* model the union bargains with the firm over the wage, although the firm still has complete control over employment as in the simple monopoly union model. In the *efficient bargains* model the union and the firm bargain over both wages and employment. In the fourth model, the *insider-dominated* model, the union is not prepared to trade wages for employment. These are examined in turn below.

The Simple Monopoly Union

The situation in which the union is powerless to influence the employment level while the firm is powerless to control the wage rate is called the 'simple monopoly union' model. The union sets the wage which enables it to reach the highest indifference curve, subject to the constraint that employment takes place on the labour demand curve. This outcome is shown in Figure 2 as point E.

If the firm's revenue, expressed as a function of employment, n, is written as $R(n)$, then profit maximization requires $w - R'(n) = 0$. The demand curve for labour is defined by $w = R'(n)$, and the simple monopoly union outcome is given by maximization of the Lagrangean, L, given by:

$$L = n\{U(w) - U(x)\} + m\bar{U} + \lambda\{w - R'(n)\}. \quad (8)$$

Setting the partial derivative of L with respect to w equal to zero gives $\lambda = -nU'(w)$, and substituting into $\partial L/\partial n = 0$ gives, with $w = R'(n)$, the result that:

$$\frac{wU'(w)}{U(w) - U(x)} = \frac{-R'(n)}{nR''(n)}. \quad (9)$$

The left-hand side of (9) is the wage elasticity of the net utility from work, ϵ, defined in Section II, while the right-hand side is interpreted as the negative of the wage elasticity of demand for labour, denoted θ. Hence the first-order condition can be rewritten simply as:

$$\epsilon = \theta. \quad (10)$$

Notice that this could be obtained simply by setting the slope of the union's indifference curve, $-w/n\epsilon$, equal to the slope of the labour demand curve, given by $R''(n)$.

Wage Bargaining

The more general case of bargaining over wages while the employer retains unilateral control over employment, has been called the 'right to manage' model by Nickell (1982). In this case, where the wage is jointly determined by the union and the firm through bargaining, a bargaining solution concept is required. The bargaining solution usually used is the asymmetric Nash solution, given by the values of w and n which maximize the weighted geometric mean of the union's and the firm's payoffs. In the case of wage bargaining the Nash solution is subject to the constraint that bargains are on the firm's labour demand curve. The union's payoff has already been considered in Section III above. If the firm's 'threat point' is assumed to be zero profits, the payoff is simply the value of profits, $R(n) - wn$. The Lagrangean for this problem is:

$$L = [n\{U(w) - U(x)\}]^{\phi/(1+\phi)}[R(n) - wn]^{1/(1+\phi)} + \lambda\{w - R'(n)\} \quad (11)$$

The weights $\phi/(1+\phi)$ and $1/(1+\phi)$ reflect the bargaining power of the union and the firm respectively. When $\phi = \infty$, all the bargaining strength is in the hands of the union, and maximizing (11) is equivalent to the simple monopoly union model of (8). Using the interpretation of Binmore, Rubinstein and

Wolinsky (1986, p. 187), ϕ is positively related to the speed of response of the union to the firm's offers and inversely related to the speed of the firm's response to the union's offers. Furthermore, ϕ is inversely related to the union's estimate of the probability that the bargaining process will break down and positively related to the firm's estimate that the bargaining process will break down.

Differentiation of (11) with respect to n, w and λ, setting the resulting partial derivatives equal to zero and rearranging, gives the first-order condition that:

$$\epsilon = \left[\phi\left\{\frac{R(n)}{nR'(n)} - 1\right\}\right]^{-1} + \left[\frac{-R'(n)}{nR''(n)}\right] \quad (12)$$

The second term in (12) is the elasticity θ. The term $nR''(n)/R'(n)$ is the ratio of the marginal revenue product to the average revenue product, and is the elasticity of revenue with respect to employment, which will be denoted α. Equation (12) can therefore be rewritten as:

$$\epsilon = \frac{\alpha}{\phi(1-\alpha)} + \theta. \quad (13)$$

Bearing in mind that ϵ is a function of the wage, equation (13) determines the bargained wage. The level of employment is determined by the labour demand function. In terms of Figure 2, the outcome under wage bargaining will lie on the labour demand curve somewhere between E and F. If the union has complete power over wages then $\phi = \infty$, the first term on the right-hand side of (13) is zero and (13) reduces to the simple monopoly union result given by (10). The wage-employment outcome would be at point E in Figure 2. If the union has no power over wages then $\phi = \infty$, the value of the term on the right-hand side of (13) is infinite and, for ϵ to be infinite the wage has to equal x. The wage-employment outcome would be at point F in Figure 2. Intermediate values for union power yield solutions on the labour demand curve between E and F in Figure 2.

Efficient Bargains

When the union and the firm bargain over both the wage rate and the employment level, the bargains are no longer constrained to take place on the labour demand curve. Hence the Nash bargaining solution is given by the unconstrained maximization of:

$$L = [n\{U(w) - U(x)\}]^{\phi/(1+\phi)}[R(n) - wn]^{1/(1+\phi)} \quad (14)$$

Appropriate differentiation and manipulation gives

the first-order conditions as:

$$\epsilon = \frac{w}{w - R'(n)} \qquad (15)$$

$$w = \frac{1}{1+\phi}\left[\frac{\phi R(n)}{n} + R'(n)\right] \qquad (16)$$

Equation (16), which may be called the 'power locus', shows that the wage is equal to a weighted average of the average and marginal revenue products of labour, with weights equal to $\phi/(1+\phi)$ and $1/(1+\phi)$ respectively. Equation (15) defines the contract curve of efficient bargains, which is the locus of points of tangency between the union's indifference curves and the firm's iso-profit curves. This result can be confirmed by equating the slope of an indifference curve, $-w/n\epsilon$, with the slope of the iso-profit curve. The latter is obtained, from total differentiation of $\Pi = R(n) - wn$, as:

$$\frac{dw}{dn} = \frac{\{w - R'(n)\}}{n} \qquad (17)$$

The efficient bargains model is presented graphically in Figure 3. The iso-profit curves have a slope of zero where they cut through the curve of $R'(n)$. The contract curve of tangencies of the iso-profit curves and the indifference curves is the upward sloping curve from A to B. At A, where, because $w = x$ the indifference curve is horizontal, the contract curve touches the $R'(n)$ curve. At B, where the level of profits is zero, the contract curve ends. The power locus runs from C to D. It can be seen from the equation of the power locus, (16), that for the level of employment at which $R'(n) = R(n)/n$, the power locus goes through the wage and employment levels given by $w = R'(n) = R(n)/n$, whatever the value of the union power parameter. This is point C on the power locus. Because the bargaining solution is assumed to be at $n \le m$, the power locus ends at point D where $n = m$. For an analysis of outcomes that occur at $n > m$ see Carruth and Oswald (1987).

To derive an expression determining the bargained wage, substitute (16) into the contract curve (15). This gives the resulting first-order condition that:

$$\epsilon = \frac{\phi\frac{R(n)}{nR'(n)} + 1}{\phi\left\{\frac{R(n)}{nR'(n)} - 1\right\}} \qquad (18)$$

Using the definition of α to substitute for

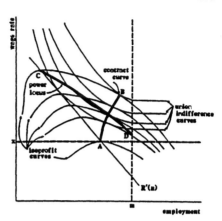

FIGURE 3
The Efficient Bargains Model

$nR'(n)/R(n)$, equation (18) becomes

$$\epsilon = \frac{\phi + \alpha}{\phi(1 - \alpha)} \qquad (19)$$

Notice that the wage elasticity of the demand for labour, θ, does not appear in (19). This is not suprising in view of the fact that efficient bargains for which $m > n$ are not on the labour demand curve. The fact that efficient bargains (with $m > n$) are on the contract curve and require bargaining over wages *and* employment was first stated by Edgeworth (1881) and clarified by Dunlop (1944), although its discovery is often attributed to Leontief (1946).

Insider-Dominated Bargains

The insider-dominated model of trade union behaviour, as explained in Section II, applies to a union which is concerned only with a sub-group of the employed, and corresponds to a situation in which $m < n$. This has been contrasted with the 'insider' model, in which $m = n$ and which produces a 'travelling' kink in the indifference curves at the current level of employment. The Nash solution for insider dominated bargains is therefore given by the values of w and n which maximize:

$$L = [\{U(w) - D - U(s)\}]^{\phi/(1+\phi)}[R(n) - wn]^{1/(1+\phi)} \qquad (20)$$

Appropriate differentiation and rearrangement

gives the first-order conditions as:

$$w = R'(n) \tag{21}$$

and
$$\epsilon = \left[\phi\left\{\frac{R(n)}{nw} - 1\right\}\right]^{-1} \tag{22}$$

It should be recognized that ϵ differs slightly from its earlier definition in (5), and is now equal to $wU'(w)/\{U(w) - D - U(s)\}$. Thus for the insider-dominated case, ϵ refers to the elasticity, with respect to the wage, of the excess of utility from working over *utility from being on strike*. As explained in Section II, for the insider-dominated case, x is defined by $U(x) = D + U(s)$. Calling x layoff pay now means the income equivalent of being on strike. For the other three cases ϵ is the elasticity, with respect to the wage, of the excess of utility from working over utility gained from the alternative activities to which workers turn if they fail to gain employment at the firm after the completion of the bargain; that is, $U(x) = D + U$.

Equation (21) shows that efficient insider-dominated bargains are on the labour demand curve. The same is true of the 'insider' model, a result which was first stated by Leontief (1946), somewhat elliptically, and Fellner (1949), and later rediscovered by Oswald (1987).

As can be seen from Figure 4, the horizontal indifference curves are tangential with the iso-profit curves where the latter cut the labour demand curve. The contract curve is the segment of the labour demand curve running from A, where the level of profit is zero, to B, where $w = x$. A powerful union can achieve the outcome at A, whilst a powerless union will have to accept the outcome at B (remember that the outside option was assumed earlier not to be a binding constraint). Intermediate values of the union power parameter yield outcomes between A and B on the contract curve in Figure 4.

By substitution of (21) and using the definition of α, (22) can be simplified to:

$$\epsilon = \frac{\alpha}{\phi(1 - \alpha)} \tag{23}$$

Equation (23) shows that the bargained wage is related to the elasticity of the revenue function and the power parameter, the same variables that are important when the union trades employment for wages; compare (23) with equations (19), (13) and (10). This similarity in the results of the models is a basis of the synthesis put forward in this paper.

The similarity between the insider-dominated model and the other three models is in marked

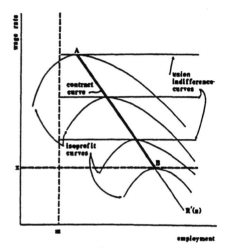

FIGURE 4
The Insider-Dominated Model

contrast to some of the recent literature dealing with 'insider' models. For example, Nickell (1990, p. 418) states that 'the foundation of the insider-outsider model' is that 'wages are inversely related to initial membership'. However, the insider-dominated model of this section has no relation between wages and initial membership. Any such relation is a consequence, not of the general idea that insiders may dominate trade union decision-making, but of the assumption concerning the size of the dominating group of insiders. In the model referred to by Nickell the dominating group of insiders do not have secure employment. This is the underlying reason why, in that model, wages are inversely related to initial membership. On the other hand in the insider-dominated model presented here insiders have secure employment and so the relationship emphasized by Nickell does not hold.

IV The Four Models Compared
General Functional Forms

The previous section derived the equations determining the behaviour of wages and employment for four bargaining models: the simple monopoly union; wage bargaining; efficient bargains and insider-dominated bargains. In the first three models the trade union's objective included both employment and wages while for insider-dominated bargains the trade union was only concerned with the level of wages. Table 1 summarizes the results for the four models. The sixth column, labelled employment, shows that for three models employment is on the marginal revenue product of labour curve. For the simple monopoly union and for the wage-bargaining models this outcome is inefficient; the outcome for efficient bargains lies to the right of the marginal revenue product curve. For insider-dominated bargains, efficient bargains are on the marginal revenue product of labour curve. In that case the union places no value on employment and ₂o is not prepared to offer a lower wage in return for the employer giving higher employment.

Wages in the four models are determined by equations (10), (13), (19) and (23). These four equations may be written in general form as:

$$\epsilon = \psi \tag{24}$$

where ϵ takes the value given by the relevant row in column 2 of Table 1 and ψ takes the value given by the relevant row of column 3 in Table 1. For example, for the simple monopoly union the value of ϵ is $wU'(w)/\{U(w) - D - \bar{U}\}$ and the value of ψ is θ.

McDonald and Solow (1981) emphasized that shifts in the demand for labour will not change the bargained wage if α, θ, ϕ and lay off pay remain constant. Instead employment would bear the brunt of changes in demand. This was for the simple monopoly union and efficient bargains cases, but as Table 1 makes clear, this conclusion can be extended to encompass the wage-bargaining model and insider-dominated bargains. However, in making the extension to the insider-dominated model it should be remembered that the definition of layoff pay in that model differs from the other three models. In the insider-dominated model layoff pay is composed of strike-pay and the disutility of work. So for the insider-dominated model it is constancy in $D + U(s)$ that implies, when α and ϕ remain constant, that shifts in the demand for labour will not change the bargained wage.

Changes in the values of α, θ, ϕ and x will change the bargained wage. The bargained wage may be expected to vary negatively with the elasticity of the revenue function, α, and the elasticity of the labour demand curve, θ, and to vary positively with union power, ϕ, and layoff pay x; that would be a 'normal' relationship. It can be seen from Table 1 that in each of the four models, increases in θ and α and decreases in ϕ will raise ψ (if they

influence ψ at all). So for a normal relation between these parameters and the bargained wage the partial derivative of ϵ with respect to w, denoted ϵ_w, has to be negative. Furthermore, for given values of θ, α and ϕ, an increase in x will raise wages if $\epsilon_w < 0$.

Differentiation of (5) and substitution yields

$$\epsilon_w = -\frac{U'(w)}{U(w) - U(x)} (1 - r - \epsilon) \tag{25}$$

where r measures the Arrow-Pratt measure of relative risk aversion, and $r = wU''(w)/U'(w)$. Clearly $r > 1$ is sufficient for the normal relation. So is $r = 0$, since this implies $\epsilon = w/(w - x)$ which is greater than unity. Another sufficient condition for a normal relation is $\psi > 1$ since, in equilibrium, $\epsilon = \psi$. Pursuing this condition, it can be seen from Table 1 that $\theta > 1$ is sufficient for $\psi > 1$ in the simple monopoly union and the wage-bargaining model and $\alpha < 1$ is sufficient for $\psi > 1$ with efficient bargains. From these conditions, there is a strong presumption for a normal relation in the general case. It will be seen below that with a constant elasticity utility function the normal relation between the bargained wage and α, θ, ϕ and x can be proved for all values of r that yield a positive value for the bargained wage.

Further insight into the models can be gained by considering the value of the bargained wage at each of the extreme values of the power parameter, ϕ. At $\phi = 0$, where the union has no power, the value of ψ is infinity for each of the models of wage bargaining, efficient bargains and insider-dominated bargains. This implies an outcome where the wage is equal to x. At the other extreme of an all powerful union, ϕ is infinite. In this case, the wage-bargaining model reverts to the simply monopoly union model, where the union's willingness to increase wages is moderated by the employment losses it would face as it moves up the labour demand curve. By contrast, an insider dominated union places no value on employment losses. For that union an infinite value for ϕ would imply, as long as $\alpha < 1$, a value of ψ of zero and thus an infinite wage demand. This is not realistic, since it is more likely that for most firms that there is a finite wage at which profits are zero. At the wage where profits are zero, α is equal to one (as $\alpha = R'(n)n/R(n) = wn/R(n)$, zero profits occur when $wn = R(n)$ and thus when $\alpha = 1$). The combination of $\alpha = 1$ and $\phi = $ infinity makes ψ indeterminate for the insider-dominated bargain, and then the wage is simply the zero profit wage, that is $w = R(n)/n$. For efficient bargains a value

TABLE 1
Determination of Wages and Employment in the Four Models of a Trade Union

Model	Wages Determined by ε = ψ				Employment
	ε	ψ			
		General case	Constant Elasticity Revenue Function		
			Using α	Using θ	
Simple Monopoly Union	$\dfrac{wU'(w)}{U(w)-U(x)}$ with $U(x)=D+\bar{U}$	θ	$\dfrac{1}{1-\alpha}$	θ	$w=R'(n)$ $n<m$
Wage Bargaining	$\dfrac{wU'(w)}{U(w)-U(x)}$ with $U(x)=D+\bar{U}$	$\dfrac{\alpha}{\phi(1-\alpha)}+\theta$	$\dfrac{\phi+\alpha}{\phi(1-\alpha)}$	$\dfrac{\theta(1+\phi)-1}{\phi}$	$w=R'(n)$ $n<m$
Efficient Bargains	$\dfrac{wU'(w)}{U(w)-U(x)}$ with $U(x)=D+\bar{U}$	$\dfrac{\alpha}{\phi(1-\alpha)}+\dfrac{1}{1-\alpha}$	$\dfrac{\phi+\alpha}{\phi(1-\alpha)}$	$\dfrac{\theta(1+\phi)-1}{\phi}$	$w=\dfrac{1}{1+\theta}\left[\phi\dfrac{R(n)}{n}+R'(n)\right]$ $n<m$
Insider-dominated Bargains	$\dfrac{wU'(w)}{U(w)-U(x)}$ with $U(x)=D+\bar{U}(s)$	$\dfrac{\alpha}{\phi(1-\alpha)}$	$\dfrac{\alpha}{\phi(1-\alpha)}$	$\dfrac{\theta-1}{\phi}$	$w=R'(n)$ $n>m$

of ϕ of infinity implies $\psi = 1/(1-\alpha)$. The expression $1/(1-\alpha)$ is the elasticity of the iso-profit curve of zero profits (taken positively). In the efficient bargains model, an all-powerful union forces the firm to operate along its zero-isoprofit curve. So that is the wage-employment trade-off that the union faces. That is why, in the expression for ψ for efficient bargains, $1/(1-\alpha)$ appears, instead of, in the expression for ψ for wage bargaining, θ.

A Constant Elasticity Revenue Function

Suppose now that the employment elasticity of revenue, α, is constant. This implies that the revenue function is such that $R(n) = kn^\alpha$ where k is a constant. The wage elasticity of demand for labour is equal to $-1/(1-\alpha)$. The negative of this elasticity has already been defined as θ, so that $\theta = 1/(1-\alpha)$, and the first-order conditions in Section III can be expressed either in terms of α or θ. These are shown in the fourth and fifth columns of Table 1. Note that, with a constant α, the wage rate is precisely the same for both

wage bargaining and efficient bargains; in the latter case employment is higher. In Figure 5 the outcome from wage bargaining is at point E and with efficient bargains is at point F. However, one should not make too much of this equivalence. The institutional processes for wage bargaining differ from the institutional processes for efficient bargains. In the latter case, bargaining is over employment as well as wages. Because of this difference in the variables to be bargained over, it is not clear whether 'equal power' in wage bargaining compared with wage and employment bargaining means that the power parameter should have the same value.

A Constant Elasticity Utility Function

Explicit expressions for the wage rate can only be obtained when a particular form for the utility function has been chosen. Consider the constant relative risk-aversion function given by:

$$U(w) = \frac{w^{1-r}}{1-r} \qquad r \geq 0 \qquad (26)$$

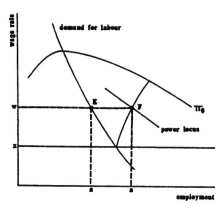

E wage bargaining
F   efficient bargaining
Π₀ zero iso-profit curve

FIGURE 5
Constant Elasticity Revenue Function

and r measures the degree of relative risk aversion, defined earlier. With this function a useful general expression for the wage can be obtained, given by:

$$w = x h^{-1/(1-r)} \qquad (27)$$

with $h = 1 - (1-r)/\psi$.   (28)

In the case of constant relative risk aversion the results in (27) and (28) provide completely general expressions covering the four models of trade union behaviour that can be used to determine the wage rate. It is only necessary to substitute the appropriate value of ψ, taken from Table 1, into (28). For the bargained wage to be positive, h has to be positive. From (28), the condition for $h > 0$ is $r + \psi > 1$, which places a lower limit on $r + \psi$. As $r + \psi$ approaches one from above the bargained wage approaches infinity. Furthermore, given that at the bargained wage $\psi = \epsilon$, it follows that with constant relative risk aversion ϵ_w, as given by (25), is negative if the bargained wage is positive. So with constant relative risk aversion there is a normal relation between the bargained wage and the exogenous variables α, θ, ϕ and x.

The similarity between the models in which the union's objective trades employment for wages, and the insider-dominated union in which the union is only concerned with wages, is remarkable. For the insider-dominated union the wage outcome is the result of a power struggle between the union and the firm. While the union only cares about wages, the firm's profit objective depends on both wages and employment. It is because of this dependence that the insider-dominated model yields similar results to the other models. As explained above, the insider models in McDonald and Solow (1984), Blanchard and Summers (1986), Carruth and Oswald (1987), Lindbeck and Snower (1988) and McDonald (1989) are 'travelling kink' models, and are not easily brought into the framework of this paper.

V *The Effects of Taxation*
A General Tax Function

There have been relatively few studies of the effects of taxes on unions. Early examples include the brief discussions in Oswald (1982, 1985) and papers by Hersoug (1984) and Sampson (1983). These studies make the assumption either that x is untaxed or that any tax change is accompanied by a policy which ensures that the real after-tax value of x remains unchanged. This approach is appropriate to those situations where x is thought to be dominated by transfer payments. Even if such payments are taxable, it can be argued that it is sensible to concentrate on the single policy of a tax change, rather than combining it with a policy to reduce the real value of transfer payments. For example, when value added tax was significantly increased in the UK in 1979, transfers were simultaneously increased to maintain their real value. Alternatively, it can be argued that there are situations in which x is affected by changes in taxation. Not surprisingly, the implications for wage bargains of tax changes are sensitive to the assumption made about x; for a detailed treatment, see Pemberton (1991).

In general any tax structure can be represented by a relationship between post-tax income, y, and the pre-tax wage, w, so that:

$$y = y(w) \qquad (29)$$

It is useful to introduce the concept of the elasticity of the post-tax wage with respect to the pre-tax wage, denoted ξ where:

$$\xi = \frac{w y'(w)}{y} \qquad (30)$$

The advantage of the synthesis presented here is that with taxation, the first-order condition determining the bargained wage can be written as a simple modification of the general form given in equation (24). It can be expressed as:

$$\epsilon\xi - \psi \qquad (31)$$

where ϵ has to be redefined in terms of y rather than w, so that it is now $yU'(y)/\{U(y) - U(x)\}$, and the appropriate value of ψ is taken from Table 1. Thus all four models are covered by (31), irrespective of whether or not taxes are assumed to affect x.

The impact on bargained wages of changes in the tax structure can be examined using comparative static analysis based on the first-order condition in (31). Suppose that τ is one (unspecified) parameter of the tax function and that x does not depend on τ; there may be other parameters but the following considers the general comparative static effect of a change in any parameter. Equation (31) gives rise to a solution for w given by w^*, where $w^* - w^*(x, \tau)$. Substitution into (31) gives the identity:

$$\epsilon(w^*(x, \tau), x, \tau)\ \xi(w^*(x, \tau), \tau), \tau) - \psi(w^*(x, \tau)) \qquad (32)$$

where ϵ, ξ and ψ are written as functions of w^* and the exogenous variables x and τ. Differentiating (32) with respect to the tax parameter and rearranging gives:

$$w_\tau^*(\epsilon_{w^*}\xi + \epsilon\xi_{w^*} - \psi_{w^*}) - -(\epsilon_\tau\xi + \epsilon\xi_\tau) \qquad (33)$$

where $w_\tau^* - dw^*/d\tau$ and so on. The term in brackets on the left-hand side of (33) is strictly negative if the second-order condition is satisfied, so that the sign of $dw^*/d\tau$ is given by the sign of the term in brackets on the right-hand side of (33). From the definition of ϵ given above, it can be seen that $\epsilon_\tau - \epsilon_y y_\tau$. The analysis in Section IV yielded a strong presumption that ϵ_w is negative. In the present context this carries over, suggesting that $\epsilon_y < 0$. This leaves the signs of y_τ and ξ_τ to be determined.

Further progress can be made by considering certain types of tax function. The most simple tax function is proportional, by which $y - (1-t)w$ with t being both the average and the marginal tax rate. With this tax function, $\tau - t$, ξ is equal to one, $\xi_t - 0$ and $y_t - -w$. Substituting these expressions into (33), it can be concluded that:

$$\text{sign}(w_t^*) - \text{sign}(-\epsilon_y w) - \text{positive.} \qquad (34)$$

Thus an increase in the average and marginal tax rate will increase wage demands.

A simple progressive tax function is the linear function with a tax-free threshold, a, whereby $y - w-(w-a)t$. This function is the one-step version of the income tax scales in general use. With this

function, $\tau - a$ or t, $y_a - t$, $\xi_a - -\xi^2(1/w)(t/(1-t)) < 0$ and so:

$$\text{sign}(w_a^*) - \text{sign}(\epsilon_y t\xi + \epsilon\xi_a) - \text{negative.} \qquad (35)$$

By (35) a decrease in a, which represents an increase in the average rate of tax holding the marginal rate constant, will increase the trade union's wage demand. However, the effect on wages of increasing the marginal rate of tax is not clear. With the linear progressive function, $y_t - (w-a) < 0$, assuming that the wage exceeds the threshold a, and $\xi_t - -\xi(a/w)(1-t)^{-2} < 0$, and so:

$$\text{sign}(w_t^*) - \text{sign}(-\epsilon_y(w-a)\xi - \epsilon\xi^2(a/w)(1-t)^{-2}) \qquad (36)$$

which is ambiguous.

Finally, consider the constant elasticity function, by which $y - \mu w^\beta$ with $\mu > 0$ and $0 < \beta < 1$. This function seems to have been first used by Edgeworth (1925), and has been used in the analysis of trade union wage determination by Hersoug (1984) and Creedy and McDonald (1990). The main attractions of this function concern the neat analytic results that can be derived from it, as is so often the case with constant elasticity functional forms. The parameter β may be regarded as a measure of the progressivity of the function. Under this convention a decrease in μ represents an increase in the average rate of tax, holding progressivity constant. The derivatives of y and ξ are $y_\mu - w^\beta > 0$, $y_\beta - y \log(w)$, $\xi_\mu - 0$ and $\xi_\beta - 1$. Using these derivatives, gives:

$$\text{sign}\ w_\mu^* - \text{sign}(\epsilon_y w^\beta\beta) - \text{negative} \qquad (37)$$

implying that an increase in the average rate of tax will increase wages. For changes in the elasticity of the tax function,

$$\text{sign}\ w_\beta^* - \text{sign}(\epsilon_y\beta \log(w) + \epsilon) \qquad (38)$$

which is ambiguous.

For each of the three tax functions considered, a change in the average rate of tax increases the trade union wage. However, for the two tax functions which can allow for a progressive tax structure, the impact on trade union wages of a change in the marginal rate of tax is ambiguous. The effect of a change in the tax structure will therefore typically require the precise specification of the utility function.

It is often required to examine changes in a tax structure, such as a change in marginal tax rates, which are in some sense 'revenue neutral'. One reason is that the imposition of revenue neutrality allows a clearer comparison of alternative tax rates and structures. Furthermore revenue neutrality can remove income effects and allow the analyst to concentrate on the impact of substitution effects. Hersoug (1984) and Sampson (1983) have interpreted revenue neutrality to mean an unchanged average tax rate for the particular union under consideration. Suppose that $y = y(w, t, a)$ where t and a are two tax parameters such that $y_t < 0$ and $y_a > 0$, and t is the marginal tax rate; the linear schedule considered earlier is a special case of such a tax function in which $a = 0$. A change in t which leaves the average tax rate unchanged leads to a change in the bargained wage given by:

$$\frac{dw^*}{dt} + k\left(\frac{dw^*}{da}\right)$$ (39)

where $k = da/dt$, calculated under the assumption that the average rate, $(w-y)/w$, remains constant. As t is increased it is necessary to raise the other parameter, a, in order to keep the average rate constant. An alternative approach may require not simply that the average tax rate facing a group of workers remains fixed but that the total tax revenue of all workers in the economy remains constant, thereby complicating the expression for k. For a non-technical discussion of a variety of tax changes which impose aggregate revenue neutrality, see Creedy and McDonald (1989). In general, under various specifications of revenue neutrality, increases in marginal rates of tax decrease trade union wages. However, Pemberton (1991) has shown that this result may be modified if x depends on the tax structure.

The Constant Elasticity Utility Function and the Linear Progressive Tax Function

It has been suggested above that clear results concerning the direction of wage changes in response to tax changes usually require the utility function to be specified. This subsection briefly combines the constant elasticity utility function with the linear progressive function, considered earlier. For this case the bargained wage can no longer be solved explicitly, as it could be in the case without tax shown in (27), but is the solution to the non-linear equation:

$$w(1-t)h + at - y^r x^{1-r} = 0,$$ (40)

where $h = 1-(1-r)/\psi$. In the special case where the tax is proportional, that is if $a = 0$, then (40) can be solved explicitly for w, which is equal to the right-hand side of (27) divided by $(1-t)$.

The earlier analysis has already proved that $dw/da < 0$. But the sign of dw/dt is ambiguous.

However, the case of $r = 0$, that is of risk-neutrality, yields a condition for $dw/dt > 0$, which is easy to interpret. Furthermore, the use of numerical methods of solving (40) for cases with $r > 0$ reveals a very close similarity with the risk-neutral case, so that the risk-neutral case is a good guide to the more complicated cases where $r > 0$. A microcomputer program to examine these alternatives can be obtained from the authors.

With $r = 0$, equation (40) reduces to the following expression:

$$w = \frac{(x-at)\psi}{(1-t)(\psi-1)}$$ (41)

from which:

$$\frac{dw}{dt} = \frac{x-a}{(x-at)(1-t)} > 0 \text{ if } x > a.$$ (41)

Hence $dw/dt > 0$ if $x > a$. If, as is realistic, x is greater than the threshold, a, then the bargained wage is increased by an increase in the marginal rate of tax.

Employment Effects of Tax Changes

In three of the four wage determination processes summarized in Table 1, employment occurs on the demand curve for labour. Hence the employment effects of tax changes are easily obtained in the partial equilibrium context in which the firm's revenue function is assumed to remain unaffected by the wage tax. For efficient bargains (with $n < m$) the tax change will cause the contract curve to shift, while leaving the power locus unchanged. This is because the power locus is obtained by differentiating the Nash maximand (the product of the pay offs) with respect to employment, and the introduction of taxation has no influence on this relationship. Hence employment will in this case expand or contract along a fixed power locus.

Consider the special case where the employment elasticity of revenue is constant. Appropriate substitution of $R(n)$ and $R'(n)$ into the power locus given by (17), and rearrangement to make n the subject of the resulting equation, gives:

$$n = bw^{-1/(1-a)}$$ (42)

with $b = \{k(\alpha+\phi)/(1+\phi)\}^{1/(1-a)}$.

This result shows that the wage elasticity of employment along the power locus is precisely the same as that along the demand curve. Hence any given change in wages, induced by tax change, will have the same employment effect in all models.

VI Conclusion

In analyzing the economic behaviour of trade unions, writers have tended to contrast the basic assumptions of alternative models. One contrast is between bargaining over wages and bargaining over both wages and employment. The latter assumption leads to efficient bargains. Another contrast is between a union's objective based on wages and employment and a union's objective based on wages alone. The latter assumption captures the notion of insider power. All these alternative assumptions are covered by the four models of trade union behaviour examined in this paper. The synthesis put forward here shows that these four models are sufficiently similar to be fitted into a general framework. In each model, the bargained wage is inversely related to the elasticity of the firm's revenue function and/or the elasticity of the labour demand function, the elasticity of the union member's utility function and the marginal rate of tax on workers and positively related to the opportunity cost of labour, the power parameter of the trade union and the average rate of tax on workers. Furthermore shifts in the demand for labour have their major effect on employment and little or no effect on wages, as emphasized in McDonald and Solow (1981). This behaviour is consistent with the results of empirical studies on the cyclical pattern of real wages, which show little correlation between real wages and recent employment. Kennan (1988) provides a recent study of six OECD countries and Ackland and Borland (1990) provide a recent study of the Australian pattern.

The one qualification to the similarity of wage behaviour between the four models is that layoff pay has a different definition for the insider-dominated models than for the other three models. For the insider-dominated model layoff pay is the income equivalent of strike pay plus the disutility of work. For the other three models layoff pay is the income equivalent of not being employed by the firm *after* the completion of negotiations plus the disutility of work. In this latter definition, layoff pay is more sensitive to market opportunities, through their influence on alternative employment prospects, than in the definition derived from the insider-dominated model.

The emphasis in this paper has been on the behaviour of wages. The similarity in this behaviour for the four models of trade unions holds even although in one model outcomes are not on the labour demand curve. As Edgeworth (1881) pointed out a long time ago, if a union places a positive value on additional employment then efficient bargains lie to the right of the labour demand curve. The major contribution of the modern literature on the economics of trade unions has been to elucidate the nature of wage behaviour.

REFERENCES

Ackland, R. and Borland, J.L. (1990), 'Real Wages over the Business Cycle in Australia', University of Melbourne, mimeo.

Ashenfelter, O. and Johnson, G.E. (1969), 'Bargaining Theory, Trade Unions and Industrial Strike Activity', *American Economic Review* 59(1), 35–49.

Binmore, K., Rubinstein, A. and Wolinsky, A. (1986), 'The Nash Bargaining Solution in Economic Modelling', *Rand Journal of Economics* 17(2), 176–88.

Bishop, R. (1964), 'A Zeuthen-Hicks Theory of Bargaining', *Econometrica* XXXII, 410–17.

Blanchard, O.J. and Summers, L.H. (1986), 'Hysteresis and the European Unemployment Problem' in S. Fischer (ed.), *NBER Macroeconomics Annual* (MIT press, Cambridge, Massachusetts).

Booth, A. (1984), 'A Public Choice Model of Trade Union Behaviour and Membership', *Economic Journal* 94, 883–98.

Borland, J.L. (1985), 'The Economic Analysis of Trade Unions', Master of Arts Thesis, University of Melbourne.

Carruth, A.A. and Oswald, A.J. (1987), 'On Union Preferences and Labour Market Models: Insiders and Outsiders', *Economic Journal* 97, 431–45.

Corden, W.M. (1981), 'Taxation, Real Wage Rigidity and Employment', *Economic Journal* 91, 309–30.

———— and Dixon, P.B. (1980), 'A Tax-Wage Bargain in Australia: Is a Free Lunch Possible?', *Economic Record* 56(154), 209–21.

Creedy, J. and McDonald, I.M. (1989), 'Trade Unions Wages and Taxation,' *Fiscal Studies* 10, 3, 50–9.

———— and ———— (1990), 'Income Tax Changes and Trade Union Wage Demands', University of Melbourne, mimeo.

Dunlop, J.T. (1944), *Wage Determination Under Trade Unions*, Macmillan, New York.

Edgeworth, F.Y. (1881), *Mathematical Psychics*, Kegan Paul, London.

———— (1925), *Papers Relating to Political Economy*, 3 vols, Macmillan, London.

Farber, H.S. (1986), 'The Analysis of Union Behaviour', in O.C. Ashenfelter and R. Layard (eds), *Handbook of Labor Economics*, Volume 2, North-Holland, Amsterdam, 1039–89.

Fellner, W. (1949), *Competition Among The Few*, Alfred Knopf, New York.

Grossman, G. (1983), 'Union Wages, Seniority and Unemployment', *American Economic Review* 73, 277–90.

Grout, P.A. (1984), 'Investment and Wages in the

Absence of Legally Binding Labour Contracts: A Nash Bargaining Approach', *Econometrica* 52, 449–60.

Hersoug, T. (1984), 'Union Wage Responses to Tax Changes', *Oxford Economic Papers* 36, 37–51.

Kennan, J. (1988), 'Equilibrium Interpretations of Employment and Real Wage Fluctuations', *NBER Macroeconomics Annual* 3, MIT press, Cambridge, Massachusetts.

Layard, R. and Nickell, S. (1990), 'Is Unemployment Lower if Unions Bargain over Employment', *Quarterly Journal of Economics*, CV (3), 773–87.

Leontief, W. (1946), 'The Pure Theory of the Guaranteed Annual Wage Contract,' *Journal of Political Economy* 56, 76–9.

Lindbeck, A. and Snower, D.J. (1988), 'Cooperation, Harassment, and Involuntary Unemployment: An Insider-Outsider Approach', *American Economic Review* 78(1), 167–88.

McDonald, I.M. (1991), 'Insiders and Trade Union Wage Bargaining', Manchester School of *Economic and Social Studies* (forthcoming).

——— (1989), 'The Wage Demands of a Selfish, Plant-Specific Trade Union', *Oxford Economic Papers* 41, 506–27.

——— (1984), 'Anti-Stagflationary Tax Cuts and the Problem of Investment', *Economic Record* 60(170), 284–93.

——— and Solow, R.M. (1981), 'Wage Bargaining and Employment', *American Economic Review* 71, 891–908.

——— and Solow R.M. (1984), 'Union Wage Policies:

Reply', *American Economic Review* 74(4), 759–61.

Nickell, S. (1982), 'A Bargaining Model of the Phillips Curve', Centre of Labour Economics Discussion Paper No. 130, *London School of Economics*.

——— (1990), 'Unemployment: A Survey', *Economic Journal* 100, 391–439.

Oswald, A.J. (1982), 'The Microeconomic Theory of the Trade Union', *Economic Journal* 92, 576–95.

——— (1984), 'On Union Preferences and Labour Market Models: Neglected Corners', Institute for International Economic Studies Paper 296, University of Stockholm.

——— (1985), 'The Economic Theory of Trade Unions: An Introductory Survey', *The Scandinavian Journal of Economics* 87(2), 160–93.

Oswald, A.J. (1987), 'Efficient Contracts are on the Labour Demand Curve: Theory and Facts', Discussion Paper No. 284, Centre of Labour Economics, London School of Economics.

Pemberton, J. (1991), *Taxation and wage bargaining*, University of Reading.

Pitchford, J.D. (1981), 'Taxation, Real Wage Rigidity and Employment: The Flexible Price Case', *Economic Journal* 91, 716–20.

Sampson, A.A. (1983), 'Employment Policy in a Model with a Rational Trade Union', *Economic Journal* 93, 297–311.

Ulph, A. and Ulph D. (1990), 'Union Bargaining: A Survey of Recent Work' in D. Sapsford and Z. Tzannatos (eds), *Current Issues in Labour Economics*, Macmillan, Basingstoke, UK, 86–125.

5

The Economics of Ageing
Edited by John Creedy

Introduction

This volume collects 32 journal papers concerned with a variety of economic aspects of individual and population ageing. They have been arranged under four main headings as follows: individual ageing and the life cycle; population ageing; ageing and social insurance, and macroeconomic effects. The present Introduction makes no attempt to summarize the articles or to survey the wider literature (much of which is contained in books rather than journal articles). Rather, it aims to set the context and discuss some of the major issues. In view of the central role of population dynamics, it seems useful to provide a discussion of the systematic demographic changes that have taken place over time, along with an examination of the basic analytics of population change. The implications for social expenditure are then discussed.

The fundamental role of individual ageing is something that everyone is necessarily aware of, and the division of the life cycle into a number of distinct stages has been recognized for many centuries. The best known statement of these stages is perhaps that of Jaques in Shakespeare's *As You Like It*. He described the 'seven ages of man', beginning with 'the infant, mewling and puking in the nurse's arms' and ending with 'the last scene of all, that ends this strange eventful history ... sans teeth, sans eyes, sans taste, sans everything'. While the ageing process has for long played a prominent role in some other disciplines, extensive investigations into the economics of ageing are relatively recent. Few published data contain decompositions according to age or life-cycle stages, so that there are still large gaps in knowledge of cross-sectional age comparisons, never mind knowledge about true cohort variations.

An important distinction must be drawn between individual and population ageing. The latter concerns the age distribution of the population and is influenced more by fertility patterns than by mortality or longevity characteristics of individuals. It might be thought that, in view of the importance of the population model associated with the famous work by Malthus, concern with population ageing would stem at least from the early classical economists. However, the major area of interest was rapid population growth, even though changes in death rates were recognized as important; concern for ageing is also relatively modern. The analytics of population growth and age structure were not explored at length until the early years of the present century. Furthermore, in view of the early age of death of the large majority of people, population growth was regarded by the classical economists as being synonymous with labour force growth, so that no independent role was attached to the age distribution.

Demographic Transitions

It is possible to distinguish several demographic stages or transitions through which most industrialized societies have been observed to pass. The time taken to move through the various stages has varied between countries, however, and there is evidence to suggest that more recently industrialized countries have passed through some later stages relatively more quickly.

The different stages are characterized mainly by their birth and death rates (expressed per 1000 of the population) and the associated age distribution of the population. They are shown in Table 1 under four main headings. The figures given in the table must be regarded simply as representative values rather than indicating precise orders of magnitude for a particular country.

The pre-modern stage is characterized in Table 1 by quite high fertility and high mortality. The expectation of life at birth is only about 25 years, so there are very few individuals in the 'over 60' age group. The high birth rate, while imposing very heavy burdens on families, is nevertheless associated with a growth rate of the total population of only about half of one per cent, so that reproduction is sometimes described as being very inefficient.

The middle two stages are shown as 'early transition' and 'later transition' periods, though they are sometimes amalgamated into a single demographic transition or movement towards the 'modern' period. The early transition period is characterized by a fall in mortality, particularly infant mortality, which is associated with a rise in the expectation of life to about 30 years. In the later transition period, improved health conditions reduce mortality and increase longevity further, while the birth rate continues to be high. This period is thus associated with a high 'youth dependency' ratio, with about 45 per cent of the population under the age of 15 years. Despite the much higher expectation of life at birth, the proportion of people over 60 years remains relatively low, while the population growth rate is increased to about 3 per cent. Indeed, it can be shown that the extent of population ageing is more sensitive to fertility than to mortality changes.

Table 1   Demographic Transitions

	Pre-modern	Early transition	Later transition	Modern
Births/1 000	45	45	45	20
Deaths/1 000	40	33	15	10
% ≤ 15	36	38	45	26
% ≥ 60	5	5	5	15
Expectation of life at birth	25	30	50	70
Population growth rate	.5	1	3	1

Despite increased longevity, the later transitional period is one in which the idea of retirement from employment does not really exist. Individuals continue to work, unless illness prevents labour market participation. For example, during this transitional period in Britain, the various Friendly Societies were able to cope with the requirements of such sickness insurance for their members and were also well placed to handle the potential moral hazard problems. Hence increased longevity did not lead to a breakdown of family support systems, despite the high 'youth' burden already faced.

As shown in Table 1, the modern period experiences a continued reduction in mortality and an increase in the expectation of life at birth to about 70 years. A significant feature is the reduction in the birth rate so that, despite the extra longevity, the population growth rate falls to about 1 per cent. The age composition of the population shifts dramatically, with a reduction in the proportion below 15 years and an increase in the proportion aged over 60 years. Given the difficulty of making life cycle savings, these later transitions place great strain on family support systems, despite the reduction in the youth burden. In Britain, the significance of these changes was not at first fully appreciated by the Friendly Societies, who were initially opposed to the introduction of government Old Age pensions; however, the demand for some kind of government pension became irresistible in the major industrialized countries at the turn of the century. The shift from family support to government support in the form of a tax and transfer system involves a complex range of factors, including the very high costs – particularly health costs – of supporting the aged relative to those of the young. Hence the overall burden of dependency increased despite the reduction in birth rates.

The modern period shown in Table 1 corresponds to the industrialized countries around 1960 and must be augmented by a yet 'more modern' period through which many countries are currently passing. The expectation of life at birth has increased further, and it has been found that support costs (again particularly health costs) rise dramatically for individuals over 75 years who form a growing proportion of the population. The birth rates have also fallen further, implying significant population ageing in the early years of the 21st century. This prospect is also associated with the ageing of members of the post-war baby boom. The implications of the more recent demographic transition are, however, more complicated than is often portrayed in popular debate.

The recent 'post-modern' period has also seen a substantial increase in the labour force participation rate of women (partly associated with the lower birth rate) along with a certain amount of variability in unemployment rates. Following a shift of the 'aged burden' to the tax and transfer system during the modern period, the commonly expressed fear is that future working populations will renege on the 'implicit social contract' between generations. Inter-generational equity issues are therefore now receiving some attention from economists. It is also of interest that, despite the much lower birth rate, more recent times have seen increased pressure from some quarters for a further shift of the 'youth burden' to the tax and transfer system. Others have expressed concern over such a shift, partly associated with what some commentators have referred to as a breakdown of the nuclear family. The potential costs associated with population ageing are considered further below, following a brief discussion of the analytics of population dynamics.

Population Projections

It is useful to appreciate some of the basic determinants of the population age structure and population growth. There are of course well-established models developed by demographers and used by, among others, actuaries. However, their notation and methods are less familiar to economists, and for this reason the present discussion presents a social accounting framework. The analysis makes use of matrix methods which are more widely known among economists.

Population flows can be represented by a social accounting framework as follows.

Table 2 Demographic Flows

t+1 \ t		Ages 1 2 3............N	Births	In migration	Total
Ages	1	0 0 0............ 0	b_1	v_1	p_1
	2	f_{21} 0 0............ 0	0	v_2	p_2
	3	0 f_{32} 0............ 0	0	v_3	p_3
	:	:	:	:	:
	N	0 0 0............ 0	0	v_N	p_N
Deaths + out migration		d_1 d_2 d_3............d_N			
Total		p_1 p_2 p_3............p_N			

The square matrix of flows (from columns to rows) has $N-1$ non-zero elements which are placed on the diagonal immediately below the leading diagonal. No one is assumed to survive beyond the age of N. Define the coefficients, a_{ij}, showing the proportion of people in the jth age who survive in the country to the age i, as:

$$a_{ij} = f_{ij}/p_j \qquad (1)$$

only the $a_{i+1,i}$, for $i=1,...,$ N-1 are non-zero. This framework applies to males and females separately, distinguished by subscripts m and f. The 'forward equations' corresponding to this framework are therefore:

$$p_{m,t+1} = A_m\, p_{m,t} + b_{m,t} + v_{m,t} \qquad (2)$$

$$p_{f,t+1} = A_f\, p_{f,t} + b_{f,t} + v_{f,t}. \qquad (3)$$

Given population age distributions in a base year and information about the relevant flows, equations (2) and (3) can be used to make projections. In general the matrices A_m and A_f, along with births and inward migration flows, may be allowed to vary over time. Changes in the As can arise from changes in either mortality or outward migration.

Further specification can be added to the model by considering births. Suppose that c_i represents the proportion of females of age i who give birth per year. Many elements, for young and old ages, of the vector, c, will of course be zero, and in general the c_is may vary over time. Suppose that a proportion, δ, of all births are male, and define the N-element vector τ as the column vector having unity as the first element and zeros elsewhere. Then births in any year can be represented by:

$$b_m = \delta\tau c' p_f \qquad (4)$$

$$b_f = (1-\delta)\tau c' p_f \qquad (5)$$

where c' is the transpose of the vector c (that is, the column vector written as a row). The b vectors contain only one non-zero element, of course. Equations (2) to (5) can thus be used to make population projections for assumed immigration levels.

Stable Populations

If all the coefficients, represented by the elements of the A matrices and the c and v vectors, remain constant over time, the population should eventually reach a stable level and age distribution. The age distribution of males and females will be such that total 'entrants' are exactly matched by total 'exits' from the country. In practice, such a stable population is unlikely ever to be experienced, given the time required for convergence from some initial non-stable distribution, so that the coefficients are bound to change before stability is reached. Yet it is sometimes useful to have an idea of the population structure towards which any given system may be thought to be approaching.

First, consider the female population. Combine (3) and (5) and set $p_{f,t+1} = p_{f,t} = p_f$. With constant migration $v_{f,t} = v_f$ per year, so that:

$$p_f = [A_f + (1-\delta)\,\tau c']p_f + v_f. \tag{6}$$

Notice that the matrix $\tau c'$ takes the simple form:

$$\tau c' = \begin{bmatrix} c_1 & \cdots\cdots & c_N \\ 0 & \cdots\cdots & 0 \\ \vdots & & \vdots \\ 0 & \cdots\cdots & 0 \end{bmatrix} \tag{7}$$

Rearranging (6) gives:

$$[I - A_f - (1-\delta)\tau c']p_f = v_f \tag{8}$$

where I is the unit matrix. It is convenient to denote the matrix in square brackets in (8) as M, so that:

$$Mp_f = v_f. \tag{9}$$

This matrix takes the form:

$$M = \begin{bmatrix} 1-(1-\delta)c_1 & -(1-\delta)c_2 & -(1-\delta)c_3 & \cdots\cdots \\ -a_{21} & 1 & 0 & \cdots\cdots \\ 0 & -a_{32} & 1 & 0\cdots \\ \cdots\cdots\cdots & \cdots\cdots & \cdots\cdots & \cdots\cdots \end{bmatrix} \tag{10}$$

The first few terms c_i (for $i=1,\ldots,N$) will, as noted above, be zeros. However, this matrix will in general be non-singular, so that the stable female distribution is given by:

$$p_f = M^{-1} v_f. \tag{11}$$

The model has the property that if there are no inward female migrants, so that $v_f=0$, then equation (9) represents a set of linear homogeneous equations. Given the non-singularity of M, this means that the model has only the trivial solution whereby the stable population is $p_f=0$.

If $v_f=0$, and denoting the matrix in square brackets in equation (6) as A_f^*, then:

$$p_{f,t+1} = A_f^* \, p_{f,t}$$

$$= (A_f^*)^t \, p_{f,1}. \tag{12}$$

Therefore with constant birth and death rates and no migration, the total population will grow at a constant geometric rate (which may be positive or negative), while the relative age distribution will settle down to be constant whatever the form of $p_{f,1}$. The population growth will be either 'explosive' or will converge to zero, which again confirms the earlier result. The population grows steadily if the largest characteristic root of A_f^* is greater than unity, and declines steadily if the largest root is less than one. The process shown in equation (12) can converge to a stable value of p_f only if the matrix A_f^* has a largest characteristic root of exactly unity, which is extremely unlikely.

The stable male population is determined by substituting (4) into (2) and setting the coefficients constant, so that

$$p_m = A_m \, p_m + \delta \tau c' \, p_f + v_m. \tag{13}$$

Substituting for p_f from (11) and further rearranging gives:

$$p_m = [1-A_m]^{-1} \, [\delta \tau c' \, M^{-1} v_f + v_m]. \tag{14}$$

A stable non-trivial solution for p_m does not therefore require any male migrants.

Social Expenditure

It has been mentioned earlier that an increase in longevity in the industrialized countries led to a demand for the introduction of some kind of government age pension and health 'insurance' scheme. The difficulty of providing adequate personal savings for old age, combined with the strain placed both on family support and the existing sickness support schemes (which anyway covered only a small minority of workers), resulted in a situation in which the aged formed the vast majority of those found to be living below a designated poverty level. At around the same time, there was much wider recognition of a role for the government in other areas of social insurance, such as sickness and unemployment. It is no accident that this movement coincided with wider support for redistribution, involving also the use of progressive income taxation.

Social insurance schemes are typically financed on a pay-as-you-go (PAYG) basis – that is, from current taxation – with pensions forming by far the largest component of social expenditure. A variety of market failure arguments have been advanced to justify the use of such social insurance. In addition, the inter-generational transfers involved in PAYG pension schemes are often described in terms of an implicit social 'contract' between three generations: each generation stands to gain from such an arrangement so long as there is sufficient productivity and population growth. The increased ageing of the population (expected to be most prominent in the early years of the next century) has been widely anticipated as placing great strain on this metaphorical contract. It is possible that the post-war 'baby boom' generation will once again be squeezed.

Pensions and health are not, however, the only age-related forms of social expenditure. Indeed, given the many elements involved, the implications of population ageing for aggregate social expenditure are far from clear. Many projections can perhaps be criticized for not providing sufficient sensitivity analyses, given the wide range of assumptions and the many uncertainties involved. A basic projection framework, which formalizes the approach used by a number of investigators, may be described as follows.

The population is divided into, say, N age groups and the numbers in each group at time t are placed in a vector p_t, where $p_t = p_{m,t} + p_{f,t}$. The per capita social expenditures within each group are placed in a matrix with N rows and k columns, where there are k items of social expenditure (education, medical care, pensions and so on). If this matrix is denoted S, then the i, j th element s_{ij} measures the per capita cost of the j th type of social expenditure in the i th age group. Suppose that the j th type of social expenditure per capita is expected to grow in real terms at the annual rate ψ_j in each age group. Then define g_t as the k-element column vector whose j th element is equal to $(1 + \psi_j)^{t-1}$. Aggregate social expenditure at time t, C_t, is thus equal to:

$$C_t = g'_t \, S' \, p_t \tag{14}$$

where, as above, a dash indicates transposition. This could of course be complicated by allowing for expenditure per person in each category and age to differ for males and females, but such information is rarely available.

The relevant cost is not, however, the absolute value as in (14), but the ratio of this cost to GDP in each year. Projections of Gross Domestic Product depend on assumptions about five factors: initial productivity defined as GDP per employed person, productivity growth, employment rates, participation rates and the population of working age. Total employment is the product of the population, participation rates and the employment rate. Employment is calculated by multiplying the labour utilitization rate by the labour force. If U_t is the total unemployment rate in period t, the utilization rate is $1-U_t$. The aggregate unemployment rate is calculated by dividing the total number of unemployed persons in period t, V_t, by the total labour force in that period, L_t. The value of V_t is in turn calculated by multiplying the age distribution of unemployment rates by the age distribution of the labour force, where these differ according to both age and sex. Let the vectors U_m and U_f be the N-element age distributions of male and female participation rates. If the symbol â represents diagonalization, whereby the vector is written as the leading diagonal of a square matrix with other elements equal to zero, the total number of people unemployed in period t is

$$V_t = U'_{m,t} \, \hat{L}_{m,t} \, p_{m,t} + U'_{f,t} \, \hat{L}_{f,t} \, p_{f,t}. \tag{15}$$

The labour force in period t, L_t, is given by:

$$L_t = L'_{m,t} \, p_{m,t} + L'_{m,t} \, p_{f,t}. \tag{16}$$

Suppose productivity grows at the constant rate, θ. Then GDP in period t is calculated as the product of the utilization rate, $1 - U_t \ (= 1 - V_t/L_t)$, the labour force, L_t, and productivity, whence:

$$GDP_t = \left[\frac{GDP_1}{(1 - U_1) \, L_1} \right] (1 + \theta)^{t-1} \, (1 - U_t) \, L_t. \tag{17}$$

If the population age distribution, along with the sex and age specific participation and unemployment rates, are constant, then the social expenditure to GDP ratio will remain constant if all items of expenditure grow at the same rate as productivity; that is, if $\theta = \psi_j$ for $j = 1, \dots, k$.

This framework illustrates that there are many assumptions required to make projections, as well as many potential interdependencies which are not easy to model. For example, productivity may itself depend on social expenditures and the age distribution of workers. Furthermore, participation rates and population growth are interdependent. The changing age distribution is just one component of the ratio of aggregate social expenditure to GDP, and its effects may be swamped by changes in unemployment rates, for example.

Hypothetical Examples

The approach outlined above can be illustrated by considering a hypothetical example where, for simplicity, there are just five age groups. Suppose the constant survival rates for males and females, and fertility rates, are as shown in Table 3. With no migration and the additional assumption that half of all births are male, the application of the above population projection method gives a constant rate of population growth of 1 per cent, with age distributions as shown also in Table 3. Suppose there are just four categories of social expenditure, nominally defined as education, labour market related (including unemployment benefits), health and pensions. Hypothetical costs per capita are shown in Table 4. Suppose male participation rates are zero for ages 1 and 5, and 0.95 for the other ages, and female participation rates are 0.7, 0.7 and 0.4 for the middle three age groups. Furthermore, assume that unemployment rates are 0.05 for all age groups for males and females. If labour productivity is initially 180 units, and if both productivity and all social expenditures per capita grow at a constant rate of 0.018, then total social expenditure as a rate of GDP is found to be constant at 0.2185.

Consider the alternative survival and fertility rates shown in Table 5. These rates represent lower mortality and fertility and imply a steady rate of population growth which is negligible, as well as a stable relative age structure as shown in Table 5. It can be seen that the population in this alternative case is substantially older than in Table 3. With the same assumptions about productivity, unemployment and so on as in the first case, this new population structure implies a ratio of social expenditure to GDP of 0.2394. Hence population ageing in these examples implies increased total expenditures as a proportion of GDP. These orders of magnitude reflect those of the major industrialized countries.

Table 3   Hypothetical Population Structure 1

Age	Survival rates		Fertility	Age distribution		
	M	F	rates	M	F	Total
1	.99	.99	0	0.2484	0.2453	0.2468
2	.955	.955	.95	0.2434	0.2403	0.2418
3	.755	.775	.755	0.2300	0.2272	0.2286
4	.625	.655	.55	0.1719	0.1742	0.1731
5	0	0	0	0.1063	0.1130	0.1097

Table 4   Social Expenditure Per Capita

Age	Education	Labour	Health	Pensions
1	10	0	5	0
2	8	5	4	0
3	0	5	5	0
4	0	5	12	5
5	0	0	20	25

Table 5   Hypothetical Population Structure 2

Age	Survival rates		Fertility	Age distribution		
	M	F	rates	M	F	Total
1	.99	.99	0	0.2335	0.2215	0.2274
2	.955	.955	.9	0.2312	0.2193	0.2251
3	.8	.9	.75	0.2208	0.2094	0.2150
4	.78	.855	.47	0.1767	0.1885	0.1828
5	0	0	0	0.1378	0.1612	0.1498

The higher expenditure requires correspondingly higher tax revenues and, depending on the tax structure, increases in tax rates. This may perhaps generate pressure for some items of social expenditure to be reduced, for example by cutting state pensions and government health benefits.

It is, however, most unlikely that changes in the population structure would occur without any other changes, for example in participation rates. Furthermore, social expenditures are also influenced by productivity and other variables. If the participation rates of women in the middle three age groups are increased to 0.8, 0.8 and 0.5 respectively, the social expenditure ratio would become lower, at 0.2247. If, in addition, all unemployment rates were 0.04, the ratio would again be lower, at 0.2223. Higher productivity would of course reduce the ratio further, though a differential between the expenditure growth of each category and productivity means that the ratio falls steadily over time. What is clear is that population ageing is just one component of the aggregate social expenditure-to-GDP ratio, which is sensitive to a wide range of variables. Some of the variables (such as unemployment rates) may be independent of ageing, but there are several interdependencies about which very little is known.

Many industrialized countries may be regarded as entering a largely unfamiliar territory whose characteristics are very difficult to predict. The present collection of articles is intended to provide an initial reference source for those wishing to examine the varied and important issues relating to the economics of individual and, particularly, population ageing.

PART III

DEMAND AND EXCHANGE

[6]
Demand Analysis: An Introduction

John Creedy

1 Introduction

This paper provides a brief review of some of the main results in consumer theory. No attempt is made to provide a comprehensive survey or to prove all the results, or even to state them with complete rigour. It aims to provide an informal collection of results that are useful in a variety of contexts, particularly in welfare economics. For more detailed treatments see, for example, Anderson (1980), Cornes (1992), Deaton and Muellbauer (1980), Gravelle and Rees (1992), Varian (1992) and Weymark (1980).

Attention is restricted to single-period models. The foundation of consumer theory is the theory of optimising behaviour, and an important role is played by duality results. Direct and indirect utility functions are examined in sections 2 and 3 respectively. The concepts of expenditure and distance functions are presented in section 4, and compensated demand functions are examined in section 5. Demand elasticities are presented in section 6, which is followed by a brief examination of aggregation over consumers, in section 7.

Most of the discussion concerns a single individual, assumed to face prices, p_i, for the ith good ($i = 1, ..., n$). Where x_i denotes the consumption of good i, and m is the budget, or 'income', then the budget constraint facing the individual is $m \geq \sum_{i=1}^{n} p_i x_i$.

1

2 The Direct Utility Function

The direct utility function is denoted $U(x)$, where U represents a preference ordering of consumption bundles, and is defined up to a monotonic increasing transformation, so that utility is ordinal. For interior, or tangency, solutions maximisation of $U(x)$ subject to the budget constraint, $m = \sum_{i=1}^{n} p_i x_i$, gives the Lagrangian:

$$L = U(x) + \lambda \left(m - \sum_{i=1}^{n} p_i x_i \right) \tag{1}$$

and the $n+1$ first-order conditions are $\partial U / \partial x_i = \lambda p_i$ for $i = 1, ..., n$, along with the budget constraint. These are used in order to determine the quantities consumed and the Lagrange multiplier, λ. For any pair of goods, this means that interior solutions must satisfy:

$$\frac{\partial U / \partial x_i}{\partial U / \partial x_j} = \frac{p_i}{p_j} \tag{2}$$

giving the familiar equi-marginal condition that marginal utility per unit of money devoted to each good, $(\partial U / \partial x_i) / p_i$, must be the same for all goods. This is equivalent to the tangency of an indifference curve with the budget line, shown as follows.

Along an indifference curve:

$$dU = \sum_{i=1}^{n} \frac{\partial U}{\partial x_i} dx_i = 0 \tag{3}$$

Hence, for any pair of goods, the marginal rate of substitution of good i for good j, denoted $MRS_{i,j}$, is:

$$MRS_{i,j} = -\frac{dx_j}{dx_i} \bigg|_U = \frac{\partial U / \partial x_i}{\partial U / \partial x_j} \tag{4}$$

This gives the tangency condition that the marginal rate of substitution of good i for j, the (absolute) slope of an indifference curve in a diagram with x_j on the vertical axis and x_i on the horizontal axis, is equal to the price

2

ratio, p_i/p_j, which is the (absolute) slope of the budget constraint. This gives the equi-marginal condition stated above. The marginal rate of substitution is obviously not affected by monotonic transformations of $U(x)$.

2.1 Homothetic Preferences

A function, $f(x)$ is homogeneous of degree k if $f(\theta x) = \theta^k f(x)$. For linear homogeneous functions, where $k = 1$, differentiation with respect to θ and setting $\theta = 1$ immediately gives Euler's law, $\sum_{i=1}^{n} x_i \frac{\partial f(x)}{\partial x_i} = f(x)$.

Differentiating $f(\theta x) = \theta^k f(x)$ with respect to x_i gives the result that $\partial f(x)/\partial x_i$ is homogeneous of degree $k - 1$. In the linear homogeneous case, then:

$$\frac{\partial f(\theta x)}{\partial x_i} = \frac{\partial f(x)}{\partial x_i} \tag{5}$$

In the context of a linear homogeneous utility function, $U(x)$, this implies that marginal utility, and hence the marginal rate of substitution, is constant along a ray from the origin; an equal proportionate increase in all x_i has no effect on the slope of the indifference curves. Hence budget shares are independent of both m and U. This implies that Engel curves are straight lines through the origin and all income elasticities are unity.

These results have important implications for aggregation over individuals. In view of the ordinal nature of utility, it would be undesirable to be restricted to utility functions that are linear homogeneous. However, this property also holds for functions that are positive monotonic transformations of linear homogeneous functions; such functions are known as homothetic functions.

2.2 Endowments

Suppose that the individual holds an endowment, s_i, of good i, in addition to the fixed income, m. The budget constraint becomes:

3

$$\sum_{i=1}^{n} p_i x_i = m + \sum_{i=1}^{n} p_i s_i \tag{6}$$

and it is convenient to define 'full income', M, as the budget that is available if the endowments are converted into money. From the resulting optimal values of x_i in relation to s_i it is possible to find whether the individual is a net demander or supplier of the good. In this context an increase in the price of a good increases the value of the individual's endowment. For a net supplier of the good, this can therefore produce an increase in demand, or reduction in supply. This gives rise to a 'backward bending' supply curve, which in turn creates the possibility of multiple equilibria in exchange models.

A popular context is the case where the individual has an endowment, H, of time and the net wage rate is w per unit of time. If the utility function is augmented to include leisure, h, then $U(x, h)$ is maximised subject to the constraint $\sum_{i=1}^{n} p_i x_i + wh = m + Hw = M$, and the supply of labour is given by $H - h$. In this case, an increase in the net wage, by increasing the value of the endowment, may lead to a reduction in labour supply despite the higher opportunity cost of leisure.

2.3   Marshallian Demands

The first-order conditions can in principle be solved to express the demand for each good as a function of m and the prices, p, giving the Marshallian demand functions, $x_i^M(p, m)$. These are homogeneous of degree zero, since $x_i^M(\theta p, \theta m) = x_i^M(p, m)$ and an equal proportional increase in all prices and income leaves demands unchanged. However, except for some standard cases, the first-order conditions are too nonlinear to be solved explicitly for the Marshallian demands.

In some contexts it is appropriate to regard the price, or willingness to pay for each good, as the endogenous variable. This gives rise to the inverse Marshallian demand function, $p_i^M(x, m)$, which is more easily obtained from the direct utility function than the ordinary demand function. Multiplying each first-order condition by x_i and summing over all goods gives $\sum_{i=1}^{n} x_i \left(\partial U / \partial x_i \right) = \lambda \sum_{i=1}^{n} p_i x_i = \lambda m$. Solving for λ and substituting into each first-order condition then gives:

$$p_i^M \left(x, m \right) = m \left\{ \frac{\partial U / \partial x_i}{\sum_{j=1}^{n} x_j \left(\partial U / \partial x_j \right)} \right\} \tag{7}$$

Hence, the inverse demand function can be expressed in terms of normalised prices, $\tilde{p}_i = p_i / m$, so that:

$$\tilde{p}_i^M \left(x \right) = \frac{\partial U / \partial x_i}{\sum_{j=1}^{n} x_j \left(\partial U / \partial x_j \right)} \tag{8}$$

This is sometimes referred to as the Hotelling-Wold identity.

3   The Indirect Utility Function

Substituting the demands $x_i^M \left(p, m \right)$ into the direct utility function gives the indirect utility function, $V \left(p, m \right)$, which is also expressed as a function of p and m. The indirect utility function is nondecreasing in m and nonincreasing in p. It is homogeneous of degree zero, so that $V \left(\theta p, \theta m \right) = V \left(p, m \right)$, implying that an equal proportional increase in prices and income has no effect on utility.

In view of the difficulty of solving for the demands from U, it is often useful to begin the analysis by specifying a form for the indirect utility function. The corresponding indifference curves are given in a diagram in which prices appear on the axes. In terms of normalised prices, $\tilde{p}$, indirect utility can be written as $V = V \left(\tilde{p} \right)$ and along an indifference curve:

$$dV = \sum_{i=1}^{n} \frac{\partial V}{\partial \tilde{p}_i} d\tilde{p}_i = 0 \tag{9}$$

The minimisation of indirect utility subject to the budget constraint then gives a corresponding tangency solution in terms of the inverse demands, or willingness to pay, expressed as:

$$\frac{\partial V/\partial p_i}{\partial V/\partial p_j} = \frac{x_i}{x_j} \tag{10}$$

If the indirect utility function is available, the associated direct utility function can be obtained by solving the problem of finding the prices to minimise $V(p,m)$, subject to the constraint that $\sum_{i=1}^{n} p_i x_i = m$, remembering that $V(p,m)$ is nonincreasing in p. The Lagrangian is thus $L = -V(p,m) + \lambda (m - \sum_{i=1}^{n} p_i x_i)$, giving $-\partial V(p,m)/\partial p_i = \lambda x_i$, where λ is the Lagrange multiplier for this problem. Solving for the inverse demands, that is the ps, and substituting into $V(p,m)$ gives the direct utility function. However, solving for the inverse demands from the indirect utility function can prove to be intractable, just as solving for the Marshallian demands from the direct utility function is often intractable.

3.1 Marshallian Demand Functions

The Marshallian demands are readily obtained from the indirect utility function, just as the inverse Marshallian demands are readily obtained from the direct utility function. Multiplying the first-order conditions by $\tilde{p}_i$ and summing gives $\lambda = -\sum_{i=1}^{n} (\partial V/\partial \tilde{p}_i)\, \tilde{p}_i$, so that substituting for λ gives the Marshallian demand:

$$x_i^M(p,m) = \frac{\partial V/\partial \tilde{p}_i}{\sum_{j=1}^{n} (\partial V/\partial \tilde{p}_j)\, \tilde{p}_j} \tag{11}$$

This is sometimes referred to as the Ville-Roy identity. An alternative form, usually known as Roy's identity, gives the demands as:

$$x_i^M(p,m) = -\frac{\partial V(p,m)/\partial p_i}{\partial V(p,m)/\partial m} \tag{12}$$

This follows from the fact that for fixed V, total differentiation with respect to p_i and m gives $(\partial V/\partial p_i)\, dp_i + (\partial V/\partial m)\, dm = 0$, combined with the requirement that $dm = x_i dp_i$.

6

4   The Expenditure and Distance Functions

4.1   The Expenditure Function

Consider the problem of finding the minimum expenditure, $\sum_{i=1}^{n} p_i x_i$, re-quired in order to reach a specified indifference curve or level of utility, U^*, at prices, p. The Lagrangian for this problem is $L = -\sum_{i=1}^{n} p_i x_i + \lambda (U - U^*)$. This is in fact the dual problem to that of utility maximisation subject to a budget constraint. It is easily seen that the first-order conditions for this problem are precisely the same as with the dual problem of utility maximisation. However, the optimal values of x are expressed in terms of the given level of utility and prices: these are the Hicksian or compensated demands, $x_i^H (p, U)$. Substitution of these demands into $\sum_{i=1}^{n} p_i x_i$ gives the minimum expenditure, expressed also as a function of U and p; this is the expenditure function, $E (p, U)$. This is concave and linear homogeneous in prices, since an equal proportional increase in all prices increases the minimum expenditure required to attain a given level of utility by the same amount; hence $E (\theta p, U) = \theta E (p, U)$.

However, if the indirect utility function $V (p, m)$ is available, the required minimum expenditure is obtained simply by inverting V in order to express m as a function of V and the prices, p, and then replacing V with U and m with $E (p, U)$. More formally, the two useful relationships used here can be stated as $U = V (p, E (p, U))$ and $m = E (p, V (p, m))$. Since $V (p, m)$ is nondecreasing in m, the required inversion can always, at least in principle, be carried out.

The expenditure function can also be used to define a constant-utility price index number, P_U, for price changes from p^0 to p^1, given by:

$$P_U = \frac{E (p^1, U)}{E (p^0, U)} \tag{13}$$

The Laspeyres and Paasche forms of this index are defined respectively for

7

pre- and post-change utility.

For a linear homogeneous direct utility function, an equal proportionate increase of θ in all x_i produces a θ-fold increase in utility; for fixed prices, this costs θ times as much. Since utility is ordinal, this result may not be regarded as interesting. However, it suggests that the expenditure function can be written as:

$$E\left(p, U\right) = UE\left(p, 1\right) = Ue\left(p\right) \tag{14}$$

where $e\left(p\right) = E\left(p, 1\right)$. Similarly:

$$V\left(p, m\right) = mV\left(p, 1\right) = mv\left(p\right) \tag{15}$$

The application of Roy's identity then gives the result that Marshallian demand functions are linear in m, with all income elasticities equal to unity. This has implications for aggregation, discussed below. For homothetic preferences, the constant-utility price index number is independent of U.

4.2   Money Metric Utility

The expenditure function can be used to define the concept of a 'money metric' utility function. This is motivated by the need for a money measure which, unlike ordinal utility, can be added over consumers. The major candidate is a system of labelling indifference curves based on the cost, at specified prices, of getting on to a specified indifference curve. Such a cost measure is clearly independent of monotonic transformations of the utility function, which simply change the utility index given to each indifference curve.

The money metric utility arises from considering the question of what amount of money an individual would require, at a set of prices, p, in order to be as well-off as when consuming a bundle of goods given by x. The amount, which may be denoted $m\left(p, x\right)$, is given by the money that would place the individual on the same indifference curve that passes through x.

8

Hence it is given directly from the expenditure function in terms of direct utility, since:

$$m(p, x) = E(p, U(x)) \tag{16}$$

If x is fixed, then $m(p, x)$ behaves just like an expenditure function and has the same properties. Alternatively, when p is fixed, $m(p, x)$ is a monotonic transformation of the direct utility function, and is therefore itself a utility function.

Another money metric can be defined by considering the question of how much money the individual would need, at some reference set of prices, p_r, in order to be as well-off as when facing the prices p and having an income of m. This amount, denoted $m_e(p_r, p, m)$, is given from the expenditure function in terms of indirect utility, since:

$$m_e(p_r, p, m) = E(p_r, V(p, m)) \tag{17}$$

This behaves just like an expenditure function with respect to variations in p_r for fixed V. However, for fixed p_r it is a monotonic transformation of the indirect utility function. The money metric indirect utility is in some contexts also referred to as 'equivalent income'.

4.3 The Distance Function

The function that is 'dual' to the expenditure function is the distance function, $D(x, U)$. This expresses the extent to which each of a set of xs must be adjusted (divided) in order to bring consumption on to a specified indifference curve, associated with utility of U. For given U, say U', and x, suppose the scalar adjustment is denoted by δ. Then $U' = U(x_1/\delta, ..., x_n/\delta)$, so that the solution for δ is given simply by the process of inverting the direct utility function. The distance function is then given by replacing U' with U, and δ with $D(x, U)$. Hence the distance function is obtained by inverting the direct utility function, just as the expenditure function is obtained by inverting the indirect utility function.

The distance function is homogeneous of degree 1 in x, so that $D\left(\theta x, U\right) = \theta D\left(x, U\right)$. It is increasing (and concave) in x and decreasing in U. It is sometimes referred to as the 'transformation' function.

5   Compensated Demands

The expenditure, or cost, function is extremely convenient in demand and welfare analysis when considering the demands as endogenous (depending on price changes), while the distance function is extremely convenient when considering the willingness to pay (or normalised prices) as endogenous. They can be used to obtain the associated compensated or Hicksian demands.

For changes in prices the Hicksian or compensated demands, $x_i^H\left(p, U\right)$, that is the demands that occur when changes are restricted to take place along a given indifference curve, have been defined above. They are the solutions to the dual problem of minimising expenditure subject to reaching an indifference curve. However, a valuable result is that they can also be obtained directly from the expenditure function by using Shephard's lemma, such that:

$$x_i^H\left(p, U\right) = \frac{\partial E\left(p, U\right)}{\partial p_i} \tag{18}$$

For unchanged total expenditure when prices change:

$$dE\left(p, U\right) = \sum_{i=1}^{n}\left(\partial E / \partial p_i\right) dp_i = \sum_{i=1}^{n} x_i dp_i = 0 \tag{19}$$

giving the tangency solution in price space, such that:

$$\left. \frac{dp_j}{dp_i}\right|_E = -\frac{x_i}{x_j} \tag{20}$$

A useful pair of results link the Hicksian and Marshallian demands, since:

$$x_i^M(p,m) = x_i^M(p, E(p,U)) = x_i^H(p,U) \tag{21}$$

$$x_i^H(p,U) = x_i^H(p, V(p,m)) = x_i^M(p,m) \tag{22}$$

The Hicksian demand at U is therefore the same as the Marshallian demand at income $E(p,U)$, and the Marshallian demand at m is the same as the Hicksian demand at $V(p,m)$.

5.1 Inverse Demands

The compensated, or Hicksian, inverse demands, $\tilde{p}_i^H(x,U)$, that is the willingness to pay for goods when changes are restricted to take place along a given indifference curve (with normalised prices on the axes), can be obtained from the distance function, just as the compensated demands are obtained from the expenditure function. Shephard's lemma can again be used, whereby:

$$\tilde{p}_i^H(x,U) = \frac{\partial D(x,U)}{\partial x_i} \tag{23}$$

This result is sometimes referred to as the Shephard-Hanoch lemma. The compensated inverse demands are homogeneous of degree zero in x, so that $\tilde{p}_i^H(\theta x, U) = \tilde{p}_i^H(x,U)$. Hence, associated with each level of U and with a set of quantity *ratios,* there is a set of expenditure-normalised 'shadow prices'. For unchanged total utility when consumption changes:

$$dD(x,U) = \sum_{i=1}^{n}(\partial D/\partial x_i)\,dx_i = \sum_{i=1}^{n}\tilde{p}_i dx_i = 0 \tag{24}$$

This gives the familiar tangency solution in quantity space, given earlier.

5.2 Budget Shares

The logarithmic form of Shephard's lemma is also very useful, since this gives the budget shares, $w_i = p_i x_i/m$, and again links the expenditure and distance functions. This gives:

$$w_i = \frac{\partial \log E(p, U)}{\partial \log p_i} = \frac{\partial \log D(x, U)}{\partial \log x_i} \qquad (25)$$

6   Price Changes and Demand Elasticities

Differentiate the Hicksian demand for good i, making use of the relationship given above between Hicksian and Marshallian demands, to give:

$$\frac{\partial x_i^H}{\partial p_j} = \frac{\partial x_i^M}{\partial m} \frac{\partial E}{\partial p_j} + \frac{\partial x_i^M}{\partial p_j} \qquad (26)$$

so that, using Shephard's lemma:

$$\frac{\partial x_i^H}{\partial p_j} = \frac{\partial x_i^M}{\partial m} x_j + \frac{\partial x_i^M}{\partial p_j} \qquad (27)$$

This is the famous Slutsky theorem. This can be converted into the following relationship among elasticities:

$$\sigma_{ij} = w_j e_i + \eta_{ij} \qquad (28)$$

where e_i is the income (total expenditure) elasticity:

$$e_i = \frac{\partial x_i^M}{\partial m} \frac{m}{x_i} \qquad (29)$$

η_{ij} is the Marshallian price elasticity of demand for good i, for a change in the price of good j, and is given by:

$$\eta_{ij} = \frac{\partial x_i^M / x_i^M}{\partial p_j / p_j} = \frac{\partial x_i^M}{\partial p_j} \frac{p_j}{x_i^M} \qquad (30)$$

and σ_{ij} is the corresponding compensated elasticity relating to movements along a Hicksian demand curve, given by:

$$\sigma_{ij} = \frac{\partial x_i^H}{\partial p_j} \frac{p_j}{x_i^H} \qquad (31)$$

12

From Shephard's lemma, $x_i^H = \partial E\left(p, U\right)/\partial p_i$, so the compensated elasticities can be written as:

$$\sigma_{ij} = \frac{\partial^2 E\left(p, U\right)}{\partial p_i \partial p_j} \frac{p_j}{x_i^H} \tag{32}$$

The matrix of compensated elasticities is therefore not symmetric. However, the substitution elasticities, s_{ij}, are defined as $s_{ij} = \sigma_{ij}/w_j$, and these are symmetric, in view of the symmetry of the $\partial^2 E\left(p, U\right)/\partial p_i \partial p_j$.

Other restrictions on elasticities arise from the budget constraint, giving the results that $\sum_{i=1}^{n} w_i = 1$, $\sum_{i=1}^{n} w_i e_i = 1$. The condition that $\sum_{j=1}^{n} \eta_{ij} = -e_i$ arises from the fact that the demand functions are homogeneous of degree zero, so that Euler's law gives $\sum_{j=1}^{n}\left(\partial x_i/\partial p_j\right) dp_j + \left(\partial x_i/\partial m\right) dm = 0$. In addition, the homogeneity conditions give $\sum_{j=1}^{n} w_j \sigma_{ij} = 0$ and $\sum_{j=1}^{n} s_{ij} = 0$.

The matrix $\left[\frac{\partial^2 E(p,U)}{\partial p_i \partial p_j}\right]$ is known as the Slutsky matrix, while the symmetric matrix $\left[\frac{\partial^2 D(x,U)}{\partial x_i \partial x_j}\right]$ is known as the Antonelli matrix.

7 Aggregation Over Consumers

The above analysis has considered only a single consumer. But the question arises of whether it is possible to aggregate over consumers, such that aggregate consumption can be expressed as a function of aggregate income and the aggregate function looks just like the individuals' functions. For this to be possible, an immediate requirement is that aggregate demand must not be affected by a change in the distribution of income, with the total income unchanged. If a change in income distribution is not to affect the total consumption of a good, then the changes arising from income gains must exactly off-set changes arising from income losses of individuals. Hence the demand functions must at least be linear, with each individual having the same marginal propensity to consume. This is satisfied for identical homothetic preferences, which imply linear demand curves having the same slope through the origin for each individual. However, this restriction is extremely

13

strong.

7.1   Quasi-homothetic Preferences

Consider the following special form of indirect utility function, given by:

$$V(p, m) = a(p) + b(p)m \tag{33}$$

where $a(p)$ and $b(p)$ are functions of the prices. This extends the homothetic form through the addition of the term $a(p)$, and is also known as the Gorman form. This could just as well have been written in terms of the expenditure function, the inverse of the indirect utility function, by expressing $E(p, U)$ as a linear function of U, with slope and intercept depending on prices. In this case, the intercept can then be interpreted as the cost of subsistence.

The application of Roy's identity gives the Marshallian demands:

$$x_i^M(p, m) = \alpha_i(p) + \beta_i(p)m \tag{34}$$

where:

$$\alpha_i(p) = -\frac{\partial a(p)/\partial p_i}{b(p)} \tag{35}$$

and:

$$\beta_i(p) = -\frac{\partial b(p)/\partial p_i}{b(p)} \tag{36}$$

Hence the Engel curves are straight lines but, unlike the homothetic case, are not required to go through the origin.

Suppose that there are T consumers, each with Gorman indirect utility functions where the $a(p)$ can vary but the $b(p)$ are the same for each individual. The latter requirement arises because, as suggested above, exact aggregation requires that the marginal propensities of all individuals must be the same. Variations in the $a(p)$ can arise because of demographic differences, such as household composition effects. The consumption of the ith good by the jth person can be expressed as:

$$x_{i,j}^M(p, m_j) = \alpha_{i,j}(p) + \beta_i(p) m_j \qquad (37)$$

and aggregate consumption is:

$$\sum_{j=1}^{T} x_{i,j}^M(p, m_j) = \sum_{j=1}^{T} \alpha_{i,j}(p) + \beta_i(p) \sum_{j=1}^{T} m_j \qquad (38)$$

These total demands could therefore be generated by a 'representative consumer', with income, $Y = \sum_{j=1}^{T} m_j$, equal to aggregate income and with the indirect utility function:

$$V(p, Y) = \sum_{j=1}^{T} a_j(p) + b(p) Y \qquad (39)$$

The Gorman form is in fact both necessary and sufficient for such exact aggregation to be possible. However, less restrictive conditions are needed if the nature of the aggregation requirement is relaxed.

8 Conclusions

This paper has provided a brief review of some of the results in demand analysis, concentrating on those that are useful for welfare measurement. There are four types of demand function. These include the pair of Marshallian ordinary and inverse demand curves, and the associated pair of compensated or Hicksian demand and inverse demand curves. In each case the demand curve is associated with a constrained optimisation problem, yet it is possible to avoid the difficulties of working with first-order conditions based on Lagrangians by making use of duality results.

15

References

[1] Anderson, R.W. (1980) Some theory of inverse demand for applied demand analysis. *European Economic Review*, 14, pp. 281-290.

[2] Cornes, R. (1992) *Duality and Modern Economics*. Cambridge: Cambridge University Press.

[3] Deaton, A.S. and Muellbauer, J. (1980) *Economics and Consumer Behaviour*. Cambridge: Cambridge University Press.

[4] Gravelle, H. and Rees, R. (1992) *Microeconomics*. London: Longman.

[5] Varian, H. (1992) *Microeconomic Analysis*. New York: Norton.

[6] Weymark, J.A. (1980) Duality results in demand analysis. *European Economic Review*, 14, pp. 377-395.

16

Multiple equilibria and hysteresis in simple exchange models

John Creedy and Vance Martin

This paper presents a simple two-good general equilibrium model of exchange in which demands are linear functions of relative prices. The solution of the model is represented by a cubic equation which can have either a single root which corresponds to a unique equilibrium price or three roots corresponding to multiple equilibria. The major properties of the model are that the relative price can make large discrete jumps in response to small parameter changes, and can display hysteresis. The paper shows how recent developments in non-linear methods can be used to examine the equilibrium properties of the model and establish conditions under which multiple equilibria can arise. The model is compared with that used by Shapley and Shubik.

Keywords: Exchange; Multiple equilibria; Hysteresis

ere has been much interest in recent years in n-linear economic models which give rise to multiple uilibria. See Dodgson [7] and Fischer [10] for a neral discussion, Venables [17] for an example the context of international trade, Fischer and mmeragg [9] for an application to the Phillips curve, nanno [3] and Creedy and O'Brien [6] for cussion of multiple equilibria in monopoly and Lye d Martin [13] for an application to exchange rates. r a survey of multiple equilibria and its relationship chaos theory see Creedy and Martin [5]. Of rticular interest is the behaviour of such models in ponse to small perturbations, which can generate ge jumps in the dependent variables rather than ooth continuous changes. This class of models may o give rise to the phenomenon of hysteresis, whereby urther small perturbation in the opposite direction es not cause the model to return to its initial sition. Models of hysteresis have been used by, for mple, Baldwin and Lyons [1] to explain the lack movement in the real US dollar.

The identification of zones of multiple equilibria important implications for economic policy since smooth relationship between policy targets and truments, which is a feature of linear models, breaks wn. For an economy operating at the knife edge of multiple equilibria zone, a small perturbation of the system can lead to the existing stable equilibrium position becoming unstable, resulting in the system jumping to a new stable equilibrium. In this situation the target variable is very sensitive to changes in policy instruments. In a linear analysis the high degree of sensitivity between instruments and targets would not be recognized, so that changes in instruments would probably be too large, thus causing an overshooting of policy targets. In the case where multiple equilibria give rise to hysteresis, the optimal policy needed to restore an economy to its original position may be both opposite in sign and larger in magnitude than previous policies.

It does not seem to be recognized that several of the early neoclassical economists were fully aware of, and even stressed, the problem of multiple equilibria in the context of simple exchange models. A feature of the 'marginal revolution' in economics of the 1870s was an emphasis on exchange, rather than simply the utility analysis of demand which is emphasized by modern texts. Such an emphasis leads naturally to a general equilibrium treatment which indicates very readily the possibility of multiple equilibria. In particular, even for the simplest case where linear demand functions are specified in a general equilibrium framework, multiple equilibria can be generated. The neglect of this early insight may perhaps be attributed to the dominance of partial equilibrium analysis. With partial equilibrium demand and supply curves it seems that special conditions are required for them to intersect more than once. General equilibrium characteristics were exploited by J.S. Mill [15] in his famous

: authors are with the Department of Economics, iversity of Melbourne, Parkville, Victoria 3052, Australia.

al manuscript received 22 March 1993.

-4-9993/93/040339-09 © 1993 Butterworth-Heinemann Ltd

339

analysis of international values. The first mathematical statement of Mill's analysis was produced by Whewell [19] who also demonstrated the possibility of multiple equilibria in situations where the demands are elastic: see Creedy [4].

The purpose of this paper, then, is to examine multiple equilibria in a simple model of exchange. The basic approach is set out in the next section, which concentrates on a model with linear demand schedules, similar to that of Walras [18]. This section also derives the utility functions implied by linear demand functions. These can be contrasted with alternative utility functions, such as those used by Shapley and Shubik [16], to generate multiple equilibria; their model is considered in the appendix. The following section provides an alternative representation of the model by using non-linear methods of analysis. This alternative formulation is then applied to show how the model can display hysteresis. Brief conclusions are finally drawn in the last section.

A basic model

Reciprocal demand and supply

The basis of a simple two-person two-good exchange model is the recognition that demand functions must be written in terms of relative prices, combined with the fact that a demand for one good is associated with a supply, or offer, of the other good. These features imply that only the demand functions need to be specified. The approach can be presented more formally as follows. Consider two goods X and Y exchanged by individuals A and B. Let

$x_d = B$'s demand for good X (from A)

$y_d = A$'s demand for good Y (from B)

Both x_d and y_d depend on the price ratio p_x/p_y, where p_x and p_y are respectively the price per unit of goods X and Y. In this context it is useful to interpret the price ratio p_x/p_y in terms of amounts of goods; it is the amount of good Y that has to be given up in order to obtain one unit of good X. Hence the demand by B for x_d units of good X carries with it an implied supply of $x_d(p_x/p_y)$ units of good Y. In equilibrium this must be equal to the amount of good Y demanded by A, that is, y_d. Thus in equilibrium:

$$x_d(p_x/p_y) = y_d \qquad (1)$$

This is, of course, precisely the usual condition that in equilibrium the amount of money that B wishes to spend on X is exactly the same as the amount of money A wishes to spend on Y, since $x_d p_x = y_d p_y$. In the context

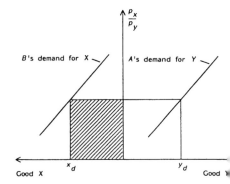

Figure 1. Price taking equilibrium.

of international trade, for example, this would give t[] required trade balance. But the formulation in (1) useful in bringing out the reciprocal nature of supp[] and demand in exchange.

The equilibrium is illustrated in Figure 1. In th[] back-to-back diagram the relative price is shown [] the vertical axis while quantities of X and Y a[] measured along the two horizontal axes. If A's dema[] for good Y is assumed to decrease as the price of [] increases, the demand curve on the right hand side [] upward sloping. From (1), it follows that the equi[] brium price ratio is such that the area of the shad[] rectangle in Figure 1 (equal to x_d multiplied by p_x/p_y[]) is equal to the length y_d. The same type of relationsh[] obviously applies when looking at the situation fro[] the point of view of the supply of X. If A demands [] the amount of X offered in return is equal to [] multiplied by the ratio p_y/p_x (the amount of X need[] to pay for one unit of Y). But as the price axis measu[] p_x/p_y, there is no longer a simple relationship betwe[] the area of the rectangle under the demand curve [] Y and the horizontal distance along the X axis.

Linear demand functions

The simple but important insight provided by []] concept of reciprocal demand was exploited by Wal[] [18], who took the step of writing the dema[] functions explicitly as functions of the relative pri[] Suppose that the two demand schedules are linear a[] downward sloping. Hence B's demand for X and []. demand for Y are:

$$x_d = a - b(p_x/p_y)$$

$$y_d = \alpha - \beta(p_y/p_x) = \alpha - \beta(p_x/p_y)^{-1}$$

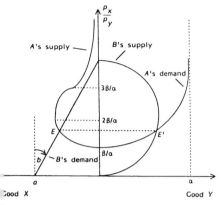

Figure 2. Linear demand curves.

where $a, b, \alpha, \beta > 0$. The supply of Y by B, y_s, is given by:

$$y_s = x_d(p_x/p_y) = a(p_x/p_y) - b(p_x/p_y)^2 \qquad (4)$$

Similarly, A's supply of X, x_s, associated with a demand for Y of y_d, is given by:

$$x_s = y_d(p_y/p_x) = \alpha(p_x/p_y)^{-1} - \beta(p_x/p_y)^{-2} \qquad (5)$$

The four schedules (2)–(5) are shown in Figure 2. In view of the quadratic nature of (4) the supply curve of good Y is backward bending. The turning point of , where the elasticity of supply is zero, occurs where the relative price p_x/p_y is equal to $a/2b$. This corresponds to the point where the demand for X, x_d, has unit elasticity, since the elasticity of demand is $-b/\{a/(p_xp_y) - b\}$, and is -1 when $p_x/p_y = a/2b$. For a partial equilibrium demand curve it is well known that expenditure is a maximum when the elasticity is unity. For the general equilibrium demand curve, the (reciprocal) supply behaves in the same way as does expenditure in the partial equilibrium curve. As the elasticity of demand for X moves from (minus) infinity the point a on the X axis, through minus unity and zero at the point a/b on the price axis, the elasticity supply moves from infinity at the origin, through zero (where the curve is vertical) to minus one at a relative price of a/b. The elasticity of demand is (minus) one, plus the elasticity of supply. The supply of X is also backward bending, having a maximum where the relative price of X is $2\beta/\alpha$; it has a point of inflexion where the relative price is $3\beta/\alpha$.

The equilibrium price ratio is point E on the left hand side of the diagram, corresponding to E' on the right hand side, where the supply and demand

schedules intersect. However, the existence of backward bending supply schedules gives rise to the possibility of more than one equilibrium position. This can also be seen by substituting (3) and (4) into the equilibrium condition $y_d = y_s$, which gives, after rearrangement:

$$\beta - \alpha(p_x/p_y) + a(p_x/p_y)^2 - b(p_x/p_y)^3 = 0$$

By writing $p = p_x/p_y$ this now becomes:

$$p^3 - (a/b)p^2 + (\alpha/b)p - \beta/b = 0 \qquad (6)$$

The equilibrium price ratio is thus represented as the root of a cubic, which can have up to three roots, though they need not necessarily be real or distinct. It has been seen that the supply schedules become backward bending where the demand schedules become elastic. Hence a necessary, but not sufficient, condition for the existence of three equilibria is the existence of a range of the demand schedules over which the elasticity of demand is numerically greater than unity.

Diagrams similar to the left hand side of Figure 2 were presented by Walras [18]. The first form of the back-to-back diagram was presented by Launhardt [13], and reproduced by Wicksell [20, 21], but since then has been neglected.

Offer curves

Marshall first produced his offer curves when 'translating' Mill's trade analysis into diagrams and used them to stress the possibility of multiple equilibria. He later referred to Walras's independent analysis; see Guillebaud ([12], II, p 804). These separate contributions, the French and English, nevertheless involve precisely the same basic model. Marshall's offer curves provide a direct relationship between supply and demand by eliminating the relative price. Consider, for example, the offer curve of B who offers good Y in exchange for good X. Solve for the price ratio, using (2), to get:

$$p_x/p_y = (a - x_d)/b \qquad (7)$$

Then substitute (7) into (4), giving:

$$y_s = (ax_d - x_d^2)/b \qquad (8)$$

The offer curve of B is thus quadratic in x_d. The turning point occurs where $dy_s/dx_d = 0$; that is, when $x_d = a/2$. Since the demand for X has unit elasticity where the relative price is $a/2b$, the corresponding value of x_d is

Multiple equilibria and hysteresis in simple exchange models: J. Creedy and V. Martin

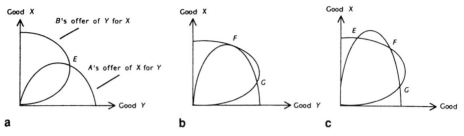

Figure 3. Offer curves.

$a/2$. Hence the turning point of the offer curve occurs at the point of unit elasticity of demand; beyond this, the demand is elastic. This result is intuitively clear; the offer curve will only bend back on itself where the supply curve is backward bending and the latter is only backward bending where the corresponding (reciprocal) demand curve is elastic. The slope of any ray drawn from a point on the offer curve to the origin measures the amount of one good that has to be given up in order to obtain the other good; hence it measures the rate of exchange.

Quadratic offer curves are shown in Figure 3 for three cases corresponding to alternative parameter configurations. In Figure 3a, a unique equilibrium price ratio is established at point E. The more interesting case of three equilibria is given in Figure 3c. Consider point F and suppose that the price of good X falls relative to that of Y. This means that the ray from the origin, representing the relative price, becomes steeper (the same quantity of X will 'purchase' a lower quantity of Y). It can be seen that the supply or offer of X increases as a result of the price fall. Thus a rise in the price of good Y leads A to 'spend' more on the good – which can only be done by offering more of good X. The demand for X also expands, but by less than the increase in supply. Hence the reduction in the price of X from the equilibrium at F leads to an excess supply of X, which reduces the price yet further from its equilibrium position; thus F represents an unstable equilibrium. Similar reasoning shows that the other two points of equilibrium are stable in the sense that a small change in the price ratio away from the equilibrium leads to changes that would be expected to reverse the disturbance rather than reinforce it. A different case is given in Figure 3b where two equilibria are established. From the discussion above, the equilibrium positions represented by points F and G are unstable and stable respectively. Any statement about Figure 3 can be translated into an equivalent statement about Figure 2.

Utility functions

It is of interest to examine the utility functions tha would give rise to the above exchange mode Following Edgeworth [8], the offer curve can t defined as the locus of points of tangency betwee indifference curves and price lines. It is convenient t redefine x and y as amounts exchanged, rather tha consumed, and to write the utility function as

$$U = U(x, y)$$

Transforming to polar coordinates, with $x = \rho \cos$ and $y = \rho \sin \theta$, the equation of the offer curve is:

$$\frac{dU}{d\rho} = 0 \tag{1}$$

For this to be a quadratic, it is required that:

$$ay - by^2 - x = 0 \tag{1}$$

where a and b are parameters. Substituting for x ar y this becomes:

$$a\rho \sin \theta - b\rho^2 \sin^2 \theta - \rho \cos \theta = 0 \tag{1}$$

So that substituting (12) into (10) and integrating give

$$U = \int (a\rho \sin \theta - b\rho^2 \sin^2 \theta - \rho \cos \theta) d\rho$$

$$= \frac{\rho^2}{2}(a \sin \theta - \cos \theta) - \frac{b\rho^3}{3} \sin^2 \theta \tag{1}$$

Transferring back to Cartesian coordinates, usi $\rho = (x^2 + y^2)^{1/2}$ and so on, and rearranging, gives:

$$U = 0.5(x^2 + y^2)^{1/2}\{y(a - 2by/3) - x\} \tag{1}$$

the individual is assumed to hold an amount, S, of ᴐod X before exchange, then consumption is $S - x$. edefining x as the amount consumed gives:

$$U = 0.5\{(S - x)^2 + y^2\}^{1/2}\{y(a - 2by/3) - (S - x)\} \quad (15)$$

his utility function may be compared with the form ᵴed in the exchange model of Shapley and Shubik ᵼ5], discussed in the appendix below.

ᴐn-linear demand functions

, has been seen that linear demand functions give rise ᴐ quadratic offer curves, which can produce three ᴐistinct equilibria. It is necessary to consider how the ᵴults may alter if higher order polynomials are used ᴐ specify the demand functions. If x_d and y_d are ᵴsumed respectively to be quadratic functions of p ᴐd $1/p$, where p is the relative price, it can be shown ᴐat the equation corresponding to (6) is a polynomial ᵼ order five in p. But only the downward sloping ᵴgment of the quadratic demand functions (with $y > 0$) can be regarded as feasible; when this is taken ᴐto account only three of the roots can be found to ᵥve rise to feasible equilibria, even though there may ᴐ five real and positive solutions to p.

The offer curves corresponding to such quadratic ᴐmand curves are rather awkward to obtain, since it necessary to eliminate p. However, if the alternative ᵴsumption is made that p and $1/p$ are quadratic ᴐnctions of x_d and y_d respectively, cubic offer curves ᴐ obtained. After much tedious manipulation it can ᴐ found that the equilibrium condition is an eighth ᴐder polynomial in p. Consideration of the cᴐnstraint ᴐat x_d and y_d must be non-negative eliminates five of ᴐ solutions, so that at most there can be three feasible ᴐuilibria. Continuing this type of approach shows ᴐat both cubic and fourth order polynomial demand ᴐnctions can give rise to at most five feasible equi ᵼria (along with many others that are not feasible). ᴐe cost of increasing the non-linearity of the ᴐmand functions is thus to add considerable algebraic ᴐmplexity.

ᴐn alternative representation of the model

was demonstrated above that alternative parameter ᴐnfigurations could change the number of equilibria ᴐd that a necessary but not sufficient condition for ᴐree equilibria is that the demand schedule be elastic. this section more formal conditions needed for ᵤltiple equilibria are established. The equilibrium ᵼlues of p, the relative price, are given by the roots ᴐ the polynomial in (6). This function represents a ᵤr-dimensional relationship between the three para ᴐters (a/b, α/b, and β/b) and the relative price p. It

is convenient to transform (6) in order to reduce the number of parameters from three to two. This is achieved by using a simple transformation of the relative price which preserves the qualitative properties of the solution. The treatment of models which do not result in polynomials is discussed, in the context of the Shapley and Shubik model, in the appendix. Without loss of generality, define w as the adjusted relative price, where:

$$w = p - a/3b \quad (16)$$

The term $-a/3b$ is simply the coefficient on p^2, in (6), divided by three. This transformation is known as a diffeomorphism which is a generalization of a linear transformation. In general, for polynomials of degree n, the $(n-1)$ degree term can be eliminated by generalizing (16) to $w = p + \phi$, where ϕ is a simple function of the coefficient corresponding to p^{n-1}. See Gilmore [11] for further discussion of diffeomorphisms in higher order polynomials. Substituting (16) in (6) for p gives:

$$(w + a/3b)^3 - (a/b)(w + a/3b)^2$$
$$+ (\alpha/b)(w + a/3b) - \beta/b = 0$$

which reduces to:

$$w^3 + \tau_1 w + \tau_0 = 0 \quad (17)$$

where

$$\tau_1 = \alpha/b - a^2/3b^2$$
$$\tau_0 = -\beta/b - 2a^3/27b^3 + a\alpha/3b^2$$

The transformation given by (16) provides a more parsimonious representation of the model as its parameters are now summarized by τ_0 and τ_1. Equation (17) represents a cubic in w which has the same qualitative properties as the cubic equation given in (6). Although τ_0 and τ_1 have no clear economic interpretation, both parameters are related to the structural parameters (a, b, α and β) of the model as given by the expressions in (17). Thus, it is possible to analyse the effects of structural parameter perturbations on relative prices, via the expressions given in (16) and (17).

It is useful to consider the relationship between w and τ_0, for alternative values of τ_1. Taking the total differential of (17) while holding τ_1 constant gives:

$$(3w^2 + \tau_1)dw + d\tau_0 = 0$$

Multiple equilibria and hysteresis in simple exchange models: J. Creedy and V. Martin

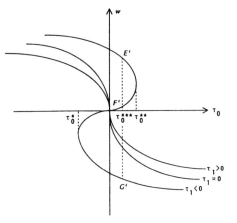

Figure 4. Equilibrium properties: relationship between τ_0 and w.

The slope of the relationship between w and τ_0 is thus:

$$\frac{dw}{d\tau_0} = -\frac{1}{(3w^2 + \tau_1)} \qquad (18)$$

Three separate cases can be distinguished according to whether τ_1 is negative, zero or positive. These are illustrated in Figure 4. First, when $\tau_1 > 0$, $dw/d\tau_0 < 0$ and a unique inverse relationship between w and τ_0 exists. The explanation for this relationship is that a shift in the demand schedule for good Y caused for example by a decrease in β, leads to an increase in the price of Y and therefore a fall in the relative price p. The decrease in β involves, from (17), an increase in τ_0, while the fall in p is associated, from (16), with a fall in w. Hence an increase in τ_0 is associated with a reduction in w.

Secondly, when $\tau_1 = 0$, (18) reduces to:

$$\frac{dw}{d\tau_0} = \frac{-1}{3w^2} \qquad (19)$$

As with the case where $\tau_1 > 0$, there is an inverse relationship between w and τ_0 except at the point $w = 0$, in which case the slope approaches (minus) infinity. This property is demonstrated in Figure 4.

The two cases discussed above show that for $\tau_1 \geqslant 0$, the model has a unique equilibrium. The more interesting case is when $\tau_1 < 0$, since multiple equilibria may now arise. The relationship between w and τ_0 when $\tau_1 < 0$ is depicted in Figure 4 by the inverted S-shaped schedule. The two points τ_0^* and τ_0^{**} are referred to as the threshold points and correspond to

the points when the slope of the line approaches (minus) infinity. From (18), this occurs when

$$w = \pm(-\tau_1/3)^{1/2} \qquad (20)$$

For $\tau_0^* > \tau_0 > \tau_0^{**}$, there is a unique inverse relationship between w and τ_0 and as with the cases discussed above, the model has a unique equilibrium. However, for $\tau_0^* < \tau_0 < \tau_0^{**}$, there is no unique relationship between w and τ_0, as the slope of the line given by (18) can be negative ($w^2 > -\tau_1/3$) as well as positive ($w^2 < -\tau_1/3$). This is the zone of multiple equilibria where the stable equilibria are given by the upper and lower schedules in Figure 4 and the unstable equilibrium points are given by the interior schedule. Thus the point $\tau_0 = \tau_0^{***}$ yields three equilibrium points, E, F' and G' which correspond to the three equilibrium points E, F and G depicted in Figure 3. For values of τ_0 at the threshold points, there are two equilibria, one stable and one unstable. This situation corresponds to the two equilibria case highlighted in Figure 3.

It is helpful to state the conditions of the equilibrium properties of the model more formally by looking at the relationship between τ_0 and τ_1. Consider the case of two equilibrium points when, for a particular (negative) value of τ_1, τ_0 is at one of the threshold points. From (20):

$$\tau_1 = -3w^2 \qquad (21)$$

Substituting (21) into (17) and rearranging gives:

$$\tau_0 = 2w^2 \qquad (22)$$

Solving both (21) and (22) for w, and equating yields:

$$(-\tau_1/3)^{1/2} = (\tau_0/2)^{1/3}$$

Rearranging this expression yields the following relationship between τ_0 and τ_1, which holds when there are two equilibria:

$$27\tau_0^2 + 4\tau_1^3 = 0 \qquad (23)$$

This relationship is shown in Figure 5, which gives the combinations of τ_0 and τ_1 resulting in the model having two equilibrium points. These lines can be derived from Figure 4 by mapping the threshold points for different (negative) values of τ_1 onto the (τ_0, τ_1) surface in Figure 5.

To see how the number of equilibria change for different combinations of τ_0 and τ_1, consider Figure If τ_0 increases above the threshold point τ_0^*, while holding τ_1 constant, the number of equilibria reduce

Multiple equilibria and hysteresis in simple exchange models: J. Creedy and V. Martin

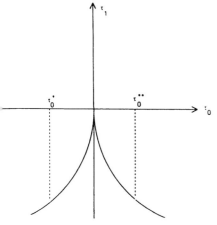

ure 5. Equilibrium properties: relationship between τ_0
d τ_1.

m two to one. Comparing this result with Equation
3), this implies that the model has a unique
uilibrium when:

$$27\tau_0^2 + 4\tau_1^3 > 0 \qquad (24)$$

milarly, if τ_0 is decreased below τ_0^{**}, such that
$< \tau_0 < \tau_0^{**}$, there are three equilibria. Again, com-
ring this result with (23) implies that for three
uilibria:

$$27\tau_0^2 + 4\tau_1^3 < 0 \qquad (25)$$

e equilibrium properties of the model can be
mmarized as follows. A necessary condition for
ltiple equilibria is that $\tau_1 < 0$. A necessary and
fficient condition for multiple equilibria is that
$\tau_0^2 + 4\tau_1^3 \leqslant 0$. The necessary condition has a simple
terpretation in terms of the demand and supply
rves shown in Figure 2. For $\tau_1 < 0$ it is seen that
$a^2/3b$. Now α is the asymptotic value to which the
mand for Y approaches as the price ratio p_x/p_y
creases. The elasticity of the demand for X is unity
en the price ratio is $a/2b$, which implies that the
ximum supply of good Y is, from (4), equal to $a^2/4b$.
nce the necessary condition for two or more
uilibria to occur requires that the maximum demand
good Y is less than $1\frac{1}{3}$ times the maximum supply
good Y. The necessary and sufficient condition does
t, however, seem to generate such a clear condition,
ce it requires that τ_1 is no greater than the (negative)
be root of $27\tau_0^2/4$.

Hysteresis

To highlight the equilibrium properties of the model
as summarized in Figures 4 and 5, this section applies
the results to the analysis of hysteresis. Assume that
$\tau_1 < 0$ and that the economy is operating at point A
in Figure 6, which is both stable and unique. Consider
a shock to the system which increases τ_0 (while leaving
τ_1 still negative). The adjusted relative price variable
w starts decreasing smoothly until reaching point C.
The economy has moved from a unique equilibrium
point at A to a zone of multiple equilibria. At the
point C, however, the existing equilibrium position is
unstable. If τ_0 is further increased, the economy jumps
to the new stable equilibrium position identified by
point D on the lower surface. Additional increases in
τ_0 will still lead to falls in w but such changes will be
smooth.

Suppose that after the shock in τ_0 which forced the
adjusted relative price variable to jump from the upper
to the lower surface, that is from points C to D, the
shock is reversed in the opposite direction. The process
does not jump from D to C, but w increases gradually
until reaching point E. The process is irreversible as
an offsetting shock does not restore the equilibrium
position. Further decreases in τ_0 cause the process to
jump again from the lower to point B on the upper
surface.

The definition of hysteresis used here can be
contrasted with the definition used by Blanchard and
Summers [2] and Baldwin and Lyons [1], where
hysteresis is captured by a non-mean reverting process
such as a random walk. While both approaches

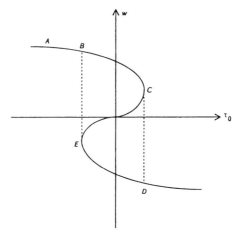

Figure 6. Demonstration of hysteresis.

attempt to explain how processes can become 'sticky', the approach used in the present paper captures the essential characteristic of hysteresis; namely that a process exhibits multiple equilibria and fails to move from one equilibrium to another equilibrium.

Conclusions

Neoclassical economists such as Walras and Marshall stressed the possibility of multiple equilibria in simple models of exchange. The later emphasis on partial equilibrium methods, combined with the analytical problems of dealing with multiple equilibria, meant that for a long time economists tended to ignore the more interesting and important issues, such as discrete jumps and hysteresis, that arise when models do not have a unique equilibrium. It has been shown with the aid of recent developments in non-linear methods, that the basic properties of simple exchange models can be examined using a relatively simple and convenient approach. The approach also yields more insights into the nature of the models than the cumbersome analysis of the roots of polynomials, which typically requires the application of numerical methods. The paper has therefore combined the rediscovery of a much neglected exchange model with the application of modern techniques of analysis. The present paper is also an attempt to encourage the wider use of these techniques.

References

1 R. Baldwin and R. Lyons, *Exchange Rate Hysteresis: The Real Effects of Large vs Small Policy Misalignments*, NBER Working Paper Series, No 2828, 1989.
2 O.J. Blanchard and L.H. Summers, *Fiscal Increasing Returns, Hysteresis, Real Wages and Unemployment*, Harvard Institute of Economic Research, Discussion Paper No 1266, 1986.
3 G. Bonanno, 'Monopoly equilibria and catastrophe theory', *Australian Economic Papers*, Vol 27, 1987, pp 197–215.
4 J. Creedy, 'Whewell's "translation" of J.S. Mill', *Scottish*

Journal of Political Economy, Vol 36, 1989, pp 266–28
5 J. Creedy and V.L. Martin, *Chaos and Non-Line Models in Economics*, Edward Elgar, Aldershot, 199
6 J. Creedy and D.P. O'Brien, 'Marshall, monopoly a rectangular hyperbolas', *Australian Economic Pape* Vol 29, 1990, pp 141–153.
7 J.S. Dodgson, 'Kinks and catastrophes: a note the relevance of catastrophe theory for economi *Australian Economic Papers*, Vol 21, 1982, pp 407–415
8 F.Y. Edgeworth, *Mathematical Psychic*, Kegan Pa London, 1881.
9 E.O. Fischer and W. Jammeragg, 'Empirical inves gation of a catastrophe theory extension of the Philli curve', *Review of Economics and Statistics*, Vol 68, 19 pp 9–17.
10 S. Fischer, 'Recent developments in macroeconomic *Economic Journal*, Vol 98, 1988, pp 294–339.
11 R. Gilmore, *Catastrophe Theory for Scientists a Engineers*, John Wiley, New York, 1981.
12 C.W. Guillebaud, *Marshall's Principles of Economi* Vol 2, 9th edn, Macmillan, London, 1961.
13 W. Launhardt, *Mathematical Principles of Economi* originally published 1885, translated by H. Schmidt a edited by J. Creedy, Edward Elgar, Aldershot, 1993.
14 J.L. Lye and V.L. Martin, 'Non-linear time ser modelling and distributional flexibility', *Journal of Ti Series Analysis*, forthcoming, 1993.
15 J.S. Mill, *Essays on Some Unsettled Questions Political Economy*, originally published 1844, reprint by LSE in Series of Scarce Works in Political Econom No 7, J.W. Parker, London, 1948.
16 L.S. Shapley and M. Shubik, 'An example of a tradi economy with three competitive equilibria', *Journal Political Economy*, Vol 85, No 4, 1977, pp 873–875.
17 A.J. Venables, 'Multiple equilibria in the theory international trade with monopolistically competiti commodities', *Journal of International Economics*, V 16, 1984, pp 103–121.
18 L. Walras, *Elements of Pure Economics*, origina published 1874, translated by W. Jaffe, Allen a Unwin, London, 1954.
19 W. Whewell, *Mathematical Exposition of Some Doctri of Political Economy*, Gregg International Publishe 1968.
20 K. Wicksell, *Value Capital and Rent*, translated by S Frowein, Allen and Unwin, London, 1954.
21 K. Wicksell, *Lectures on Political Economy*, translat by E. Classen and edited by L. Robbins, Routled London, 1934.

Appendix
The Shapley–Shubik model

Consider two individuals who exchange two goods X and Y, where x and y denote amounts consumed. Suppose that person 2 initially holds all the initial stock of good Y, denoted D, and that person 1 holds all the stocks of good X, denoted R. The utility functions are:

$$U_1(x, y) = x + \alpha_1(1 - e^{-y/\beta_1}) \qquad (26)$$

$$U_2(x, y) = y + \alpha_2(1 - e^{-x/\beta_2}) \qquad ($$

where all parameters are positive. Shapley and Shubick [examined special cases of these utility functions which ga rise to multiple equilibria. For comparison with the mo considered in this paper it is useful to examine the dema functions implied by (26) and (27).

346

Consider person 2, and form the appropriate Lagrangean, for maximization of $U_2(x, y)$ subject to the budget constraint. Then:

$$L = U_2(x, y) + \lambda(D - y - px) \tag{28}$$

From the first order conditon $\partial L/\partial y = \partial U_2/\partial y - \lambda = 0$, substitution of the appropriate partial derivative shows that the Lagrangean, λ, is simply equal to unity. Substitution into the first order condition $\partial L/\partial x = \partial U_2/\partial x - \lambda p = 0$ gives:

$$p = (\alpha_2/\beta_2) e^{-x/\beta_2} \tag{29}$$

which yields person 2's demand for good X given by:

$$x = -\beta_2 \log(p\beta_2/\alpha_2) \tag{30}$$

since for $x \geqslant 0$ it is required to have (for $\beta_2 > 0$), $\beta_2 p/\alpha_2 < 1$, $p < \alpha_2/\beta_2$. Substitution for x, from (30), into the budget constraint and rearranging gives the demand for good Y as:

$$y = D + p\beta_2 \log(p\beta_2/\alpha_2) \tag{31}$$

To derive person 1's demand functions, form the Lagrangean:

$$L = U_1(x, y) + \lambda(R - y - px) \tag{32}$$

The first order condition $\partial L/\partial x = \partial U_1/\partial x - \lambda p$ gives $p = 1/\lambda$. The condition $\partial L/\partial y = \partial U_1/\partial y - \lambda = 0$ then gives the demand by person 1 for good Y as:

$$y = \beta_2 \log(p\alpha_1/\beta_2) \tag{33}$$

For $y \geqslant 0$, with $\beta_1 > 0$, this requires $p > \beta_1/\alpha_1$. Substitution into the budget constraint of person 1, gives 1's demand for X as:

$$x = R/p - (\beta_1/p) \log(p\alpha_1/\beta_1) \tag{34}$$

It is not, of course, necesssary to consider both goods, since an excess demand for one good will imply an excess supply of the other good. For good X, the sum of (30) and (34) must equal the amount available, R; while for good Y, the sum of (31) and (33) must be equal to D. In the case of good Y, for example, it can be found that:

$$(\beta_1 + \beta_2 p) \log p = \beta_1 \log(\beta_1/\alpha_1) - \beta_2 \log(\beta_2/\alpha_2) \tag{35}$$

This is non-linear in p. To analyse its equilibrium properties, it is convenient to approximate (35) by a polynomial. By taking a Taylor series expansion around the parity value $p = 1$, including only the first two terms, (35) can be written as

$$(\beta_1 + \beta_2 p) \left[(p-1) - \frac{(p-1)^2}{2} + \dots \right] = \phi \tag{36}$$

where $\phi = \beta_1 \log(\beta_1/\alpha_1) - \beta_2 \log(\beta_2/\alpha_2)$. Expanding and rearranging gives the cubic equation

$$p^3 + \left[\frac{\beta_1}{\beta_2} - 4 \right] p^2 + \left[3 - \frac{4\beta_1}{\beta_2} \right] p + \left[\frac{3\beta_1}{\beta_2} + \frac{2\phi}{\beta_2} \right] = 0 \tag{37}$$

which is of the same form as Equation (6). Using the transformation given by (16), similar expressions to (17), (18) and (23) can be derived.

[8]

EXCHANGE EQUILIBRIA: BARGAINING, UTILITARIAN AND COMPETITIVE SOLUTIONS*

JOHN CREEDY

University of Melbourne

I. INTRODUCTION

The purpose of this paper is to provide a simple exposition of three alternative solution concepts in the context of exchange. It is well known that with barter between just two traders, the rate of exchange cannot be determined given only the assumption of rational egotistical behaviour; additional structure must be added to the model. The approach followed by most early studies of exchange, up to Edgeworth (1881), was to avoid the question by explicitly concentrating on competitive or price-taking behaviour. A major contribution of Edgeworth was to show that as the size of the market (in terms of the number of traders) increases, a barter process which allows recontracting will replicate price-taking behaviour. Alternatively, it was sometimes argued that a principle of arbitration, involving value judgements, would be required in practice. A third approach, now widely used, involves the formulation of bargaining solutions. The three approaches are described below. Section II examines the widely used *bargaining* solution associated with Nash (1950). Section III considers a particular rule, that of the utilitarian principle of maximum total utility, for *arbitration* between traders. The utilitarian criterion is of course often used also as a 'social evaluation' function. Finally, Section IV examines *competitive* equilibria where the two individuals are regarded as just two representative traders who take prices as given in a large market consisting of many similar pairs of traders.

The three approaches have several features in common. First, they are based not surprisingly on the maximisation of some objective function. The Nash maximand is the weighted geometric mean of the traders' payoffs. The utilitarian maximand is the unweighted arithmetic mean utility of individuals. The competitive solution involves each individual independently maximising utility subject to the given prices and endowments. Only the utilitarian approach requires an interpersonal comparison of utility. Secondly, each solution is Pareto efficient, so that a movement away from an equilibrium involves a loss of utility for at least one person. This is a fundamental requirement; with zero transaction costs and full information, there would otherwise be an incentive for traders to find an alternative arrangement. Thirdly, each approach is static in that it concentrates on the properties of the solution without investigating the process by which equilibrium may be reached. This is obvious in the case of the utilitarian arbitration, but with the other two approaches it is a question of the great difficulty of handling even simple dynamic processes in which trades take place out of equilibrium. (A special case of an adjustment process

* I should like to thank a referee for constructive suggestions.

34

will, however, be examined in Section IV.) Fourthly, the first-order conditions required for each optimisation problem are deceptively simple. In general they can be stated very succinctly, but except for special cases it is necessary to solve non-linear equations, which requires the use of numerical procedures. Nevertheless, comparative static results can be obtained using standard analytical methods, but these are not discussed here. It is argued that the use of specific functional forms helps to provide further insights into the nature of the problems and the properties of their solutions, so that examples are given in each section. First, the following subsection describes the basic model of exchange which is used throughout the paper.

The exchange model

The following analysis concentrates on the 'pure exchange' case, where traders are endowed with given stocks of each good. There are two traders, denoted A and B, and two goods, X and Y. The pre-trade stocks held by each trader are as follows:

> Person A holds a_A and b_A of X and Y respectively
> Person B holds a_B and b_B of X and Y respectively.

It will be supposed that these stocks are such that person A holds most of X and person B holds most of Y, and that trade involves A giving up x of X in exchange for y of Y from B. After trade the utilities U_A and U_B are given by:

$$U_A = U_A(a_A - x, b_A + y) \tag{1}$$

$$U_B = U_B(a_B + x, b_B - y) \tag{2}$$

This statement of the model essentially follows that of Jevons (1871), although Edgeworth (1881) added general rather than additive utility functions. It is worth noting that, for example, A's marginal utility of good X is not simply the first derivative of (1) with respect to x, but is $-\partial U_A / \partial x$ since the amount held decreases as x, the amount exchanged, increases. In examining this model, Edgeworth's concepts of indifference curves and the contract curve have been invaluable.

It is well-known that Pareto efficiency, requiring equality of the marginal rates of substitution, defines a *range* of allocations along the contract curve, between the pre-trade indifference curves which go through the endowment point. For differentiable utility functions, the contract curve is defined for interior solutions by:

$$\frac{\partial U_A / \partial x}{\partial U_A / \partial y} = \frac{\partial U_B / \partial x}{\partial U_B / \partial y} \tag{3}$$

The rate of exchange, the rate at which one good is given up for the other, is equivalent to the slope of a line from the endowment point to the place on the contract curve where trade takes place. The *price* of a good essentially measures such a ratio of amounts of two goods traded (where one of the goods may be money). This reflects the fundamental property of 'reciprocal demand' which is inherent in a statement of a price (ratio). Since there are infinitely many points on the contract curve, Edgeworth (1881) described the situation as reflecting 'indeterminacy' of the exchange rate. It is therefore necessary to introduce addition structure into the model.

II The Bargaining Solution

This section presents the Nash bargaining solution and applies it to exchange with Cobb-Douglas utility functions and the special case of constant marginal utilities, requiring the treatment of corner solutions. An exchange context which has received much attention is that of bargaining between a firm and a union, and this is examined in the final subsection.

The general Nash solution

The Nash (1950) solution involves the use of each trader's 'threat point'. This is the utility in the worst situation possible, so in the trading context it is the utility obtained from the individual's pre-trade endowment of goods. The 'payoff' to each individual is defined as the excess of utility in the bargained outcome to that in the threat point; it is thus the net gain from trade. The approach allows for the relative bargaining power of each trader through the use of a 'power parameter', though the sources of such power are not usually specified. The Nash solution can be shown to arise in a situation in which each rational and fully informed individual maximises his or her payoff given the behaviour of the other trader. Nash did not consider the *process* by which agreement is reached. For extensive discussion of the various axioms, see de Menil (1971). For present purposes it is sufficient to state that the Nash solution is the outcome which maximises the weighted geometric mean of the payoffs, with weights equal to the respective power parameters. The payoffs can be denoted P_A and P_B for A and B respectively, and are obtained as:

$$P_A = U_A(a_A - x, b_A + y) - U_A(a_A, b_A) \tag{4}$$

$$P_B = U_B(a_B + x, b_B - y) - U_B(a_B, b_B) \tag{5}$$

The power parameters for traders A and B are denoted ϕ and $1 - \phi$ respectively.

The solution is given by the values of x and y which maximise L, given by:

$$L = P_A^\phi P_B^{1-\phi} \tag{6}$$

The first-order conditions are obtained by differentiating L with respect to x and y, and are, after rearranging, given by:

$$\phi \frac{\partial U_A}{\partial x} P_B + (1 - \phi) \frac{\partial U_B}{\partial x} P_A = 0 \tag{7}$$

$$\phi \frac{\partial U_A}{\partial y} P_B + (1 - \phi) \frac{\partial U_B}{\partial y} P_A = 0 \tag{8}$$

Equations (7) and (8) give two non-linear equations in x and y. They may have no solution or more than one solution, and will typically require numerical methods. Combining (7) and (8) to eliminate the payoffs, P_A and P_B, gives the equation of the contract curve as shown in (3). Hence a Nash solution is a point of tangency between indifference curves and is Pareto efficient.

Consider the extreme situations where either $\phi = 0$ or $\phi = 1$. When $\phi = 0$, then on the assumption of monotonicity, so that the partial derivatives of utility functions are non-zero, the solution requires $P_A = 0$. This condition specifies the equation of the pre-trade indifference curve of person A, which is the indifference curve going through the endowment point. Hence the solution is the intersection of the contract curve with A's pre-trade indifference curve. When $\phi = 1$, the first order conditions require $P_B = 0$, giving the equation of the pre-trade indifference curve of person B. Hence the solution is at the other extreme of the contract curve where trader A obtains all the gains from trade. However, without these extreme assumptions, all that can generally be said from the first-order conditions about a Nash solution is that for each good the ratio of marginal utilities is proportional to the ratio of payoffs. It is therefore instructive to turn to a special case.

Cobb-Douglas utility functions

Consider the special case of Cobb-Douglas utility functions, such that:

$$U_A = (a_A - x)^\alpha (b_A + y)^\beta \tag{9}$$

$$U_B = (a_B + x)^\gamma (b_B - y)^\delta \tag{10}$$

For convenience, write the pre-trade utilities of each person as U_A^* and U_B^*. Note that in this case, the utility functions do not have positive partial derivatives if the amount held of any good is zero. After appropriate differentiation and substitution into (7) and (8), the first-order conditions for the Nash solution are:

$$\frac{-\phi\alpha}{a_A - x} U_A (U_B - U_B^*) + \frac{(1-\phi)\gamma}{x + a_B} U_B (U_A - U_A^*) = 0 \tag{11}$$

$$\frac{\phi\beta}{b_A + y} U_A (U_B - U_B^*) - \frac{(1-\phi)\delta}{b_B - y} U_B (U_A - U_A^*) = 0 \tag{12}$$

Even for this special case the first order conditions are non-linear in x and y, and cannot be solved analytically. Suppose that $\alpha = 0.3$, $\beta = 0.5$, $\gamma = 0.2$, $\delta = 0.4$, with initial endowments given by $a_A = b_B = 0.9$ and $b_A = a_B = 0.1$. The solution is illustrated in Figure 1, which shows other solution concepts and will be used in later sections of this paper. The endowment point is shown as point E in the Edgeworth box shown in Figure 1, where indifference curves U_A^* and U_B^* are the pre-trade indifference curves. Assuming that $\phi = 0.5$, the loci defined by equations (11) and (12) may be obtained numerically and are shown by the lines marked N_1 and N_2. These intersect at the point on the contract curve where x and y, the amounts exchanged, are equal to 0.473 and 0.283 respectively. A higher value of ϕ would move the Nash equilibrium in a north-easterly direction.

A further simplification

The problem of finding the Nash solution is considerably simplified if it is assumed that trader A initially holds all of good X, while trader B initially holds all the stocks of good Y, so that $U_A^* = U_B^* = 0$. The stocks may then conveniently be normalised to unity, so that:

$$a_A = 1, \quad b_A = 0, \quad a_B = 0, \quad b_B = 1 \tag{13}$$

This means that, for example, A's indifference curve through the endowment (now the bottom right hand corner) effectively coincides with the base of the box. The terms U_A and U_B can be eliminated from the first order conditions (11) and (12), which can be arranged to give:

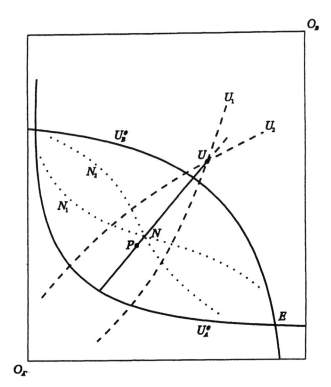

FIGURE 1
Alternative equilibria with Cobb-Douglas utility functions

$$x = \left\{1 + \frac{\alpha\phi}{\gamma(1-\phi)}\right\}^{-1} \tag{14}$$

$$y = \left\{1 + \frac{\delta(1-\phi)}{\beta\phi}\right\}^{-1} \tag{15}$$

From (14) it can be seen that if $\alpha \geq \gamma$, then $x \leq 1 - \phi$. Similarly, from (15), if $\beta \geq \delta$, then $y \geq \phi$. If trader A has all the bargaining power, that is where $\phi = 1$, equations (14) and (15) show that $x = 0$ and $y = 1$, so that B gives up all the stock of good Y without gaining any of good X in return. Where B has all the power, that is where $\phi = 0$, the situation is reversed. This extreme situation arises because each person has zero utility before trade and, as noted earlier, with Cobb-Douglas utility functions, positive utility requires individuals to hold at least some of *both* goods. With extreme asymmetry in the bargaining power, the effective price of the good held by the strong trader can be raised infinitely high.

In the more normal situation where $0 < \phi < 1$, the effective rate of exchange, p_N or price ratio of good X for Y, is the ratio of the amount of Y given up per unit of good X, or the ratio of (14) to (15), and is thus given by:

$$p_N = \frac{y}{x} = \frac{1 + \alpha\phi/\{\gamma(1-\phi)\}}{1 + \delta(1-\phi)/\beta\phi} \tag{16}$$

In the special case where tastes are identical, $\alpha = \gamma$, $\delta = \beta$, and the implicit rate of exchange depends only on the relative bargaining power and is simply equal to $\phi/(1-\phi)$.

Constant marginal utilities

In view of the widespread use of an assumption of constant marginal utilities, it is useful to examine the implications for the Nash solution. In the appropriate context, this assumption implies risk neutrality (that is, zero relative risk aversion). For the same initial endowment as in the previous case, given by (13), suppose that the utility functions are linear, whereby:

$$U_A = \alpha(1-x) + \beta y \tag{17}$$

$$U_B = \gamma x + \delta(1-y) \tag{18}$$

The payoffs are thus $P_A = \beta y - \alpha x$ and $P_B = \gamma x - \delta y$. Unlike the Cobb-Douglas case, which generates interior solutions for the contract curve, it is necessary to allow for corner solutions. The Edgeworth box is shown in Figure 2, where the contract curve is no longer a locus of tangencies between indifference curves, but follows the boundary of the box between C and C'. First, it is clear that trade will only take place if the slope of B's indifference curves, γ/δ, exceeds that of A's indifference curves, α/β. This diagram is drawn for the case where $\alpha/\beta < 1 < \gamma/\delta$. Secondly, it is necessary to allow for the restriction that $x, y \leq 1$. The Lagrangian must therefore be written as:

$$L = P_A^\phi P_B^{1-\phi} + \lambda_1(1-x) + \lambda_2(1-y) \tag{19}$$

along with the non-negativity constraint $x, y \leq 0$. This requires the use of the Kuhn-Tucker conditions, which are:

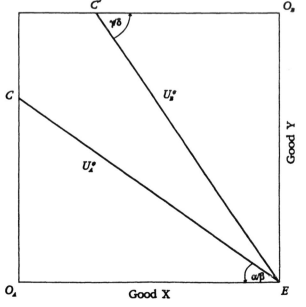

FIGURE 2

Constant marginal utilities

$$\partial L / \partial x \le 0 \quad ; \quad x \ge 0 \qquad ; \quad x\, \partial L / \partial x = 0 \tag{20a}$$

$$\partial L / \partial y \le 0 \quad ; \quad y \ge 0 \qquad ; \quad y\, \partial L / \partial y = 0 \tag{20b}$$

$$\partial L / \partial \lambda_1 \ge 0 \quad ; \quad \lambda_1 \ge 0; \qquad ; \quad \lambda_1 \partial L / \partial \lambda_1 = 0 \tag{20c}$$

$$.\partial L / \partial \lambda_2 \ge 0 \quad ; \quad \lambda_2 \ge 0 \qquad ; \quad \lambda_2 \partial L / \partial \lambda_2 = 0 \tag{20d}$$

From Figure 2 it is evident that if $\gamma/\delta > \alpha/\beta$, the solution to the first-order conditions in (20) must have either x or y equal to unity, with one individual consuming a proportion of one of the goods and the other trader consuming the remainder. Suppose that $x = 1$, so that from (20c) $\lambda_1 > 0$, and that $y < 1$, so that from (20d) $\lambda_2 = 0$. A necessary condition for this to arise is that A's indifference curves are flatter than 45°, so that $\alpha/\beta < 1$. Substitution into $\partial L/\partial y = 0$ and rearrangement gives, with $\theta = \phi/(1 - \phi)$.

$$y = (\alpha/\beta + \theta\gamma/\delta)/(1 + \theta) \tag{21}$$

When A has no power, $\phi = \theta = 0$ and substitution into (21) confirms that $y = \alpha/\beta$, and the trade takes place at the point C.

The other alternative combination is that $y = 1$ with $x < 1$, so that from (20c) $\lambda_1 = 0$. This result could only arise if B's indifference curves are steeper than 45°, so that $\gamma/\delta > 1$. Substitution into $\partial L / \partial x$ gives $\gamma P_A(1 - \phi) = \alpha P_B\phi$, so that if $\phi = 1$, $x = \delta/\gamma$, giving the other extreme of the contract curve, C'. Further rearrangement for $\phi < 1$ ($\theta < \infty$) gives:

$$x = (\beta/\alpha + \theta\delta/\gamma)/(1 + \theta) \tag{22}$$

Despite the apparent simplicity, the example of linear utility functions is therefore significantly more awkward to deal with than the Cobb-Douglas case.

Union/firm bargaining

Edgeworth (1881) argued that a major context in which indeterminacy would arise is that of bargaining between an employer and a trade union, and stated that efficiency requires bargaining over wages *and* the level of employment. If bargaining concerns only wages, with the firm having full control over the level of employment, then the result will be somewhere on the employer's offer curve (its demand curve for labour) rather than the contract curve. This argument was clarified by Dunlop (1944), Leontief (1946) and Fellner (1949). McDonald and Solow (1981) explored the nature of the Nash bargaining solution using a particular form of the union's utility function and a profit maximising employer, and there is now a large literature applying the Nash solution to trade unions; see Oswald (1985), Ulph and Ulph (1990) and Creedy and McDonald (1991).

The union's objective function was assumed by McDonald and Solow (1981) to take the form:

$$W = n\{U(w) - D\} + (m - n)U(b) \tag{23}$$

where m and n denote the (fixed) number of union members and the numbers of employed members respectively, b is the level of unemployment benefits, D is the disutility of work, and $U(.)$ is the utility function of each identical union member. If x is defined as the opportunity cost of working, so that $U(x) = D + U(b)$, W can be rewritten as:

$$W = n\{U(w) - U(x)\} + mU(b) \tag{24}$$

This approach implies that the union is prepared to trade wages and employment. If the threat point is the situation where all the union's members are unemployed, the payoff is simply $n\{U(w) - U(x)\}$. More recent approaches, following Binmore, Rubinstein and Wolinsky (1986), have taken a more sophisticated approach to the bargaining process, allowing for alternative employment opportunities and strike pay, and a richer interpretation of x; see also Layard and Nickell (1990). However, under simple assumptions, the union's payoff is still expressed as $n\{U(w) - U(x)\}$, which is the main focus here.

If the firm's objective is profit maximisation, and if $R(n)$ denotes revenue as a function of employment, then profit, Π, is given by:

$$\Pi = R(n) - wn \tag{25}$$

On the assumption that the threat point is zero profit, the firm's payoff is also equal to Π. It is worth stressing that this approach implicitly assumes constant marginal utility of profits, or risk neutrality on the part of the firm. The maximand for the Nash problem is thus:

$$L = [n\{U(w) - U(x)\}]^{\phi} [R(n) - wn]^{1-\phi} \tag{26}$$

Differentiating (26) with respect to n, setting the result equal to zero and rearranging gives the result that, with $\theta = \phi/(1-\phi)$:

$$w = \frac{1}{1+\theta}\left[\frac{\theta R(n)}{n} + R'(n)\right] \tag{27}$$

The wage is therefore the weighted mean of the average and marginal revenue products of labour. Appropriate differentiation and substitution into the equation of the contract curve, given by (8), gives the result that:

$$\varepsilon = \frac{wU'(w)}{U(w) - U(x)} = \frac{w}{w - R'(n)} \tag{28}$$

The term ε can be interpreted as the wage elasticity of the net utility from working. The problem of solving (27) and (28) for w and n is straightforward only for special assumptions about $U(w)$, in particular that it is iso-elastic (and has constant relative risk aversion). The special case where union members have constant marginal utility (and are risk neutral) is worth noting for comparison with other results in this paper. The substitution of a linear utility function in (28) gives $\varepsilon = w/(w - x)$, so that $x = R'(n)$. Hence, whatever the form of the revenue function, the contract curve is vertical, as n does not depend on w. The level of employment is always the same as that on the labour demand curve corresponding to a wage of x.

The form of the union's objective is obviously open to debate, and some authors have suggested an alternative approach in which the objective is based only on the utility of employed 'insiders'; see, for example, Carruth and Oswald (1987) and Lindbeck and Snower (1988), or the modification proposed by McDonald (1991). Edgeworth's own response to indeterminancy in bargaining was to propose a principle of arbitration, and this is the subject of the next section.

III. THE UTILITARIAN SOLUTION

The present analysis is limited to two traders who have comparable utility functions, so for the utilitarian solution the maximand is simply the sum of utilities, $U_A + U_B$. It is, however, worth recognising that in general, utilitarianism is concerned with the number of individuals in society as well as the distribution of resources. Yaari (1981) argues that if $W(x,\lambda)$ is the weighted sum $\sum_{i=1}^{N} \lambda_i U_i(x)$, utilitarianism requires the maximisation of the population, N (for choice of weights λ, subject to the requirement that the product of N and the maximum of W (for choice of x) is equal to some value $\overline{W}$ specified by scarce resources. This is equivalent to the saddlepoint value given by min (over λ) max (over x) of $W(x, \lambda)$. Yaari shows that this is equivalent to Rawls's (1971) maxi-min rule, according to which the welfare of the least well-off person is maximised.

The general case

Faced with indeterminacy in exchange, the utilitarian arbitrator would allocate the goods in order to maximise total utility, $U = U_A + U_B$. Unlike the bargaining solution of Nash, or the competitive equilibrium, interpersonal utility comparisons are required. This kind of arbitration rule in the context of exchange was first explored by Edgeworth (1881). Instead of maximising total utility subject to the constraints imposed by the stocks of the goods available, it is most convenient to write the utility functions as in (1) and (2), that is, in terms of amounts exchanged. Where utility functions are differentiable, the first-order conditions (for interior solutions) are given by:

$$\frac{\partial U_A}{\partial x} + \frac{\partial U_B}{\partial x} = 0 \qquad\qquad (29)$$

$$\frac{\partial U_A}{\partial y} + \frac{\partial U_B}{\partial y} = 0 \qquad\qquad (30)$$

It is found, by multiplying (29) by $\partial U_A/\partial y$, multiplying (30) by $\partial U_B/\partial x$, and subtracting the resulting equations, that the utilitarian solution is a position on the contract curve. This result is obvious by contradiction: any change which makes one person better off without making the other worse off (that is, a move towards the contract curve) must increase total utility. However, this property contrasts with alternative arbitration principles such as equal division, which do not typically give an allocation on the contract curve. One problem with this approach is, however, that it does not impose a constraint that the solution to (29) and (30) ensures that no trader is worse-off than before trade. This point was made most clearly by Wicksell (1893), but was implicit in Edgeworth's discussion, as acknowledged in Edgeworth (1925, ii, p.102).

If each individual is completely sympathetic towards the other, and thereby attaches equal weight to the other person's utility, they both maximise $U_A + U_B$ and agree to the utilitarian solution without any appeal to arbitration. If the weight attached to the other's utility is less than unity, then the equation of the contract curve remains unchanged and only the range of indeterminacy shrinks. This point, first noted by Edgeworth (1881, p.53, n.1), has been explored by Collard (1978).

The result that the utilitarian position is on the contract curve was described as 'momentous' by Edgeworth, and was the basis of his argument that, faced with uncertainty about the outcome in a situation of indeterminacy, and attaching equal *a priori* probabilities to the alternatives, individuals would agree to accept the utilitarian arbitrator's decision. A similar argument is involved in the later 'neo-contractarian' approaches of Harsanyi (1953, 1955) and Vickrey (1960). Extreme risk aversion, leads to the maxi-min rule, mentioned earlier, of Rawls (1971), who nevertheless refused to accept this approach as a basis for his own social contract approach; see also Atkinson and Stiglitz (1980, pp.339, 420) and Creedy (1986).

Cobb-Douglas utility functions

In order to obtain further insight into this approach, consider the special case of Cobb-Douglas utility function. Substituting the appropriate partial derivatives of (9) and (10) into (29) and (30) gives the first-order conditions:

$$\frac{\alpha U_A}{a_A - x} = \frac{\gamma U_B}{a_B + x} \tag{31}$$

$$\frac{\beta U_A}{b_A + y} = \frac{\delta U_B}{b_B - y} \tag{32}$$

These non-linear equations cannot be solved analytically, but it is easily seen that (as for any concave utility function) if individuals have identical tastes the stocks are shared equally between the two traders. For the same tastes and endowments as in the numerical example used in Section II, the *loci* defined by (31) and (32) can be obtained using numerical methods of solution and are shown as the lines U_1 and U_2 in Figure 1. The two *loci* intersect at the point on the contract curve where x and y are 0.256 and 0.501 respectively. This is a clear example of a situation where the utilitarian arbitration makes one person worse off than before trade. The assumed parameter values imply that both individuals prefer good Y to good X, but the utilitarian arrangement does not allow the person who holds the majority of good Y to exploit this advantage.

IV. COMPETITIVE EQUILIBRIA

The utilitarian solution has been discussed above in terms of a principle of arbitration, but it has also been very widely used in terms of a 'social evaluation' function (along with a variant which is in terms of a weighted sum of individual utilities, with the weights reflecting a specified degree of aversion to inequality). The idea that in some sense competition maximises total utility can sometimes be found in the earlier literature, but the condition required for there to be no excess demands or supplies (at a given price) will only coincidentally give the same allocation as the utilitarian solution. This was fully recognised by the major neoclassical economists. The present section concentrates on price-taking, or competitive, equilibria. The special cases of Cobb-Douglas and CES utility functions are examined, along with the possibility of multiple solutions. Finally, a special case of disequilibrium trading is discussed.

The price-taking assumption

Adding the common slope, dy/dx, to the equation of the contract curve in (3) gives the statement that:

$$-\frac{\partial U_A/\partial x}{\partial U_A/\partial y} = -\frac{\partial U_B/\partial x}{\partial U_B/\partial y} = \frac{dy}{dx} \tag{33}$$

The slope dy/dx may be interpreted as the rate of exchange at which the trade takes place *at the margin*. It is the extent to which good Y is given up for good X, after moving from the endowment position to the contract curve, following some unspecified sequence of trades, and is equivalent to the final price of good X divided by that of good Y. Since traders may settle anywhere along the contract curve, this price ratio is mathematically indeterminate, unless additional conditions are imposed.

Instead of trying to examine a dynamic process of trading, a considerable simplification is achieved by regarding the individuals as price-takers; that is, A and B are treated as typical traders in a market with a large number of similar individuals. Hence attention is restricted to the nature of the equilibrium which exists if all units traded are assumed to be exchanged at the equilibrium price. Hence y/x can be substituted for dy/dx, and the rate of exchange given by the ratio, $y/x = p$, is the equilibrium price. It was this simplification which Jevons (1956) clearly perceived. In his analogy with the analysis of lever, Jevons argued that although the dynamic analysis is extremely complex, the static properties can be examined much more easily. It can be noted that setting $dy/dx = y/x$ specifies the equation of a straight line; that is in fact the 'price line' which passes through the endowment point in the standard Edgeworth box diagram. Substitution into (33) therefore gives the two equations in two unknowns:

$$-\frac{\partial U_A / dx}{\partial U_A / \partial y} = \frac{y}{x} \qquad\qquad (34)$$

$$-\frac{\partial U_B / \partial x}{\partial U_B / \partial y} = \frac{y}{x} \qquad\qquad (35)$$

These two simultaneous equations are simply an alternative statement of Jevons's famous 'equation of exchange'. Jevons stated his equations using an intuitive argument, but equation (33) is also the first-order condition under which each individual maximises utility, given initial endowments and prices. For example, person A maximises $U_A = U_A(a_A - x, b_A + y)$ subject to the price-taking condition that $p = y/x$. Forming the Lagrangean $L = U_A + \lambda(y - px)$ gives the first-order conditions, $\partial U_A / \partial x = \lambda p$ and $\partial U_A / \partial y = -\lambda$, so that division gives the familiar result that the ratio of marginal utilities is equal to the price ratio (the indifference curve is tangential to the budget constraint), remembering that the marginal utility of good X is $-\partial U_A / \partial x$.

With explicit functional forms for the utility functions, the equations (34) and (35) can be solved for x and y, from which the price ratio, $p = y/x$, is obtained. This was the approach taken by Jevons, who deliberately avoided introducing 'prices' until the final state, preferring to retain y/x in order to stress the 'rate of exchange' nature of prices.

Cobb-Douglas utility functions

An explicit solution for the price-taking equilibrium can be found for the utility functions (9) and (10). Substitution of the partial derivatives into (34) and (35) gives:

$$\frac{\alpha(b_A + y)}{\beta(a_A - x)} = \frac{y}{x} \qquad\qquad (36)$$

$$\frac{\gamma(b_B - y)}{\delta(a_B + x)} = \frac{y}{x} \qquad\qquad (37)$$

By rearranging these equations, multiplying the first by $(\gamma + \delta)$ and the second by $(\alpha + \beta)$, and subtracting the resulting equations, the cross-product terms in xy can be eliminated. After some further rearrangement of the resulting equation, it can be found that the price ratio, p, is:

$$p = \frac{y}{x} = \frac{(b_A + b_B)\left\{\left(\frac{\alpha}{\alpha+\beta}\right)\left(\frac{b_A}{b_A+b_B}\right) + \left(\frac{\gamma}{\gamma+\delta}\right)\left(\frac{b_B}{b_A+b_B}\right)\right\}}{(a_A + a_B)\left\{\left(\frac{\beta}{\alpha+\beta}\right)\left(\frac{a_A}{a_A+a_B}\right) + \left(\frac{\delta}{\gamma+\delta}\right)\left(\frac{a_B}{a_A+a_B}\right)\right\}} \tag{38}$$

Given the value of y/x from (38), substitution into (36) gives the equilibrium amount of good X traded, x. The amount of good Y traded can then be obtained using $y = px$.

A much more succinct way of writing (38) is obtained by setting $b = b_A + b_B$, $a = a_A + a_B$, and then letting $a'_A = a_A/a$ and so on. Then:

$$p = \frac{bS}{a(1-R)} \tag{39}$$

where S is a weighted average of $\alpha/(\alpha + \beta)$ and $\gamma/(\gamma + \delta)$ with weights equal to a'_A and a'_B respectively, while R is a weighted average of the same terms with weights b'_A and b'_B respectively. For the utility functions and endowments used earlier, in Section II, the price-taking equilibrium rate of exchange is found to be 0.536. This is shown as point P in Figure 1. The associated indifference curves and price line are not shown in order to avoid cluttering the figure.

For completeness, the equation of the contract curve is given by:

$$y = \frac{(b_B a_A - k a_B b_A) + x(k b_A - b_B)}{k(x + a_B) + (a_A + a_B) - x} \tag{40}$$

where $k = \alpha\delta/\beta\gamma$ \hfill (41)

For the assumptions about endowments given in (13), the price ratio reduces to $\gamma(\beta+\alpha)/\beta(\delta+\gamma)$.

An alternative approach to finding the price-taking equilibrium amounts traded and the rate of exchange (price ratio) would be to derive each individual's demand and supply functions for the two goods. It was Walras who took the important step of recognising that instead of writing (34) as above, the equation $(-\partial U_A/\partial x)/(\partial U_A/\partial y) = p$ can be used to obtain A's supply of good X. Thus rewrite (36) as $\alpha(b_A/x + p)/\beta(a_A/x - 1) = p$ and rearrange to get A's supply of X in terms of the relative price: that is, $x = (\beta p a_A - \alpha b_A)/p(a + \beta)$. Similarly, (37) can be used to find B's supply of good Y and then, with $y = px$, B's demand for X. Then the equilibrium price ratio is obtained from the condition that there must be no excess demand or supply. This approach is equivalent to finding the point of intersection of offer curves. Either approach gives a unique equilibrium price in the Cobb-Douglas case. In other cases where the equilibrium price cannot be solved explicitly, it is sometimes still possible to derive the supply and demand functions explicitly and they can be used to provide further insight into the nature of the model. It seems that Launhardt (1985) was the first to produce algebraic forms of demand and supply curves in this way, based on quadratic utility functions. It was Jevons's reluctance to substitute for $p = y/x$ until the final stage that meant that he failed to consider demand and supply functions expressed in terms of relative prices.

A further property of the Cobb-Douglas case can be mentioned here. The traders have so far been assumed to be honest, in the sense that they do not conceal any of their pre-trade stocks. It can, however, be shown that with Cobb-Douglas preferences, a trader has an incentive to conceal some stocks, so long as enough is revealed to persuade the other trade to participate in exchange; for general discussion of this issue, and an illustration using other utility functions, see Postlewaite (1981).

CES utility functions

In view of the limitations of Cobb-Douglas utility functions, consider the use of constant elasticity of substitution (CES) utility functions. Suppose A holds all of good X while B holds all of good Y before trade, and utility functions take the form:

$$U_A = \left\{ (a-x)^{-\alpha} + \beta y^{-\alpha} \right\}^{-1/\alpha} \tag{42}$$

$$U_B = \left\{ x^{-\gamma} + \delta (b-y)^{-\gamma} \right\}^{-1/\gamma} \tag{43}$$

with β, $\delta > 0$ and α, $\gamma > -1$. Appropriate differentiation and substitution into (34) and (35) gives:

$$\frac{1}{\beta} \left(\frac{y}{a-x} \right)^{1+\alpha} = \frac{y}{x} - \frac{1}{\delta} \left(\frac{b-y}{x} \right)^{1+\gamma} \tag{44}$$

This direct approach shows (more quickly than deriving the demand functions and examining excess demands) that the equilibrium price cannot be solved analytically and numerical methods of solution are again required. However, it is possible to derive the demand and supply functions expressed in terms of p, and inspection of these reveals that there is only one feasible solution.

Multiple solutions

When Marshall (1879) and Walras (1874) considered exchange between two traders, they *began* with a specification of demand and supply curves in terms of relative prices, without first deriving them from utility analysis. Walras, as mentioned above, later made the link explicit. Marshall used intersecting offer curves, while Walras used demand and supply curves specified in terms of relative prices, but their approaches (based on the idea of reciprocal demand) were fundamentally similar; see Creedy (1992). They both stressed the possibility and implications of multiple intersections. For example, Launhardt's (1885) case of quadratic utility functions gives rise to a cubic equation in the equilibrium price ratio, so there may be three feasible and distinct solutions. Marshall and Walras both recognised that a necessary condition for multiple equilibria to occur was simply that demand curves are such that they have elastic and inelastic ranges. Later work has demonstrated that gross substitutability is sufficient to rule out multiple equilibria; see Kreps (1990).

An example of utility functions giving rise to multiple equilibria was provided by Shapley and Shubik (1977), who used numerical examples to generate three feasible equilibria. Atkinson and Stiglitz (1980, pp. 88-189) discussed this example and illustrated the implied demand and supply curves, using an approach and diagram that is very similar to those used by Walras (1874), though Walras was not mentioned by any of these authors. However, the Shapley and Shubik utility functions are most conveniently examined using Jevons's 'equations of exchange'. In general, they can be written as:

$$U_A = (a-x) + \alpha \left(1 - e^{-y/\beta} \right) \tag{45}$$

$$U_B = (b-y) + \gamma \left(1 - e^{-x/\delta} \right) \tag{46}$$

where A is assumed to hold all the stocks, a, of good X before trade, and B holds b of Y. Instead of deriving the demand and supply in terms of p, take the partial derivations and substitute into (34) and (35) to get:

$$\frac{\beta}{\alpha}e^{y/\beta} = \frac{y}{x} = \frac{\gamma}{\delta}e^{-x/\delta} \qquad (47)$$

Using the first equation to express x in terms of y, substituting the result into the second equation, gives, after rearrangement:

$$\log(\alpha\gamma/\beta\delta) = (y/\beta) + (\alpha/\beta\delta)ye^{-y/\beta} \qquad (48)$$

The properties of the non-linear equation in y given by (48) can be further examined by taking the expansion of $e^{-y/\beta} = 1 - y/\beta + (y/\beta)^2/2 - (y/\beta)^3/3! + \ldots$ and so on. Equation (48) then becomes a polynomial in y, with the signs alternating. Hence the number of real roots depends on the number of terms which are required in the expansion of $e^{-y/\beta}$, which depends on the size of β. For the numerical values used by Shapley and Shubik, a cubic is most appropriate. For further analysis of multiple solutions in exchange see Creedy and Martin (1993).

Price-taking and monopoly

A modification of the competitive case arises where one of the traders is treated as a price-setter (for example a monopolistic holder of one good dealing with a large number of identical suppliers of the other good). The trader is then regarded as maximising utility subject to the offer curve of the other trader or traders, so that an indifference curve is tangential to an offer curve. This corresponds to the standard analysis of the optimal tariff in foreign trade analysis, or the case of a 'simple monopoly union', which sets the wage rate, dealing with a firm that decides on the corresponding employment level. The implication is that trade does not take place on the offer curve, so that there is Pareto inefficiency. However, a perfectly discriminating monopolist is able to set a different price for each unit sold, and can push the other trader (or traders) to the extreme of the contract curve. This is equivalent to the Nash bargaining case where one party has all the power (and ϕ is either zero or unity).

A special case of disequilibrium trading

Finally, it is of interest to examine a special set of assumptions that were first investigated by Marshall (1890) and to which he attached a great deal of importance. This case became the centre of a dispute between Marshall and Edgeworth, which helped to reveal more clearly the implicit assumptions used and the properties of the model. Marshall was aware of indeterminacy in the general case. He wanted to avoid this problem as well as allowing for trades to take place at disequilibrium prices. Suppose that utility functions are additive and that the marginal utility of good Y is constant for both individuals. For convenience, suppose also that $a_B = b_A = 0$ and $a_A = a$, with $b_B = b$. Then:

$$U_A = U_1(a - x) + \beta y \qquad (49)$$

$$U_B = U_2(x) + \delta y \qquad (50)$$

Taking the appropriate partial derivatives and substituting into the equation of the contract curve (8) gives:

$$\frac{\partial U_1/\partial x}{\beta} = \frac{\partial U_2/\partial x}{\delta} \qquad (51)$$

But (51) depends only on x, so that in this special case the amount of good X exchanged is determinate, without the need for any arbitration or a bargaining solution. The contract curve, if y and x are on vertical and horizontal axes respectively, is therefore vertical. For example, if $U_1 = (a-x)^\alpha$ and $U_2 = x^\gamma$, equation (51) becomes:

$$\frac{\alpha\delta}{\beta\gamma} = \frac{x^{\gamma-1}}{(a-x)^{\alpha-1}} \tag{52}$$

This can be solved for x using numerical methods. The amount of good Y exchanged is, however, still indeterminate. This case of a vertical contract curve may be compared with the example of trade union bargaining where the firm and the union have linear utility functions, considered in Section II above.

There is a further implication of these assumptions which is worth stressing. Since, from (51), the slope of each individual's indifference curve depends only on x, the rate of exchange in turn only depends on x. This means that any process of adjustment of prices, allowing for trading at disequilibrium prices, will – if it converges to an equilibrium – always arrive at a total amount of good X traded which is equal to the value of x obtained from (51). This means that the final (equilibrium) price ratio must always be the same, whatever the intermediate path of price adjustments. Hence Marshall was able to say something about the result of a dynamic process of price adjustments, without having to write down and solve any differential equations; This example is illustrated in Figure 3. For further discussion of Marshall's model see Hicks (1939), Samuelson (1942), Walker (1967), Newman (1990) and Creedy (1992).

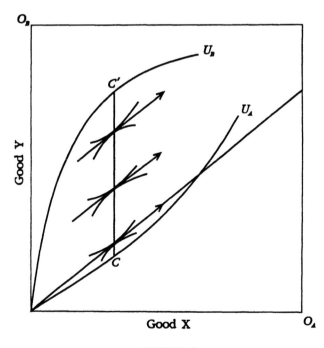

FIGURE 3

Marshall's special case

V. CONCLUSIONS

Ever since economists first began to think seriously about exchange, it was recognised that where a small number of traders is involved, the rate of exchange, or relative price, is in some sense indeterminate. With small numbers there is little reason why traders should take prices as being outside their control. The early neoclassical period saw a great deal of emphasis on the analysis of exchange, with the formal models (of, for example, Jevons, Walras and Marshall) concentrating on price-taking behaviour. It was recognised that the dynamics of adjustment towards an equilibrium present considerable problems, but the characteristics of a competitive equilibrium (or equilibria) could more readily be established.

It was Edgeworth who first clarified the role of the number of competitors, showing that with sufficiently large numbers a process of barter with recontracting would lead to a settlement that is equivalent to a price-taking equilibrium. He also clarified the efficiency property of the competitive (price-taking) outcome, showing that it corresponds to a point on the contract curve (later referred to as a Pareto efficient allocation). He also stressed the widespread relevance of indeterminacy, especially in wage bargaining with the rise of trade unions, and argued that a principle of arbitration is required. Edgeworth proposed the use of the utilitarian principle of maximum total utility.

The later emphasis on the role of strategic behaviour, in the context of small numbers, led to the analysis of bargaining solutions which are applicable in a wide variety of contexts. The bargaining solution proposed by Nash, involving the maximisation of the weighted geometric mean of payoffs, has become almost ubiquitous in economic analysis. The Nash solution also has the fundamental property that it produces a bargain which is on the contract curve.

This paper has provided a comparison of the three solution concepts in the context of the standard exchange framework. Some special cases of utility functions have been explored in each approach, and numerical methods of solution have been used where appropriate to provide further insights into the nature of the results. A characteristic of such non-linear models is that, unlike linear models, they are capable of generating multiple solutions. The need for numerical methods was clearly recognised by Jevons when he stated that, 'as soon as we attempt to draw out the equations expressing the laws of demand and supply, we discover that they have a complexity entirely surpassing our powers of mathematical treatment. We may lay down the general form of the equations... but all the functions involved are so complicated in character that there is not much fear of scientific method making rapid progress in their direction' (1909, pp.759-760). Jevons was, however, ultimately optimistic that 'immense advances' will be made, and would no doubt have welcomed the development of computers which allow for numerical results to be obtained.

REFERENCES

Atkinson, A. B. and Stiglitz, J. (1980), *Lectures on Public Economics* (London: McGraw-Hill).

Binmore, K., Rubinstein, A. and Wolinsky, A. (1986), 'The Nash Bargaining Solution in Economic Modelling', *Rand Journal of Economics*, vol. 17.

Carruth, A.A. and Oswald, A.J. (1987), 'On Union Preferences and Labour Market Models: Insiders and Outsiders', *Economic Journal*, vol. 97.

Collard, D. (1978), *Altruism and Economy* (Oxford: Martin Robertson).

Creedy, J. (1986), *Edgeworth and the Development of Neoclassical Economics* (Oxford: Basil Blackwell).

Creedy, J. (1992), *Demand and Exchange in Economic Analysis: A History from Cournot to Marshall* (Aldershot: Edward Elgar).

Creedy, J. and Martin, V. (1993), 'Multiple Equilibria and Hysteresis in Simple Exchange Models', *Economic Modelling*, vol. 10.

Creedy, J. and McDonald, I.M. (1991), 'Models of Trade Union Behaviour: A Synthesis', *Economic Record*.

de Menil, G. (1971), *Bargaining: Monopoly Power versus Union Power* (Cambridge, MA: MIT Press).

Dunlop, J.T. (1944), *Wage Determination Under Trade Unions* (New York: Macmillan).

Edgeworth, F.Y. (1881), *Mathematical Psychics* (London: Kegan Paul).

Fellner, W. (1949), *Competition Among the Few* (New York: Alfred Knopf).

Harsanyi, J.C. (1955), 'Cardinal Welfare, Individualistic Ethics, and Interpersonal Comparisons of Utility', *Journal of Political Economy*, vol. 63.

Harsanyi, J.C. (1953), 'Cardinal Utility in Welfare Economics and the Theory of Risk Taking', *Journal of Political Economy*, vol. 61.

Hicks, J.R. (1939), *Value and Capital* (London: Macmillan).

Jevons, W.S. (1909), *Principles of Science*, second edition (London: Macmillan).

Jevons, W.S. (1957), in H.S. Jevons (ed.), *The Theory of Political Economy*, fifth edition (New York: Augustus Kelley).

Kreps, D.M. (1990), *A Course in Microeconomic Theory* (London: Harvester Wheatsheaf).

Layard, R. and Nickell (1990), 'Is Unemployment Lower if Unions Bargain Over Employment?' *Quarterly Journal of Economics*, vol. 105.

Launhardt, W. (1885), *Mathematische Begründung der Volkswirtschaftslehre*, translated by H. Schmidt and edited by J. Creedy as *Mathematical Principles of Economics* (Aldershot: Edward Elgar, 1993).

Leontief, W. (1946), 'The Pure Theory of the Guaranteed Annual Wage Contact', *Journal of Political Economy*, vol. 56.

Lindbeck, A. and Snower, D.J. (1988), 'Cooperation, Harassment and Involuntary Unemployment: An Insider-Outsider Approach', *American Economic Review*, vol. 78.

McDonald, I.M. (1991), 'Insiders and Trade Union Bargaining', *The Manchester School of Economic and Social Studies*, vol. 58.

McDonald, I.M. and Solow, R. (1981), 'Wage bargaining and employment', *American Economic Review*, vol. 71.

Marshall, A. (1879), *The Pure Theory of Foreign Trade*, reprinted in J.K. Whitaker (ed.), *The Early Economic Writings of Alfred Marshall 1867-1880* (London: Macmillan).

Nash, J.F. (1950), 'The Bargaining Problem', *Econometrica*, vol. 18.

Newman, P. (1990), 'The Great Barter Controversy', in J.K. Whitaker (ed.), *Centenary Essays on Alfred Marshall* (Cambridge; Cambridge University Press).

Oswald, A.J. (1985), 'The Economic Theory of Trade Unions: An Introductory Survey', *Scandinavian Journal of Economics*, vol. 87.

Postlewaite, A. (1979), 'Manipulation via Endowments', *Review of Economic Studies*, vol. 47.

Rawls, J. (1971), *A Theory of Justice* (Oxford: Oxford University Press).

Samuelson, P.A. (1942), 'The Constancy of the Marginal Utility of Income', in O. Lange, F. McIntyre and T.O. Yntema (eds), *Studies in Mathematical Economics and Econometrics* (Chicago: University of Chicago Press).

Shapley, L.S. and Shubik, M. (1977), 'An Example of a Trading Economy with Three Competitive Equilibria', *Journal of Political Economy*, vol. 85.

Ulph, A. and Ulph, D. (1990), 'Union Bargaining: A Survey of Recent Work', in D. Sapsford and Z. Tzannatos (eds), *Current Issues In Labour Economics* (Basingstoke: Macmillan).

Vickrey, W.S. (1960), 'Utility, Strategy and Social Decision Rules', *Quarterly Journal of Economics*, vol. 74.

Walker, D.A. (1967), 'Marshall's Theory of Competitive Exchange', *Canadian Journal of Economics,* vol. 2.

Walras, L. (1874, trans 1954), *Elements of Pure Economics,* translated by W. Jaffe (London: Allen and Unwin).

Wicksell, K. (1893, trans 1934), *Value, Capital and Rent,* translated by S. H. Frowein (London: Allen and Unwin).

Yaari, M.E. (1981), 'Rawls, Edgeworth, Shapley, Nash: Theories of Distributive Justice Re-examined', *Econometrica,* vol. 24.

[9]

The Development of the Theory of Exchange*

John Creedy

The University of Melbourne

Abstract

The aim of this paper is to provide an outline of the development of
the theory of exchange, concentrating on the less well-known development
of the formal model which culminated in the contribution of Edgeworth.
The importance of exchange, viewed as the central economic problem for
the early neoclassical economists, is stressed. Instead of taking a chronological approach, non-utility approaches are first discussed. These include
the extension by Walras of Cournot's attempt to model trade between
regions, and Whewell's mathematical version of J. S. Mill's international
trade analysis, followed by Marshall's diagrammatic version. Jevons's and
Walras's utility approaches are then examined, showing the different paths
they took from the same basic equations of exchange. After a very brief
discussion of Edgeworth, the neglected but valuable contribution of Launhardt, along with the later work of Wicksell, are examined. Emphasis is
placed on the similarity of the formal structure of the exchange model used
by the various writers. This similarity has been obscured by the different
forms of presentation used and the emphasis given to various aspects and
results by each investigator.

---

*I have benefited greatly from many discussions with Denis O'Brien, along with his comments
on earlier related papers, during the long gestation period of this paper.

1

Contents

1 Introduction

A distinguishing feature of the economic analysis of roughly the last third of the 19th century was its emphasis on exchange as the central economic problem. For example, Hicks (following Edgeworth) referred to the early neoclassicals as 'catallactists' in order to emphasise the exchange focus. He stressed that, 'while the classics looked at the economic system primarily from the production angle, the catallactists looked at it primarily from the side of exchange. It was possible, they found, to construct a "vision" of economic life out of the theory of exchange, as the classics had done out of the social product. It was quite a different vision' (1984, p.250). Edgeworth (1925, ii, p.288) summarised the position by suggesting that, 'in pure economics there is only one fundamental theorem, but that is a very difficult one: the theory of bargain in a wide sense'.[1]

There are two primary ingredients of an exchange analysis: one is an appreciation of the principle of reciprocal demand and supply while the second is the concept of demand as a function of relative prices. Early examples of treatments of exchange, including Aristotle, Beccaria, Verri, Courcelle-Seneuil, Turgot, Cantillon, Canard and Isnard, show how little real progress can be made without these two elements combined, despite the useful insights provided. However, the neoclassical economists were not the first to recognise these requirements or attempt to construct a model of exchange based on them. International trade provided an important context in which exchange theories were considered; prime examples include Cournot, J.S. Mill and Whewell.[2] Only Mill and, following him, Whewell combined the two elements successfully.

The great success of the early neoclassical economists was also associated with the fact that they provided a foundation for their exchange model in the form of a utility analysis. This allowed for a deeper treatment of the gains from exchange and the wider consideration of economic welfare. Furthermore, this type of welfare analysis survived the replacement of a cardinal utility concept with an ordinal concept, or the idea of a simple preference ordering. As Hicks (1984, p.252) argued, 'I would therefore maintain that the principal reason for the triumph of catallactics – in its day it was quite a triumph – was nothing to do with socialism or individualism; nor did it even have much to do with the changes that were then occurring in the "real world". The construction of a powerful economic theory, based on exchange, instead of production and distribution, had always been a possibility. The novelty in the work of the great catallactists is just that they achieved it'.[3]

It is only when the perceived central position of exchange analysis is recognised, along with the place of the principle of utility maximisation as the foundation, that it is possible to have some appreciation of the attitude behind Edgeworth's (1881, p. 12) remark, after discussing the extension of utility analysis to subjects such as production and labour supply, that, '"Mécanique Sociale" may one day take her place along with "Mécanique Celeste", throned each upon the double-sided height of one maximum principle, the supreme pinnacle of moral as of physical science ... the movements of each soul, whether selfishly isolated or linked sympathetically, may continually be realising the maximum energy of pleasure, the Divine love of the universe'. Other writers were much more prosaic in their expressions than Edgeworth, but his view nicely encapsulates something of the pioneering spirit of the early neoclassical economists.[4]

The central role of exchange is unfortunately seldom stressed in modern texts or histories of economic analysis, where stress is placed on the idea of a 'marginal revolution' associated with the concept of marginal utility, which of course arises naturally from the first-derivatives needed in a utility maximising approach. The emphasis is such that priority of place is often given to the adjective rather than the noun (in marginal utility), with stress on the introduction of calculus methods, or at least notation.[5] The context of discussions is typically the derivation of partial equilibrium demand curves, even though such curves hardly ever appeared in the early major works of Jevons, Walras, Edgeworth, Wicksell and even Marshall. It is suggested that this view of the neoclassicals is not helpful and actually creates something of a barrier to obtaining an understanding of their approach.[6]

The aim of this paper is to provide an outline of the development of the theory of exchange. Rather than taking a purely chronological approach, the discussion is divided into three main sections, dealing with non-utility approaches, the introduction of a utility foundation, and finally expositions and extensions.

Section 2 begins by examining the non-utility approaches to exchange, beginning in subsection 2.1 with Cournot's (1927) model of trade between two regions, involving a single good and dating from 1838: reference is generally made below to the available source, in Cournot's case the translation edited by Fisher, rather than the original date of publication. Both Walras and Marshall rejected this approach and recognised that it could not be extended simply by adding more demand and supply equations; the fundamental concept of reciprocal demand and supply has to be at the heart of any exchange model. As shown in subsection 2.2, Walras took the most direct route while Marshall took Mill as his starting point. Mill's analysis, along with the mathematical model produced by Whewell, is discussed in subsection 2.3. Marshall's extension, using offer curves, is considered in subsection 2.4. An important lesson is that Walras and Marshall produced the same formal model, leading to their emphasis on multiple equilibria and stability issues, but used different diagrammatic approaches that are directly and simply linked. Indeed, reference may be made to a Mill/Whewell/Walras/Marshall model. However, they stressed different aspects of the model, so that the initial appearance is very different and the origins are not obvious.

Section 3 turns to the utility maximising foundations of exchange, starting in subsection 3.1 with the pioneering contribution of Jevons. Subsection 3.2 then examines Walras's approach, paying particular attention to their differing attitudes to the same fundamental 'equations of exchange'. Both Jevons and Walras concentrated on price-taking solutions to these equations.[7] But Jevons left the equations in terms of quantities exchanged, leaving the equilibrium price ratio to be determined by the resulting ratio of quantities exchanged. Walras instead introduced the price at an early stage and thereby showed the route by which the general equilibrium demand and supply curves that he had produced earlier (in extending Cournot's model) can be derived. Subsection 3.3 then briefly discusses Edgeworth's treatment of exchange, representing the high point in the development of formal exchange models.

Section 4 discusses two closely related contributions to the literature, by Launhardt (1993) and Wicksell (1954), dating from 1885 and 1893 respectively. These can in many ways be regarded as masterly expositions of the theory (despite their lack of familiarity with Edgeworth's major contribution), although Launhardt made a number of original extensions of his own: indeed, it can be argued that his book represents the first major treatise on welfare economics. These contributions warrant closer analysis in view of the fact that, like Walras, they were not translated into English for many years. Furthermore, Launhardt's reputation was damaged by unfair criticisms by Wicksell, who nevertheless relied heavily on the former's work. Brief conclusions are in section 5.

2   Non-utility Approaches

It is useful to begin a discussion of non-utility approaches with Cournot's (1927) attempt to examine 'trade' in a single good, involving two regions. On this analysis, Edgeworth later commented, not without sympathy, that 'the lesson of caution in dealing with a subject and method so difficult is taught by no example more impressively than by that of Cournot. This superior intelligence ... seems not only to have slipped at several steps, but even to have taken a wholly wrong direction.' (1925, ii, p.47). Its importance lies in the fact that Cournot's model provided an influential starting point for the development of a general equilibrium approach. A major value of his work seems to have been the stimulus it provided to Walras and Marshall to attempt to improve the basic model.

The formal similarity of the basic models used by Walras and Marshall, who both stressed multiple equilibria and examined stability properties, was mentioned above.[8] The 'substantially equivalent' nature of the two analyses was stressed by Hicks, who suggested that, 'One feels almost obliged to explain it by the intrinsic excellence of the path they followed. Yet in fact there is a clear historical reason for it, one decisive influence we know to have been felt by both. Each of them had read Cournot' (1934, p. 346). Hicks's statement must, however, be qualified by the recognition that while Walras explicitly extended Cournot, Marshall extended Mill's treatment which itself provided such an impressive use of the basic ingredients of an exchange model and was produced almost ten years before that of Cournot. It does indeed seem that 'intrinsic excellence' played a major role.

2.1   Cournot's Trade Model

2.1.1   The Basic Framework

Cournot's (1927) framework was one in which a single good is initially produced in two countries that are isolated from each other. When 'communication' between the markets occurs, the good is produced and exported by the country in which it is initially cheaper, allowing for transport costs. The market demand and supply curves were taken as given, and the regions have a common currency. In isolation the equilibrium price of the good is p_a and p_b in markets A and B respectively, with demand functions $F_a(p)$ and $F_b(p)$, and supply functions $\Omega_a(p)$ and $\Omega_b(p)$. The prices are given by the intersecting partial equilibrium curves and are the solutions to:

$$\Omega_a(p_a) = F_a(p_a) \tag{1}$$

and

$$\Omega_b(p_b) = F_b(p_b) \tag{2}$$

If $p_a < p_b$ and the difference exceeds the cost of transporting the good between the two markets, ε, then the good is exported from A to B. Cournot argued that trade equalises the price of the good in the two markets, except for the transport costs. If the new equilibrium price in market A is denoted p'_a, Cournot (1927, p.119) stated that this is given as the solution to:

$$\Omega_a(p'_a) + \Omega_b(p'_a + \varepsilon) = F_a(p'_a) + F_b(p'_a + \varepsilon) \tag{3}$$

so that total supply is equal to total demand in both markets combined. Cournot wrote:

$$p'_a = p_a + \delta \text{ and } p'_b = p_a + \omega \tag{4}$$

so that δ is the change in the price in market A and ω is the pre-trade absolute difference between prices in the two markets. Trade takes place only if $\omega > \varepsilon$. Substitute for $p_a = p_b - \omega$ in the first of the expressions in (4) and add ε to get:

$$p'_a + \varepsilon = p_b + \delta + \varepsilon - \omega \tag{5}$$

Equation (3) can then be re-written as:

$$\Omega_a(p_a + \delta) + \Omega_b(p_b + \delta + \varepsilon - \omega) = F_a(p_a + \delta) + F_b(p_b + \delta + \varepsilon - \omega) \tag{6}$$

This expression can be simplified using Cournot's method of 'development and reduction' which involves taking the Taylor series expansion of each function of the form $F(p + \delta)$ and neglecting squares and higher powers of δ. Thus:

$$F(p + \delta) = F(p) + \delta F'(p) \tag{7}$$

Expanding each term in (6) in this way, and using (1) and (2), Cournot (1927, p.120) obtained:

$$\delta\left\{\Omega_a'\left(p_a\right) - F_a'\left(p_a\right)\right\} = \left(\delta + \varepsilon - \omega\right)\left\{F_b'\left(p_b\right) - \Omega_b'\left(p_b\right)\right\} \tag{8}$$

Demand curves are assumed to slope downwards and supply curves to slope upwards, so the term in curly brackets on the left hand side of (8) is positive, while that on the right hand side is negative. Since $\delta > 0$, then $\delta + \varepsilon - \omega < 0$ and $\delta < \varepsilon$. Hence the increase in price in market A must be less than the difference between the initial price differential and the unit transport cost.

Cournot used this model to examine the gains from trade using the concepts of consumer and producer surplus, and investigated the conditions under which the total demand in the two markets combined would increase.[9] He also considered the question of whether the value of output would increase. In examining import or export taxes, Cournot made an algebraic slip which led him to believe that the price may fall in the importing country, although in fact price must rise in the importing, and fall in the exporting, country. This was briefly discussed by Edgeworth (1894, reprinted in 1925, ii, p.49), where he noted that Berry and Sanger, two former pupils of Marshall, had independently made the correction.[10]

2.1.2 A Diagrammatic Version

Marshall (1975, ii, pp.246-248) made an early attempt to cast Cournot's model into diagrammatic form, mainly for the purpose of examining the gains from trade using measures of producers' and consumers' surplus. The diagrammatic analysis of the model was later refined by Marshall's student Cunynghame (1892, 1903).[11] After an unsatisfactory start (1892, p.44), Cunynghame produced a 'back-to-back' diagram without any reference to Cournot but virtually paraphrasing the latter's introduction to his model (1903, p.317).

Ignoring transport costs, the diagram is shown in Figure 1 where the equilibrium price is such that $CT = EF$. Marshall's notes show the influence of Cournot on Marshall's analysis of consumers' and producers' surplus. Marshall's diagrams translate Cournot's surplus analysis into the now familiar triangles. Using the back-to-back version of Figure 1 the left hand side shows that the gains to B's consumers arising from the price reduction outweighs the loss to producers, so that the net gain is equal to the shaded area P_1CT. The price increase in A

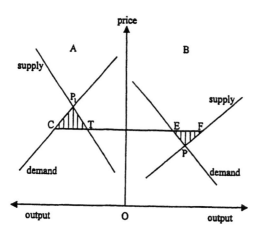

Figure 1: Cournot's Trade Model

produces a net gain equal to the shaded area EPF in the right hand side of the figure. Marshall added that if in each country the cost of production is independent of output, then the exporting country gains nothing from trade (1975, ii, pp.247-8).[12]

2.2 Walras's Extension

A fundamental criticism of Cournot's model is that it deals with only one good and the analysis ignores the fact that money is used to purchase that good. This point was acknowledged by Cournot towards the end of the *Researches*, where he wrote that, 'It will be said that it is impossible for exportation of a commodity to fail to involve importation on the exporting market of a precisely equal value; and reciprocally, importation on a market involves exportation of an equal value ... It would be necessary to consider each of these nations as acting simultaneously the part of an importing nation and that an exporting nation, which would greatly complicate the question and lead to a complex result' (1927, pp.161-162).

It was left to Walras to make the extension.[13] Walras's autobiography states that he 'soon perceived' that Cournot's approach could not be applied to exchange and, 'restricting my attention, therefore, to the case of two commodities, I rationally derived from the demand curve of each commodity the supply curve of the other and demonstrated how current equilibrium results from the intersection of the supply and demand curves' (Quoted in Jaffé, 1983, p.25). Walras's transformation of Cournot's model, using the same notation, is contained in (1954, pp.81-114). The crucial ingredient is the recognition that 'to say that a quantity D_a of (A) is demanded at the price p_a is, *ipso facto*, the same thing as saying that a quantity O_b of (B), equal to $D_a p_a$, is being offered' (1954, p.88).[14]

Suppose that there are two goods, X and Y, and comparative advantage is such that country A exports good X to country B, while the latter exports good Y to A. Assume complete specialisation, and denote the relative price of good X as p. This relative price can be interpreted as the amount of good Y that must be given in order to obtain a unit of good X. For present purposes it is necessary to express B's demand for X and A's demand for Y as $F_b(p)$ and $F_a(p^{-1})$ respectively; p^{-1} is the relative price of Y. The essential feature of an exchange model is that the demand for one good, at a given price, automatically carries with it a supply of the other good. B's supply of Y, corresponding to the demand $F_b(p)$, is thus given by:

$$\Omega_b(p) = pF_b(p) \tag{9}$$

while A's supply of X is given by:

$$\Omega_a(p) = p^{-1}F_a\left(p^{-1}\right) \tag{10}$$

The equilibrium price is that value of p for which the demand for and supply of, say Y, are equal. This requires:

$$\Omega_b(p) = pF_b(p) = F_a\left(p^{-1}\right) \tag{11}$$

which is equivalent to the equilibrium condition for good X, given by:

$$\Omega_a(p) = p^{-1}F_a\left(p^{-1}\right) = F_b(p) \tag{12}$$

The general equilibrium model therefore requires only the specification of the two demand functions in terms of the relative price, p; the associated supply curves are obtained using the reciprocal demand relationship. It was this insight that later led Wicksteed (1933) to argue that the concept of the partial equilibrium supply curve is 'profoundly misleading' and should be abandoned altogether.[15]

2.2.1 Linear Demands

In order to explore the nature of the model, suppose that demand functions are linear, such that:

$$F_b(p) = a - bp \qquad (13)$$

and

$$F_a\left(p^{-1}\right) = \alpha - \beta p^{-1} \qquad (14)$$

From A's demand for Y in (14), the corresponding supply of X is obtained using (31) as:

$$\Omega_a(p) = \alpha p^{-1} - \beta p^{-2} \qquad (15)$$

and equilibrium price is that which equates (15) and (13), giving:

$$\beta - \alpha p + ap^2 - bp^3 = 0 \qquad (16)$$

so that three equilibria, not necessarily real or distinct, exist. This approach therefore rapidly gives rise to the need to consider the stability of alternative equilibrium positions. The comparative static properties of models with multiple equilibria are of much interest, since small changes in demand conditions can lead to a large jump in the equilibrium price. The supply curve of X is 'backward bending' (if p is on the vertical axis), with supply reaching a maximum when $p = 2\beta/\alpha$ and a point of inflection where $p = 3\beta/\alpha$. Furthermore the maximum supply, where the price elasticity of supply is zero, occurs at a price for which the elasticity of demand (for Y) is minus one. It is the backward bending property that gives rise to the possibility of three equilibria.[16] The diagrammatic representation of this model, using a simple modification of Figure 1, is shown in Figure 2

The analysis may be extended by using (13) to write $p = \{a - F_b(p)\}/b$. Substituting this expression for p into equation (30) gives:

$$\Omega_b(p) = F_b(p)\{a - F_b(p)\}/b \qquad (17)$$

Equation (17) has a simple interpretation as the 'offer curve' of country B, the concept introduced by Marshall. This offer curve is quadratic, so that if both countries have linear demand curves, the offer curves may intersect three times, consistent with the result from (16). It is well-known that the turning point of an offer curve occurs at the point of unit demand elasticity.

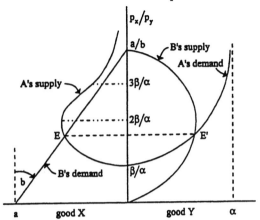

Figure 2: Exchange with Linear Demands

2.3 The Mill-Whewell Model

The previous subsection considered the path taken from Cournot to Walras. However, the same exchange model has a quite separate line of development, running from J. S. Mill and Whewell to Marshall.[17] The concept of reciprocal demand combined with the clear idea of demand as a schedule was in fact explored by Mill almost a decade before Cournot's book was published, although Mill did not publish his analysis of international trade until 1844. A mathematical analysis of Mill's model was produced by Whewell in 1850. In his first published paper, Marshall (1876) indicated his preference for the general approach of Mill rather than Cournot, and his offer curves were directly stimulated by Mill's analysis. Ironically, the precise nature of Marshall's offer curves was misunderstood by Cunynghame, who went so far as to criticise Marshall's analysis on the grounds that it should deal explicitly with more demand and supply curves (1903, p.317). Marshall commented rather tersely in a letter to Cunynghame that, 'as to international trade curves – mine were set to a definite tune, that called by Mill' (in Pigou, 1925, p.451).

2.3.1 Mill's 'Great Chapter'

In considering the determination of the terms of trade, between the comparative cost ratios of two countries, Mill was able to indicate the importance of reciprocal demand much more clearly than previous writers because of his conception of demand as a schedule.[18] But Mill did not use mathematical notation, preferring to give numerical examples. The crucial element of the analysis is the idea that demand depends on relative prices. Hence England, assumed to have a comparative advantage over Germany in the production of cloth (while Germany has a comparative advantage in linen production), has a demand for linen that depends on its price relative to that of cloth. This relative price can be expressed in terms of an amount of cloth per unit of linen. This is the basis of Mill's argument that 'all trade is in reality barter, money being a mere instrument for exchanging things' (1920, p.583).

If England demands a certain quantity of linen, there is an associated, or reciprocal, supply of cloth equal to the amount of linen multiplied by the relative price. The quantity of linen multiplied by the amount of cloth per unit of linen obviously gives an amount of cloth. Neglecting transport costs, equilibrium requires that the post-trade relative price is the same in each country and that the price is such that Germany's import demand for cloth precisely matches England's export supply (associated with its demand for linen at the corresponding relative price). After giving a numerical example, Mill added that, 'as the inclinations and circumstances of consumers cannot be reduced to any rule, so neither can the proportions in which the two commodities will be interchanged' (1920, p.587).

He then went on, when considering the gains from trade, to add that 'the circumstances on which the proportionate share of each country more remotely depends, admit only of a very general indication' (1920, p.587). It is in Mill's subsequent discussion of such 'general indications' that he used the concept of demand elasticity – although he described it with the term 'susceptibility'. Mill effectively argued (1920, p.587-8) that if the German demand for cloth is completely inelastic, then all the gains from trade go to Germany. In general, Mill was able to demonstrate that, 'If, therefore, it be asked what country draws to itself the greatest share of the advantage of any trade it carries on, the answer is, the country for whose production there is in other countries the greatest demand, and a demand the most susceptible of increase from additional cheapness' (1920, p.591).[19]

2.3.2   Whewell's Mathematical Model

Whewell (1850) produced a mathematical version of Mill's analysis, suggesting that the use of numerical examples led to the neglect of several important factors. Whewell denoted the English demand for linen and its relative price before trade as q and p respectively, with the German demand for cloth and its pre-trade relative price as Q and P respectively. After-trade prices and quantities are distinguished by the use of a dash, so that the equality of prices means that:

$$p'P' = 1 \tag{18}$$

since, for example, P' is the reciprocal of the price of linen relative to that of cloth in Germany. The reciprocal supply of cloth implied by England's demand for linen is, from the earlier argument, simply $p'q'$. Hence trade balance is achieved when:

$$p'q' = Q' \tag{19}$$

As a result of trade, the relative price of linen in England and that of cloth in Germany would fall by proportions x and X respectively, so that:

$$p' = p(1 - x) \text{ and } P' = P(1 - X) \tag{20}$$

If, in addition, the relative price of linen in Germany before trade is a proportion, k, lower than in England, then $1/P = p(1 - k)$ and combining this with (20) and (18) gives:

$$X = \frac{k - x}{1 - x} \tag{21}$$

A feature of Whewell's model is his treatment of demand. He supposed that, for the English linen demand, the proportionate fall in the relative price, x, would lead to a proportionate fall in 'revenue' (which in this context is the reciprocal supply of cloth) of mx. The coefficient m was referred to as the 'specific rate of change' of the commodity, which Whewell supposed would vary over the demand curve. In fact it is possible to show that m is simply one plus the elasticity of demand.[20] Similarly M is the 'specific rate of change' of the German demand for cloth. Hence:

$$p'q' = pq(1 - mx) \text{ and } P'Q' = PQ(1 - MX) \tag{22}$$

Substituting (21) and (22) into (19) gives, after rearranging, Whewell's result that:

$$x = \frac{n(1 - Mk) - 1}{n(1 - M) - m} \qquad (23)$$

where $n = PQ/q$ and is the value of cloth demanded in Germany before trade divided by the value of linen consumed in England before trade, measured in German prices. Alternatively n can be interpreted as the German pre-trade opportunity cost of cloth in terms of linen foregone, divided by the English demand for linen before trade. Whewell argued that when $x = 0$, England gains all the advantage from trade, and when $x = k$ (that is, when $X = 0$), Germany obtains all the advantage. It is therefore possible to obtain the limiting values of n under which trade takes place. Whewell's result gives a precise expression from which the terms of trade can be obtained in terms of the two demand elasticities and the relative 'sizes' of the two countries as measured by their demand. He also indicated that a country which receives no advantage from trade may well not specialise; that is, part of its relatively large demand for the imported good will be met from domestic production.

Whewell therefore made a significant advance over Mill's analysis. The main limitation of his approach is the highly restrictive specification of demand, which is strictly limited to small price changes. It is likely that Whewell's results provided the major impetus for Mill's supplementary sections, added in a later edition. Although Mill (1920, p.586) only mentioned Thornton, he had other 'intelligent criticism' in mind. Thornton may well have argued that the type of 'equilibrium' indicated by Mill might not be unique, a point Mill acknowledged at the beginning of the supplementary sections.[21] This might have been reinforced by the recognition, indicated by Whewell, that m and M would generally vary along the respective demand curves. Mill's attempt to deal with non-uniqueness is of interest. However, there is much stronger contextual evidence that Mill's discussion of the limits within which his 'equation' applied, his recognition of partial specialisation and emphasis on the domestic transfer of resources came directly from Whewell; see in particular Mill (1920, p.598). Mill's discussion of inelastic, unitary, and elastic demands can easily be generated by appropriate substitution into (23) above.[22]

In its essential components, Whewell's mathematical model of Mill is precisely the same as Walras's later generalisation of Cournot's one-good model. He specified only the two demand curves required, and used the concept of reciprocal demand and supply to generate the supply curves. The translation of Whewell's model into diagrammatic form gives exactly the same as Figure 2 above.[23] The major difference is that the detail of Whewell's model was more cumbersome, because of his awkward specification of the functional relationship between price and quantity changes. It meant that he arrived at an early formal statement of the concept of price elasticity to which he made good use, but the simple specification used by Walras, modified from Cournot, was much more powerful.[24]

2.4   From Mill to Marshall

It can be shown that a diagrammatic form of Whewell's model leads directly to that used by Walras, from which it is a small step to derive the offer curves devised by Marshall.[25] Marshall did not provide any statement of how he arrived at these curves, but it is of interest to compare Marshall's attempt in (1975, i, pp.260-280) with the later analysis (1975, ii, pp.117-181), and finally with the mature version (1923, pp.330-360). He began in each case with basic offer curves for each country (that are elastic over the whole length shown) and then discussed their possible shapes in terms of elasticities. In the earliest essay, Marshall used the rather clumsy expression 'guidance by the rate' for 'elasticity'. But by 1923 the analysis was clearly stated in terms of elasticities, and included a footnote giving the now standard geometrical method of finding the elasticity (1923, p.337, n.1).[26] He also provided a method of deriving consumers' surplus from the offer curves.[27]

Marshall's recognition of the possibility of his offer curves intersecting more than once, and the circumstances under which such multiple equilibria can occur, led him to devote much energy to dynamic adjustment problems and the question of which of several equilibria would be stable. Instead of presenting the mathematics of differential equations, Marshall applied, for the first time in economics, the now standard phase-diagram method. As usual, and after what must have been a great deal of thought on the question, Marshall was very sceptical about the use of mathematics to examine dynamic problems. Even if the equations of the offer curves were known precisely, he argued that, 'the methods of mathematical analysis will not be able to afford any considerable assistance in the task of determining the motion of the exchange-index. For a large amount of additional work will have to be done before we can obtain approximate laws for representing the magnitude of the horizontal and vertical forces which will act upon the exchange-index in any position' (1975, ii, p.163).[28]

Marshall came to regard his offer curve apparatus as capable of 'being translated into terms of any sort of bargains between two bodies, neither of whom is subject to any external competition in regard to those particular bargains' (1923, p.351). A major context was that of bargaining between firms and trade unions, but it was left to Edgeworth to extend the analysis to those other areas.[29] A distinguishing feature of Marshall's analysis of offer curves was that he also had variations in production in mind, rather than an exchange of fixed stocks; such variations were clarified by the later detailed treatment of Meade (1952).

Marshall can also be seen at an early stage struggling with the problem of 'triangular barter'. In some 'pages from a mathematical notebook' (1975, ii, pp.272-274), Marshall used demand curves specified in terms of relative prices (similar to those considered above) to examine the situation in which Germany exchanges linen for cloth, England exchanges cloth for fur, while Russia exchanges fur for linen. Marshall's problem was very similar to the three-country case considered by Mill, and the approach can be seen to follow Mill quite closely. As Mill suggested, 'everything will take place precisely as if the third country had bought German produce with her own goods, and offered that produce to England in exchange for hers' (1920, p.592).[30]

2.4.1 Marshall and Whewell

The question arises of whether Marshall was directly influenced by Whewell; this was first raised by Hutchison (1953, p.65). There is no reference to Whewell in any of Marshall's writings on international trade; his only reference to Whewell seems to be to the latter's role as editor of Richard Jones's works (see Pigou, 1925, p.296 and 1975, ii, p.264). However, some writers have suggested that Marshall made use of Whewell's work; these include Henderson (1985, p.422) and Cochrane (1975, p.398). One argument to support this claim is that Marshall's signature has been found on other volumes of the *Transactions* in which Whewell's papers first appeared; see Collard (1968, p.xviii). Further references by Marshall to Whewell have been collected by Vázquez (1995, p.249-250). But it does not seem possible to attribute any particular analytical contributions of Marshall to the work of Whewell.[31]

While it may seem surprising that Marshall was not influenced with Whewell's work, it is worth recalling a query raised by Hutchison (1950) in connection with Cournot's *Recherches*. The possible significance of Cournot's book was suggested to Jevons in 1875 by Todhunter who added that 'I never found any person who had read the book' (Hutchison, 1950, p.8). Yet Todhunter was, like Marshall, a Fellow of St. John's College, and Marshall stated that he read Cournot in 1868. The lack of communication between Todhunter and Marshall on the subject of Cournot must have extended to Whewell, about whom Todhunter also had considerable knowledge.[32]

3   Utility Approaches

3.1   Jevons's Equations of Exchange

Jevons, in all respects a pioneer, presented his basic exchange analysis in the context of two traders, where A and B hold endowments, a and b respectively, of goods X and Y. Where x and y are the amounts exchanged, utility after trade takes place can therefore be written as:

$$U_A = U_A\,(a - x, y) \qquad (24)$$

for trader A, while for B it is:

$$U_B = U_B(x, b - y) \qquad (25)$$

Jevons actually used additive utility functions. The 'keystone' of the theory was the result that for utility maximisation, '*the ratio of exchange of any two commodities will be the reciprocal of the ratio of the final degrees of utility of the quantities of commodity available for consumption after the exchange is complete*' (1957, p.95). This gives rise to his two famous 'equations of exchange', given using modern notation by:[33]

$$-\frac{\partial U_A/\partial x}{\partial U_A/\partial y} = \frac{dy}{dx} = -\frac{\partial U_B/\partial x}{\partial U_B/\partial y} \qquad (26)$$

The term dy/dx is the ratio of exchange of the two commodities at the margin. Jevons recognised that the integration of these differential equations presents formidable difficulties, and for this reason he restricted his attention to price-taking equilibria. He used the analogy of a lever to stress that the movement of a lever out of equilibrium also requires the difficult treatment of differential equations, but that if attention is restricted to the properties of an equilibrium, 'no such integration is applicable' (1957, p.105).

The price-taking equilibrium was examined by using his 'law of indifference', such that there are no trades at disequilibrium ratios of exchange and 'the last increments in an act of exchange must be exchanged in the same ratio as the whole quantities exchanged' (1957, p.94). This means that y/x can be substituted for dy/dx in (26), giving the two simultaneous equations:

$$-\frac{\partial U_A/\partial x}{\partial U_A/\partial y} = \frac{y}{x} = -\frac{\partial U_B/\partial x}{\partial U_B/\partial y} \qquad (27)$$

Jevons recognised that y/x is equivalent to the ratio of prices of the two goods, $p = p_x/p_y = y/x$, but he preferred to leave p out of the equations until the equilibrium values of y and x have been obtained. He recognised that in general the equations in (27) would be nonlinear and so not capable of explicit solutions. He therefore did not take their formal analysis further, although added the important but rather cryptic comment that the theory is 'perfectly consistent with the laws of supply and demand; and if we had the functions of utility determined, it would be possible throw them into a form clearly expressing the equivalence of supply and demand' (1957, p.101). He went on to discuss a number of 'complex cases', involving large and small traders, three goods and three traders, and competition between two traders, showing a very confident handling of the use of the equations of exchange.[34]

The discussion of price-taking behaviour (through the law of indifference) in the context of a two-person exchange model can be seen to create some 'tension' in view of the argument that there is no reason why two isolated traders should take prices as being outside their control. This point was raised by Jenkin before the publication of the *Theory of Political Economy* (see Black, 1977, iii, pp.166-178).[35] It may have been in response to this criticism that Jevons introduced the 'trading body', defined as 'any body either of buyers or sellers' (1957, p.88), as a rather awkward device to concentrate on representative traders who are price-takers. Edgeworth (1881, p.109) later described the idea more clearly as 'a sort of typical couple'.

3.2   Walras, Utility and Demand

Walras's extension of the Cournot model in a non-utility framework has already been discussed in section 2. As he later stated, he 'proceeded to derive the demand curve itself from the quantities possessed by each individual in the market and from each individual's utility curves for the two commodities considered' (quoted by Jaffé, 1983, p.25). Hence Walras explicitly considered the step to which Jevons had alluded, but it is important to recognised that the demand and supply curves are not partial equilibrium concepts; they refer to general equilibrium curves such as those shown in Figure 2.

What is surprising is that his approach, and associated demand and supply curves, seem to have been almost entirely 'lost'; they do not appear in any history of economics or microeconomics texts. They received their most extensive development by Launhardt (1993), whose analysis was used heavily by Wicksell (1954), and is discussed in section 4 below.[36]

3.2.1   Demand and Supply Curves

Walras was able to make the link from utility to demand following the crucial advice of his colleague Paul Piccard; see Jaffé (1983, pp.303-305) . What Piccard gave Walras was essentially the 'equations of exchange' that Jevons had earlier produced.[37] The starting point is thus each equation in (27), and for trader A, the holder of good X:

$$p = -\frac{\partial U_A/\partial x}{\partial U_A/\partial y} \qquad (28)$$

Walras made the crucial step of recognising that if the substitution $y = px$ is made where y appears anywhere on the right hand side of (28), it becomes an equation containing only p and x. Hence it may be possible to solve for x as a function of p, thereby giving A's supply curve of good X. Walras appeared to overlook the difficulty of solving the equation in practice and he did not examine any particular utility functions.

It is precisely at this point where Walras departed from Jevons, who preferred to leave the determination of the price ratio until the final stage, after obtaining the equilibrium amounts of goods X and Y traded. This created a problem because, as mentioned above, his equations are nearly always nonlinear and he fully recognised the problem of getting explicit solutions; see especially Jevons

(1909, p.759). This aspect has been ignored in the literature concerned with Jevons's 'failure' to derive demand curves from utility maximisation.

This approach of Walras gives A's supply function for good X.[38] The demand for Y is obtained using the reciprocal demand relation that $y = px$. To get B's demand for good X, it is necessary to take the result that $p = -(\partial U_B/\partial x)/(\partial U_B/\partial y)$ and again substitute for $y = px$ and solve for x as a function of p.

Although it is not always possible to solve the 'equations of exchange' for x and y, an advantage of Walras's approach is that his general equilibrium supply and demand curves can sometimes be derived explicitly. This enables the structure of the exchange model to be examined in some detail and its essential properties explored. The following subsection provides an example using the special case of constant elasticity of substitution utility functions.

3.2.2   An Example: CES Utility Functions

Suppose A has the constant elasticity of substitution utility function:

$$U_A = \left\{ \alpha_1 (a - x)^{-\rho_1} + (1 - \alpha_1) y^{-\rho_1} \right\}^{-1/\rho_1} \qquad (29)$$

where $\rho > -1$, and $\sigma_1 = 1/(1 + \rho_1)$ is the elasticity of substitution between the two goods. Differentiating with respect to x and y gives:

$$\frac{\partial U_A}{\partial x} = -\frac{\alpha_1 (a - x)^{-(1+\rho_1)} U_A}{\left\{ \alpha_1 (a - x)^{-\rho_1} + (1 - \alpha_1) y^{-\rho_1} \right\}} \qquad (30)$$

$$\frac{\partial U_A}{\partial y} = \frac{(1 - \alpha_1) y^{-(1+\rho_1)} U_A}{\left\{ \alpha_1 (a - x)^{-\rho_1} + (1 - \alpha_1) y^{-\rho_1} \right\}} \qquad (31)$$

Hence:

$$\frac{\partial U_A/\partial x}{\partial U_A/\partial y} = -\left(\frac{\alpha_1}{1 - \alpha_1} \right) \left(\frac{a - x}{y} \right)^{-(1+\rho_1)} \qquad (32)$$

Person A's supply of good X, as a function of the price ratio, p, is obtained by setting $(\partial U_A/\partial x)/(\partial U_A/\partial y)$ equal to $-p$, substituting for $y = px$ and solving for x. After some manipulation it can be found that:

$$x = \frac{a}{1 + k_A p^{1-\sigma_1}} \qquad (33)$$

where:

$$k_A = \left(\frac{\alpha_1}{1-\alpha_1}\right)^{\sigma_1} \qquad (34)$$

For person B, utility is:

$$U_B = \left\{\alpha_2 x^{-\rho_2} + (1-\alpha_2)(b-y)^{-\rho_2}\right\}^{-1/\rho_2} \qquad (35)$$

where $\sigma_2 = 1/(1+\rho_2)$ is B's elasticity of substitution. Using a similar process, it can be found that B's demand for X is given by:

$$x = \frac{b/p}{1+\left(\frac{1}{k_B}\right)p^{\sigma_2-1}} \qquad (36)$$

where:

$$k_B = \left(\frac{\alpha_2}{1-\alpha_2}\right)^{\sigma_2} \qquad (37)$$

It is not possible to solve analytically for the equilibrium price for which A's supply is equal to B's demand for good X. Inspection of the shape of the supply and demand functions shows, however, that there is only one equilibrium solution. The demand curve for X is always downward sloping and the supply curve is always upward sloping if the elasticity of substitution, σ_1, is greater than unity. If the elasticity is less than unity, then the supply curve is backward bending over the whole of the range, while the demand curve continues to slope downwards.[39]

3.2.3   Walras Lost and Found

The subsequent neglect of Walras's approach is unfortunate in view of its usefulness. For example, it shows how 'backward bending' supply curves can arise in a 'natural way'; it was in the context of the backward bending supply curve of labour that Buchanan (1971) referred to the modern treatment in terms of 'doctrinal retrogression'.[40] The backward bending curves show immediately how multiple equilibria can arise. The recognition of such multiple equilibria led Walras to his famous analysis of stability.

The usefulness of the approach is perhaps also demonstrated by the fact that similar curves have been independently reinvented several times. For example, Viner (1955, pp.538-541) used similar curves to explain an international trade argument of J.S. Mill (and in a long footnote derived the relationships between the relevant elasticities), although Viner did not show any backward bending curves. Vickrey (1964, pp.105-108) derived such curves directly from the Edgeworth box diagram. Atkinson and Stiglitz (1980, p.189) derived the general equilibrium curves directly from special utility functions suggested by Shapley and Shubik (1977); but they made no reference to Walras.

These 'rediscoveries' are of course in the context of exchange and general equilibrium. While modern general equilibrium theory has established the full conditions required for the existence and uniqueness of equilibrium, the development of the theory did not actually proceed in a direct line from Walras. Indeed, the early stimulus came from Cassel , who quickly arranged for his work to be translated into English and did not acknowledge that his simplified general equilibrium model was taken from Walras.[41]

3.3   Edgeworth: The Apogee

Edgeworth, directly stimulated by his personal contact with Jevons, provided a majestic synthesis and extension of the exchange model in his highly original *Mathematical Psychics* (1881). Jevons (1957, p.96) commented that 'it is hardly possible to represent this theory completely by means of a diagram', but of course Edgeworth provided such an apparatus with his indifference curves and contract curve contained within his 'box diagram'.[42] He also linked the offer curves directly to indifference curves. The technical device of the box diagram, after a very slow start, has now become ubiquitous in microeconomic theory.

A price-taking, or competitive, equilibrium is shown in Figure 3, which shows pre-trade indifference curves, offer curves, and the mutual tangency of indifference curves with the price line. Edgeworth emphasised the role of the number of traders, stressed that indeterminacy arises with small numbers so that there is a need for arbitration, and showed that the utilitarian objective, as a principle of arbitration, specifies a position on the contract curve and is acceptable to risk averse traders, thereby foreshadowing the later 'neo-contractarian' utilitarian approach.[43] He showed how increasing the number of traders using barter, with individuals following a recontracting process in which provisional bargains can be broken and coalitions can be formed, causes the range of indeterminacy along the contract curve to shrink until, with many traders, only the price-taking equilibria

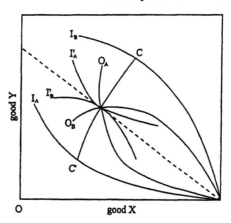

Figure 3: A Price-taking Equilibrium

remain. All this was achieved at great speed and expressed in a highly individual style; for further discussion, see Creedy (1986a)

4   Later Expositions

Two of the most comprehensive expositions of the theory of exchange were made towards the end of the century, by Launhardt (1993) and Wicksell (1954).[44] Unfortunately it was many years before their works were translated into English. The first of these was Wicksell who, despite his strong criticisms of Launhardt, made extensive use of his book and cannot properly be understood without reference to Launhardt's analysis. Walrasian supply and demand curves were first derived formally from utility functions by Launhardt (1993) in 1885, who used the assumption of quadratic utility functions and demonstrated the properties diagrammatically much more clearly than Walras. He also used the results to examine disequilibrium trading and its welfare effects. Indeed Launhardt's study can claim to be the first systematic treatise on modern welfare economics.

4.1   Launhardt's Exchange Analysis

Launhardt's analysis, starting from the exchange models of Jevons and Walras, is noteworthy for his derivation from explicit utility functions of algebraic forms of general equilibrium supply and demand curves expressed as functions of relative prices. Whereas Jevons and Walras concentrated on the price-taking equilibrium properties of their exchange models, Launhardt explored a process of disequilibrium trading in which successive trades take place at the 'short end' of the market, that is, the minimum of supply and demand at a price. His main concern was, however, to examine the welfare aspects of exchange, comparing the gains from trade under competitive and monopolistic behaviour. Launhardt has been criticised for suggesting that aggregate utility, and thus the aggregate gain from trade, is maximised at the price-taking equilibrium.[45] Launhardt nevertheless showed that a process of disequilibrium trading, in which the price initially favours the relatively poorer individual, can improve the aggregate gains from trade compared with the price-taking equilibrium.

4.1.1   Utility, Demand and Supply Functions

Instead of restricting attention to general results, Launhardt wished to illustrate the nature of the exchange model in more detail using explicit utility functions. Following Jevons, he assumed additive utility functions. As an engineer, it would have been natural to start with utility as a polynomial function of amounts consumed. The argument that marginal utility decreases steadily as consumption increases, with reference to Jevons's example of water, leads automatically to the quadratic form. Write A's utility as:[46]

$$U_A\left(a - x, y\right) = \alpha_A\left(a - x\right) - \beta_A\left(a - x\right)^2 + \gamma_A y - \delta_A y^2 \qquad (38)$$

Substituting $y = px$ in (38) gives A's utility in terms of x and p:

$$U_A = \alpha_A\left(a - x\right) - \beta_A\left(a - x\right)^2 + \gamma_A px - \delta_A\left(px\right)^2 \qquad (39)$$

A's supply function can be derived by maximising U_A with respect to x, for given relative price, p. Setting $dU_A/dx = 0$ gives, after rearrangement:

$$x = \frac{\gamma_A p - \left(\alpha_A - 2a\beta_A\right)}{2\left(\beta_A + \delta_A p^2\right)} \qquad (40)$$

A's demand for good Y is obtained by substituting into $y = px$. If B has the utility function:

$$U_B\left(x, b - y\right) = \alpha_B x - \beta_B x^2 + \gamma_B\left(b - y\right) - \delta_B\left(b - y\right)^2 \qquad (41)$$

then B's demand for X may be obtained by substituting $y = px$ into (41) and maximising U_B with respect to x, giving:

$$x = \frac{\alpha_B - p\left(\gamma_B - 2\delta_B b\right)}{2\left(\beta_B + \delta_B p^2\right)} \qquad (42)$$

Equation (40) and (42) are the equivalent of Launhardt's results in (1993, pp.36-38).

Equating (40) and (42) shows that the equilibrium relative price is the root or roots of a cubic equation, but Launhardt (1993, p.43) made the simplifying assumption that the two individuals have identical tastes, differing only in their pre-trade endowments of the goods. Setting $\alpha_A = \alpha_B = \alpha$, and so on, the denominators of both (40) and (42) become identical, so that the term in p^2 cancels and the equilibrium price is:

$$p = \frac{\alpha - \beta a}{\gamma - \delta b} \qquad (43)$$

Hence the price depends only on the parameters of the utility functions and the total stocks of the goods available.[47] This result has important implications for the following subsection.

4.1.2 Disequilibrium Trading

Whereas previous writers restricted attention to price-taking behaviour, Launhardt examined the implications of disequilibrium trading. This was in terms of 'repeated exchange' in which, starting from a disequilibrium price, there is gradual adjustment towards an equilibrium. With excess demand or supply, trade is assumed to take place at the 'short end' of the market, the minimum of supply and demand. At each stage of the price-adjustment process, there is a change in the allocation of goods between the two individuals. But in the case of identical individuals, such changes can have no effect on the final equilibrium price because, as shown by (43), this depends only on the parameters of the common utility functions and the total stocks.[48]

Another example of a situation in which trading at disequilibrium, or false, prices does not affect the equilibrium price was later produced by Marshall, although the precise structure of Marshall's example only became evident in the debate with Edgeworth.[49] If utility functions are additive and the marginal utility of one of the goods is constant, it can be shown that the final total amount

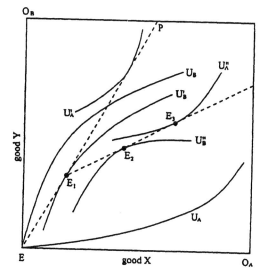

27

Figure 4: Disequilibrium Trading

of the other good traded and the final relative price are independent of the sequence of disequilibrium trades. However, the amount traded of the good for which marginal utility is constant does depend on the sequence of trades. This result holds irrespective of the form of the individuals' utility functions for the good which does not have constant marginal utility.

The type of disequilibrium trading described by Launhardt, and later by Marshall, can be illustrated by an extension of a diagram suggested by Edgeworth; see Marshall (1961, p.844). This type of process was also discussed by Johnson (1913) who made no references to earlier literature. An example is shown in Figure 4, where the endowment position moves from E to E_1, and then E_2. With the price line EP, there is an excess supply of good X and trade takes place at the demand corresponding to point E_1. At the lower price, represented by the line $E_1 P_1$ drawn through the new endowment point, the excess supply of X is lower than formerly and the new trade takes place at the point E_2, the minimum of supply and demand. Each disequilibrium trade is a Pareto improvement and the sequence of trades, bounded by the pre-trade indifference curves, must converge to an equilibrium somewhere on the contract curve.

4.1.3   Individual Gains from Trade

Launhardt emphasised disequilibrium trading in order to examine its effect on the gains from trade. The assumption of common preferences made it much easier for him to provide numerical illustrations. His main focus was on the difference between alternative allocative mechanisms. He began by comparing the price ratio that maximises an individual's gain from trade (with a single transaction taking place at that price) with the equilibrium price ratio. This is the equivalent of A's 'optimum tariff' or monopoly price. Consider A, who begins by holding all the stocks of good X, and achieves a gain in utility resulting from trade, G_A, of:

$$\begin{aligned} G_A &= U_A(a-x,y) - U_A(a,0) \\ &= \gamma_A y - \delta_A y^2 - (\alpha_A - 2\beta_A a)x - \beta_A x^2 \end{aligned} \qquad (44)$$

Substituting $y = px$ into (44) gives Launhardt's (1993, p.46) result that:

$$G_A = x\{\gamma_A p - (\alpha_A - 2\beta_A a)\} - x^2\left(\beta_A + \delta_A p^2\right) \qquad (45)$$

After producing the equivalent of (45), Launhardt substituted numerical values for the coefficients in utility functions and used the assumption of identical tastes in order to obtain G_A in terms of p and p^2. The value of p which maximises G_A turns out to be the positive root of a quadratic. However, he did not explain the precise method, giving only the numerical solution. Launhardt showed with his numerical examples that the resulting price ratio is different from the price-taking equilibrium value. However, the total gain of both A and B at that point is less than at the price-taking equilibrium.

Further insight can be obtained by differentiating (45) with respect to p, which gives, after collecting terms:

$$\frac{dG_A}{dp} = x\gamma_A - 2x^2\delta_A p + \frac{dx}{dp}\left\{\gamma_A p - (\alpha_A - 2\beta_A a) - 2x\left(\beta_A + \delta_A p^2\right)\right\} \qquad (46)$$

By taking the term $2(\beta_A - \delta_A p^2)$ outside the curly brackets in (46) it can be seen that:

$$\frac{dG_A}{dp} = \gamma_A x - 2x^2\delta_A p + 2\left(\beta_A + \delta_A p^2\right)\left\{\frac{\gamma_A p - (\alpha_A - 2\beta_A a)}{2(\beta_A + \delta_A p^2)} - x\right\}\frac{dx}{dp} \qquad (47)$$

The first term in the curly brackets in (47) is equal to A's supply of good X at price p. However, it is important to recognise that the x's in (47) must refer to the demand for good X by person B. This is because, for disequilibrium prices, trading must take place at the 'short end' of the market, and for prices that are favourable to person A, there is an excess supply of good X. By setting dG_A/dp equal to zero, and substituting for x from B's demand function in (42), the price that maximises A's gain from trade is the root of a rather complex expression. It is, however, clear that the equilibrium price, for which the term in curly brackets in (47) is zero, does not correspond to the price for which G_A is a maximum, for which the whole of the right hand side of (47) must be zero.

If individuals are identical except for their endowments of goods, the gains from trade are equal if all trade takes place at the price-taking equilibrium price. This can be seen by writing B's gains as:

$$G_B = U(x, b - y) - U(0, b)$$
$$= x\{\alpha_B - (\gamma_B - 2\delta_B b)p\} - x^2\left(\beta_B + \delta_B p^2\right) \qquad (48)$$

Substituting for the price-taking equilibrium price from (43), it can be seen from (45) and (48) and remembering that the supply and demand for X must now be equal, that $G_A = G_B$. Launhardt (1993, pp.45-46) did not give such a proof, but showed that the gains are equal using his numerical example and pointed out that the result holds only for the special assumptions.

4.1.4   Price-taking and Aggregate Utility

Launhardt's examination of exchange contained the unfortunate and incorrect argument that, 'It is simple to prove that in an exchange at equilibrium the sum of the utility for both proprietors, that is the utility achieved in an overall economic sense, has reached a maximum' (1993, p.43). Launhardt's discussion was terse, with a lack of clarity that is uncharacteristic of his work.[50] But he immediately qualified this statement, and the qualification was based on his analysis of a sequence of trades rather than a single exchange transaction. Launhardt's slip provided an easy target for later critics such as Wicksell.

Launhardt would have avoided the problem if he had attempted to solve for the values of x and y which maximise U. Total utility, as above, is given by:

$$U = U_A + U_B = U_A(a - x, y) + U_B(x, b - y) \qquad (49)$$

In view of the assumption of additivity, the partial derivatives $\partial(U_A + U_B)/\partial x$ and $\partial(U_A + U_B)/\partial y$ depend only on x and y respectively. Hence the two first-

Table 1: The Pre-trade Situation

	Person		
	A	B	Total
Stock of good X	400	0	400
Stock of good Y	0	480	480
Utility	240	576	816

order conditions for the maximisation of U can be solved explicitly for x and y, as:

$$x = \frac{(\alpha_B - \alpha_A) + 2\beta_A a}{2(\beta_A + \beta_B)} \qquad (50)$$

$$y = \frac{(\gamma_A - \gamma_B) + 2\delta_B b}{2(\delta_B + \delta_A)} \qquad (51)$$

These values of x and y do not equal the competitive equilibrium values. The competitive equilibrium involves voluntary trading on the part of individuals attempting to maximise their utility, subject to given prices, whereas alternative solutions involve the amounts traded being imposed on individuals.[51]

Launhardt assumed that the values of α, β, γ and δ, the parameters of common utility functions, are 1.0, 0.001, 1.8 and 0.00125 respectively.[52] The pre-trade situation is shown in Table 1 where, for example, A's pre-trade endowment of 400 units of good X gives utility of 240.[53] The price-taking equilibrium and the values which maximise aggregate utility, the utilitarian solution, are shown in the first two rows of 2. For identical tastes the utilitarian position involves equal sharing of the goods, and person B is worse off than before any trade takes place. Despite the fact that aggregate utility is maximised, there is no constraint requiring non-negative gains. The equilibrium price for price-taking may be obtained from equation (43) as 0.5. The assumption of identical preferences means that both individuals obtain a gains from trade of 93.33. Aggregate utility is less than with the utilitarian arrangement, as shown in the final column of 2.[54]

Launhardt contrasted the equilibrium with a sequence of trades and monopoly pricing. For the latter, substitution into A's gain from trade, given by equation (45), using B's demand for X from equation (42) to substitute for x, gives rise to A's gain in terms of the price ratio as:

$$G_A = \frac{-2520p^2 + 5040p - 1400}{4 + 5p^2} \qquad (52)$$

Table 2: Launhardt's Sequence of Trades

	p	x	y	U_A	U_B	$U_A + U_B$
Utilitarian	-	200	240	520	520	1040
Price-taking	0.5	266.67	133.33	333.33	669.33	1002.66
Trade 1.	.78	151.09	117.85	381.73	616.19	997.92
Trade 2.	.5	95.43	47.71	393.68	628.14	1021.82
Trade 1.	.43	233.12	100.24	306.91	682.07	988.98
Trade 2.	.5	41.32	20.66	309.15	684.31	993.46

Launhardt (1993, p.46) gave this equation and stated without discussion that G_A reaches a maximum for $p = 0.78$.[55] The situation after trading at this price is shown in the third row of Table 2, where person A has utility of 381.73 which exceeds that obtained from the price-taking equilibrium. Trader A gains 141.73 while B gains 40.19 from the trade at $p = 0.78$. However, aggregate utility is less than at the price-taking equilibrium.

This single trade does not exhaust all the potential gains from trade, and further trades can take place at prices lower than 0.78. Launhardt assumed that the next trade took place at the equilibrium price, and with identical tastes this is independent of the earlier trade. Hence the second trade occurs at $p = 0.5$ and the result is given in the fourth line of Table 2. The aggregate gain as a result of the two trades is 1021.82 and is higher than in the price-taking. It is indeed this result which gives Launhardt's qualification to his earlier argument. A similar approach shows that the monopoly price set by person B is $p = 0.43$. The resulting sequence of trades is shown in the last two rows of Table 2. The sequence of the two trades is shown in Figure 5.[56]

4.2 Wicksell's Examples

Wicksell (1954) relied heavily on Launhardt's treatment. However, he saw clearly that aggregate utility is not maximised at the price-taking equilibrium, and for this reason was strongly critical of Launhardt; see Wicksell (1954, p.18). However, Wicksell's discussion of disequilibrium trading can only be understood with reference to Launhardt's treatment. Wicksell produced his own numerical examples of a sequence of trades, assumed values for α, β, γ and δ of 200, 5, 10 and 0.5 respectively, and supposed that trader A holds 10 units of X while B holds 100 units of Y.[57]

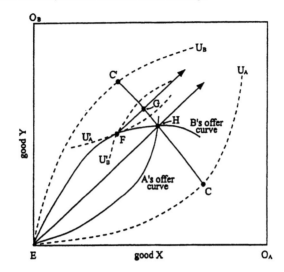

Figure 5: Launhardt's Sequence of Two Trades

Substituting into the equivalent of (43), Wicksell obtained the equilibrium price ratio of 30. Substitution for $p = 30$ into equation (40), and using $y = 30x$, gives equilibrium amounts traded as $x = 2$ and $y = 60$, where both traders gain 200 units of utility.[58] Wicksell did not present the equations of the demand and supply curves, however. Instead of goods X and Y, he used oxen and sheep respectively and stated, 'supposing that he [A] was first expected to exchange 1 ox for 13 sheep, then a second ox for $17\frac{2}{3}$ sheep, then $\frac{1}{2}$ ox for 11 sheep and finally another $\frac{1}{2}$ ox for 15 sheep, then there would remain for him after each exchange respectively a proportion of exchange between sheep and oxen [marginal rate of substitution] of more than 1 : 13, 1 : $17\frac{2}{3}$, 1 : 22 and finally of just 1 : 30, so that each single exchange would have to seem to him undoubtedly profitable, although he has in fact finally exchanged just 3 oxen for not quite 57 sheep' (1954, p. 67).

The final result is that B gets more oxen (good X) and gives up fewer sheep (good Y) in comparison with the price-taking equilibrium. Wicksell's terse discussion of this sequence of disequilibrium trades is misleading and conceals much numerical work. For example, he supposes that A is first expected to exchange 1 ox for 13 sheep. But if the price ratio is 13, it is shown in Table 3 that 1.115 units of X are traded for 14.498 units of Y. The ratio, y/x, is equal to the price ratio, but the trade that person A prefers is not quite the same as in Wicksell's example. Similarly, when the price is $17\frac{2}{3}$, A does not actually wish to trade 1

Table 3: Wicksell's Example

	p	x	y	U_A	U_B	$U_A + U_B$
Utilitarian	-	5	50	1250	1250	2500
Price-taking	30	2	60	1700	700	2400
Trade 1.	13	1.115	14.498	1516.73	706.32	2223.05
Trade 2.	$17\frac{2}{3}$	0.968	17.105	1536.05	845.05	2381.10
Trade 3.	22	0.508	11.165	1543.57	893.17	2436.74
Trade 4.	30	0.458	13.736	1554.05	903.65	2457.70

ox for $17\frac{2}{3}$ sheep, but 0.968 ox for 17.105 sheep. There is also a discrepancy in the other trades, given the prices mentioned by Wicksell, and in total 3.049 ox are traded for 56.504 sheep. Following the sequence of disequilibrium trades, A is slightly better off than in the pre-trade position, having gained 54.05 units of utility from the trades overall, but B's gain from trade is, at 403.65, over double that obtained from the price-taking equilibrium. The conclusion is similar to that of Launhardt. When the disequilibrium trades favour the poorer person, in this case trader B, total utility is greater than in the competitive solution. The fact that Wicksell did not make it clear that he had followed Launhardt and uncharacteristically poured scorn on his work simultaneously made his own contribution less transparent and damaged the reputation of Launhardt.

5 Conclusions

The aim of this paper has been to provide an outline of the development of the theory of exchange, concentrating on the less well-known development of the formal model which culminated in the contribution of Edgeworth. The importance of exchange, viewed as the central economic problem for the early neoclassical economists, was stressed. Instead of taking a chronological approach, non-utility approaches were first discussed. These included the extension by Walras of Cournot's attempt to model trade between regions, and Whewell's mathematical version of J. S. Mill's international trade analysis, followed by Marshall's diagrammatic version. Jevons's and Walras's utility approaches were then examined, showing the different paths they took from the same basic equations of exchange. After a very brief discussion of Edgeworth, the neglected but valuable contribution of Launhardt, along with the later work of Wicksell, were examined.

Emphasis was placed on the similarity of the formal structure of the exchange model used by the various writers. This similarity has been obscured by the different forms of presentation used and the emphasis given to various aspects and results by each investigator.

The pioneers of the theory of exchange fully recognised that they were dealing with pure theory rather than the 'real world'. Despite their enthusiasm over the successful development of a theory which helped to clarify the nature of alternative equilibria and provided a vehicle for the analysis of the welfare implications of exchange, they were conscious of its limitations. Indeed, Edgeworth himself managed to combine the greatest enthusiasm for the abstract results with the greatest diffidence regarding their applicability. This led to a stress on 'negative' results, or the removal of fallacies, and he quoted more than once the lines 'reason is here no guide, but still a guard'.[59] This advice was not always followed by those making further refinements to the model; but that is another story.

Notes

[1]Schumpeter (1955, p 911) wrote, 'they realised the central position of exchange value' which 'is but a special form of a universal coefficient of transformation on the derivation of which pivots the whole logic of economic phenomena'. In considering the central position of exchange theory, Fraser (1937, p.104) stated that the view of costs in terms of foregone alternatives is 'merely the extension of the exchange relationship to the whole of economic life'.

[2]As Edgworth stressed, 'the fundamental principle of international trade is that general theory which Jevons called the Theory of Exchange ... which constitutes the "kernel" of most of the chief problems of economics' (1925, ii, p.6). He added, 'distribution is the species of exchange by which produce is divided between the parties who have contributed to it' (1925, ii, p.13).

[3]Hicks also stated that 'welfare economics was captured by the catallactists and it has never got quite free' (1984, p. 253).

[4]See also Jevons's letter to his sister in Black (1977, ii, pp. 361, 410). Schumpeter argued that the utility analysis must be understood in the context of exchange as the central 'pivot', and 'the whole of the organism of pure economics thus finds itself unified in the light of a single principle – in a sense in which it never had before' (1954, p.913).

[5]The famous expression regarding adjective and noun is from Hutchison (1953).

[6]Hicks (1984, p.250) suggested that the term marginal revolution, 'is a bad term, for it misses the essence of what was involved'.

[7]It is recognised that some commentators would dispute this point, placing much stress on different interpretations of Walras's famous *tâtonnement* process. But in the formal models it is hard to escape the fact that, just as in Jevons's approach, individuals are price-takers and that in the equilibria considered, all exchange takes place at the corresponding prices; trading at disequilibrium prices is considered in section 4 below.

[8]However, some economists, including Jaffé (in Walras, 1954, p.504) have argued that the approaches were different.

[9]This can be shown to depend on the ratio of demand to supply elasticities in each country, though of course Cournot did not use the concept of elasticity himself. For further details, see Creedy (1992b).

[10]The error was later also pointed out by Fisher, in Cournot (1927, p.xxiv).

[11]He suggested that 'the method of treating economics graphically is probably due to Cournot' and added, 'the chief credit of reviving an interest in this method rests with Professor Marshall' (1892, p.36). This work culminated in Cunynghame's book (1904), reviewed at length by Edgeworth (1905). It does not seem to be widely recognised that Cunynghame's treatment stems directly from Cournot. Even Viner (1955, pp. 589), who referred to Barone's use of the same diagram to measure the gains from trade, did not seem to recognise that the diagram represents Cournot's model. The origins were, however, recognised by Samuelson (1952).

[12]Although these notes are not dated, there seems little doubt that Cournot was the sole influence and that Jenkin's (1871) analysis was quite independent, as Marshall himself always insisted.

[13]This cannot be achieved simply by adding another good and imposing a balance of payments constraint. Additional partial equilibrium demand and supply curves cannot by their very nature cope with the interdependence which is at the heart of the problem.

[14]Jaffé (1983, pp.55-77) argued that the line of filiation is instead from Isnard to Walras. Isnard recognised the important point that the price ratio is equivalent to the (inverse) ratio of quantities exchanged. He also addressed the mutual interdependence in a general equilibrium system. But his discussion was restricted merely to given quantities; there is no analysis of demand as a function of relative prices. A section from Isnard's analysis is reproduced in Baumol and Goldfeld (1968, pp.255-257), who suggest that strong claims made for him are 'somewhat over-enthusiastic' (1968, p.253).

[15]Wicksteed emphasised the role of endowments, or stocks, but surprisingly he did not use the apparatus of Walras and Jevons with which he was so familiar; see Creedy (1991a).

[16]On the equilibrium properties of this model and its implications for the distribution of prices, see Creedy and Martin (1993, 1994).

[17]Walras did not appear to be influenced by Mill's trade model, despite his familiarity with Mill's work. His published correspondence suggests that he did not become aware of Whewell's model until after he made contact with Jevons; see Jaffé (1965, I, letters 328, 375).

[18]See, for example, (1920, p.585). Mill's conception of demand in terms of a schedule is stressed by Robbins (1958, p.242) when comparing his trade analysis with that of Torrens, and by O'Brien (1975, p.183). Despite the importance of Torrens's and Pennington's work, Viner (1955, p.447) stresses the pivotal role of Mill's analysis for subsequent work. Although Pennington refers to the strength of demand when examining the gains from trade, he suggests (1840, pp.36, 39, 40-1) that the exchange rate will fluctuate between extremes, rather than tend to some determinate value. The high quality of Joplin's work in this area is now clear from O'Brien (1993, pp.211-219).

[19]Mill also introduced additional countries, transport costs, and additional goods, as well as examining the effects of technological change and shifts in demand; for further discussion of Mill and his critics, see Creedy (1990a).

[20]For a detailed analysis of Whewell's model, see Creedy (1989).

[21]Thornton's emphasis on indeterminacy in barter was also noted by Jevons and Edgeworth; see Creedy (1986a, p.48).

[22]Chipman (1965) interpreted Mill as assuming constant unit elasticites of demand; this is strongly criticised by Appleyard and Ingram (1979). On stability analysis, see Amano (1968).

[23]This was in fact the path taken by the present writer, in trying to see the link in diagrammatic terms between Mill and Marshall, without realising that the same diagram (or half of it) was in Walras.

[24]Whewell's treatment led to a certain amount of difficulty for later commentators; see Creedy (1989).

[25]For a detailed discussion and explanation of the diagrammatic links between the models, see Creedy (1990a).

[26] Consider England's offer curve in which cloth and linen are on horizontal and vertical axes respectively. If T and M are respectively the points where the tangent to the offer curve and a vertical line dropped from the point of tangency cut the horizontal axis, then the elasticity is OM/OT. The two points obviously correspond when the elasticity is unity.

[27] For further analysis of this method, see Creedy (1991b).

[28] For Samuelson's treatment of dynamics, see (1948, pp.266-269). Later treatments include Bhagwati and Johnson (1960) and Amano (1968). The latter concentrates on stability conditions.

[29] Marshall (1975, ii, p.112) contains a letter to Edgeworth of March 1891 in which Marshall discusses the application to wage bargaining. Edgeworth's application came as early as 1881, and was directly stimulated by Marshalls and Marshall (1879) and the privately printed chapters from the *Pure Theory*; see Creedy (1986a). Marshall also mentioned such applications in his 1876 paper on Mill; see Pigou (1925, pp.132-133).

[30] For further analysis of this case, see Creedy (1990a).

[31] Whewell (1850) showed that the King/Davenant 'law of demand' follows a third-order polynomial, yet when Marshall discussed the 'law' in the *Principles*, he simply reproduced some of Jevons's arguments; for further detail see Creedy (1986b). Whitaker (1975, i, p.45, n.26) noted that Marshall made no reference to Whewell's criticisms of Ricardo, but see Vázquez (1995, p.249).

[32] See, for example, Todhunter (1876). Whewell's correspondence shows that he was aware of Cournot. On the awareness of Cournot's work, see Vázquez (1997).

[33] For Jevons's version, see (1957, p.100). Jevons did not make use of constrained optimisation methods, but if utility is maximised subject to a 'price-taking' constraint, written as $y = px$ (from $yp_y = xp_x$), the Lagrangian is $L = U_A + \lambda(y - px)$. The partial derivate $\partial U_A / \partial x$ is not marginal utility, but its negative.

[34] For further discussion of these cases, see Creedy (1992a).

[35] Jevons's earlier treatment was in terms of trade between two individuals called Jones and Brown. Jenkin (1870) stimulated Jevons to publish his own work quickly, though his non-mathematical statement had been made in 1862; see (1957, appendix III).

[36] The curves were discussed very briefly, in the comprehensive review of Walras's equilibrium economics, by van Daal and Jolink (1993, p.26). They commented that 'it did not get much following', and referred to the 'undeniable complexity of the figures'. The only treatment in general works on the history of economic analysis seems to be the brief mention by Stigler (1965, p.96), who also referred to Wicksell (but not to Launhardt).

[37] Neither Jevons nor Walras made use of the Lagrangean method of constrained maximization; see Creedy (1980).

[38] An alternative approach would involve substituting $y = px$ into the utility functions, so that for example $U_A = U_A(a - x, px)$. Differentiating with respect to x and setting the result to zero also gives, after rearrangement, A's supply of good X as a function of p. This approach avoids the use of Lagrange multipliers.

[39] A richer range of possibilities exists if individuals hold some of both goods before trade takes place. For example, if person A holds a_1 and b_1 respectively of goods X and Y before trade, then in the supply curve of good X the numerator is changed from a to $a_1 - b_1 k_A p^{-\sigma_1}$. If person B holds a_2 and b_2 of X and Y respectively, then it can be found that the demand curve has a numerator of $(b_2/p) - (a_2/k_B) p^{\sigma_2-1}$ instead of simply b/p. While the demand curve is still downward sloping for all values of σ_2, the supply curve has both upward sloping and backward bending sections, so long as $\sigma_1 < 1$. In this case it is possible for multiple equilibria to occur

[40] It is possible, though unlikely, that Robbins's (1930) treatment of the supply curve of labour was influenced by Walras, indirectly through Wicksell, with whose work he was much more familiar. The direct influence of Wicksteed (1933) on Robbins is most likely, but even here there may be an indirect influence of Walras.

[41] See, for example, Weintraub (1985). Even Phelps Brown (1936) based his exposition of general equilibrium on Cassel, without being aware that it was from Walras.

[42] The treatment by Bowley (1924) is well-known, but is even more terse than Edgeworth (1881).

[43] For a comparison of alternative types of exchange equilibria, including price-taking, utilitarian and bargaining solutions, see Creedy (1994b).

[44] Neither writer seems to have read Edgeworth (1881), although Wicksell was familiar with the contract curve from Marshall's *Principles*.

[45] See for example, Wicksell (1954, p.76, n.2; 1934, p.81, n.1). For further discussion of the utilitarian optimum, along with price-taking and bargaining solutions, see Creedy (1994b).

[46] The marginal rate of substitution is a ratio of linear functions of x and y, so it is known, following the later work of Allen and Bowley (1935), that the expenditure on each good is a linear function of total expenditure, with coefficients depending on prices.

[47] Further insight into the price-taking equilibrium in this special case, not discussed by Launhardt, can be obtained by noting that A's marginal utility of good X is equal to $\alpha - 2\beta(a-x)$, while B's marginal utility is $\alpha - 2\beta x$. The arithmetic mean marginal utility is thus $\alpha - \beta a$, the numerator of (43). Similarly, the arithmetic mean utility of good Y is the denominator of (43). Hence the equilibrium price is the ratio of the arithmetic mean marginal utility of good X to that of good Y.

[48] This result does not hold if the individuals have different tastes: see Creedy (1994a).

[49] See Creedy (1990b).

[50] For further analysis of Launhardt's spurious argument, see Creedy (1994a).

[51] When criticising Launhardt, Wicksell (1934, p.81, n.1) pointed out that, with identical tastes, total utility is maximised when the parties 'simply exchange half their stocks'. This is confirmed by appropriate substitution into (50) and (51) giving a rate of exchange, y/x, of b/a, which obviously differs from that resulting from equation (43) above.

[52] He stated these in terms of fractions, which would have been more convenient when making calculations with pencil and paper.

[53]The values in the tables, obtained using a computer, show that Launhardt's own calculations were accurate, though they would have been tedious to produce.

[54]The utilitarian arrangement was not examined directly by Launhardt since he had incorrectly concluded that it coincides with the price-taking equilibrium.

[55]Differentiation of G_A with respect to p and rearrangement shows that this price can, as mentioned above, be obtained as the positive root of a quadratic.

[56]The monopoly price involves a tangency position between an indifference curve of the monopolist and the other trader's offer curve, but this is not on the contract curve so the second trade involves a movement to the contract curve. Launhardt also examined the limits of the contract curve, the intersection of the linear contract curve with quadratic pre-trade indifference curves.

[57]He stated that the equation of the contract curve is $10x + 3y = 200$.

[58]There is a misprint in Wicksell (1954, p.66) which gives $x = 30y$.

[59]The source, not of course given by Edgeworth, is Pope's *Essay on Man* (second Epistle, argument III).

References

Allen, R.G.D. and Bowley, A.L. (1935) *Family Expenditure: A Study of its Variation*, P.S. King & Son, London.

Amano, A. (1968) Stability conditions in the pure theory of international trade: a rehabilitation of the Marshallian approach. *Quarterly Journal of Economics*, 82, pp. 326-339.

Appleyard, D.R. and Ingram, J.C. (1979) A reconsideration of the additions to Mill's 'great chapter'. *History of Political Economy*, 11, pp. 459-476.

Atkinson, A.B. and Stiglitz. J.E. (1980) *Lectures on Public Economics*. London: McGraw-Hill.

Baumol, W. and Goldfeld, S.M. (1968) *Precursors in Mathematical Economics: An Anthology*. London; London School of Economics.

Bhagwati, J. and Johnson, H.G. (1960) Notes on some controversies in the theory of international trade. *Economic Journal*, 70, pp. 74-93.

Black, R.D.C. (ed.) (1977) *Papers and Correspondence of W.S. Jevons, Vols. ii and iii*. London: Macmillan.

Bowley, A.L. (1924) *The Mathematical Groundwork of Economics*. Oxford; The Clarendon Press.

Buchanan, J.M. (1971) The backbending supply curve of labour: an example of doctrinal retrogression? *History of Political Economy*, 3, pp. 383-390.

Chipman, J.S. (1965) A survey of the theory of international trade. *Econometrica*, 33, pp. 477-519.

Cochrane, J.L. (1975) *William Whewell's mathematical statements*. Manchester School, 43, pp.396-400.

Collard, D. (1968) Introduction to J.E. Tozer, *Mathematical Investigations of the Effect of Machinery* (1838). Reprinted, New York:Kelley.

Cournot, A.A. (1927) *Researches into the Mathematical Principles of the Theory of Wealth*. Translated by N.T. Bacon and introduced by I. Fisher. London; Stechert-Hafner.

Creedy, J. (1980) The early use of Lagrange multipliers in economics. *Economic Journal*, 90, pp. 371-376.

Creedy, J. (1986a) *Edgeworth and the Development of Neoclassical Economics.* Oxford; Basil Blackwell.

Creedy, J. (1986b) On the King-Davenant law of demand. *Scottish Journal of Political Economy*, 33, pp. 193-212.

Creedy, J. (1989) Whewell's translation of J. S. Mill. *Scottish Journal of Political Economy*, 36, pp. 266-281.

Creedy, J. (1990a) Marshall and International Trade. In *Centenary Essays on Alfred Marshall* (ed. by J. K. Whitaker), pp. 79-107. Cambridge: Cambridge University Press.

Creedy, J. (1990b) Marshall and Edgeworth. *Scottish Journal of Political Economy*, 37, pp. 18-39.

Creedy, J. (1991a) The role of stocks in supply and demand analysis: Wicksteed's problem. *Oxford Economic Papers*, 43, pp. 689-701.

Creedy, J. (1991b) Consumers' surplus and International trade: Marshall's example. *The Manchester School*, LIX, pp. 295-304.

Creedy, J. (1992a) Jevons's complex cases in the theory of exchange *Journal of the History of Economic Thought*, 14, pp. 55-69.

Creedy, J. (1992b) Cournot on trade between regions and the transition from partial to general equilibrium modelling. *History of Economics Review*, 18, pp. 10-19.

Creedy, J. (1994a) Launhardt's model of exchange. *Journal of the History of Economic Thought*, 16, pp. 40-60.

Creedy, J. (1994b) Exchange equilibria: bargaining, utilitarian and competitive solutions. *Australian Economic Papers*, 33, pp. 34-52.

Creedy, J. and Martin, V. (1993) Multiple equilibria and hysteresis in simple exchange models. *Economic Modelling*, pp. 339-347.

Creedy, J. and Martin, V. (1994) A model of the distribution of prices. *Oxford Bulletin of Economics and Statistics*, 56, pp. 67-76.

Cunynghame, H. (1892) Some improvements in simple geometrical methods of treating exchange value, monopoly and rent. *Economic Journal*, 2, pp.35-52.

Cunynghame, H. (1903) The effect of export and inport duties on price and production examined by the graphic method. *Economic Journal*, 13, pp.313-323.

Cunynghame, H. (1904) *A Geometrical Political Economy.* Oxford; Clarendon Press.

Edgeworth, F.Y. (1881) *Mathematical Psychics.* London; Kegan Paul.

Edgeworth, F.Y. (1894) The pure theory of international values. *Economic Journal*, 4, pp.35-50, 424-443, 606-638.

Edgeworth, F.Y. (1905) Review of Cunynghame's *Geometrical Political Economy, Economic Journal* 15, pp.62-71.

Edgeworth, F.Y. (1925) *Papers Relating to Political Economy.* London; Macmillan for the Royal Economic Society.

Fraser, L.M. (1937) *Economic Thought and Language.* London: Macmillan.

Henderson, J.P. (1985) The Whewell group of mathematical Economists. *Manchester School*, 53, pp.404-431.

Hicks, J.R. (1984) *The Economics of John Hicks* (ed. by D. Helm). Oxford: Basil Blackwell.

Hicks, J.R. (1934) Leon Walras. *Econometrica*, 2, pp.338-348.

Hutchison, T.W. (1950) Insularity and cosmopolitanism in economic ideas 1870-1914. *American Economic Association. Papers and Proceedings*, 45, pp.1-16.

Hutchison, T.W. (1953) *Review of Economic Doctrines 1870-1929.* Oxford: Oxford University Press.

Jaffé, W. (1965) *Correspondence of Leon Walras and Related Papers.* 3 Vols. Amsterdam; North Holland.

Jaffé, W. (1983) *Essays on Walras* (ed. by D.A. Walker). Cambridge; Cambridge University Press.

Jenkin, F. (1870) *The graphic representation of the laws of supply and demand.* Reprinted in 1931 in LSE Reprints of Scarce Tracts, no.9. London; Longmans, Green.

Jenkin, F. (1871) On the principles which regulate the incidence of taxes. Reprinted in *Readings in the Economics of Taxation* (ed. by R.A. Musgrave and C.S. Shaup), pp. 227-239. London: Allen and Unwin.

Jevons, W.S. (1909) *The Principles of Science.* London: Macmillan

Jevons, W.S. (1957) *The Theory of Political Economy.* (ed. by H.S. Jevons). New York: Augustus Kelly.

Johnson, W.E. (1913) The pure theory of utility curves. *Economic Journal,* 23, pp. 483-513.

Launhardt, W. (1993) *Mathematical Principles of Economics.* (Translated by H. Schmidt and edited by J. Creedy). Aldershot: Edward

Marshall A. (1975) *Early Economic Writings.* Two Vols. (ed. by J.K. Whitaker). London; Macmillan.

Marshall, A. (1876) J.S. Mill's theory of value. Reprinted in *Memorials of Alfred Marshall* (ed. by A.C. Pigou), 1925. London; Macmillan.

Marshall, A. (1923) *Money, Credit and Commerce.* London; Macmillan.

Marshall, A. (1961) *Principles of Economics* (Variorum edition). Macmillan, London.

Marshall, M. and M.P. (1879) *Economics of Industry.* London; Macmillan.

Meade, J.E. (1952) *A Geometry of International Trade.* London; Allen and Unwin.

Mill, J.S. (1844) *Essays on Some Unsettled Questions of Political Economy.* London; Parker.

Mill, J.S. (1920) *Principles of Political Economy.* (ed. by W.J. Ashley). London; Longmans, Green.

O'Brien, D.P. (1975) *The Classical Economists.* Oxford; Oxford University Press.

O'Brien, D.P. (1993) *Thomas Joplin and Classical Macroeconomics*. Aldershot: Edward Elgar.

Pennington, J. (1840) Letter to Kirkman Finlay Esq. Reprinted in *Economic Writings of James Pennington* (ed. by R.S. Sayers). 1963. London; London School of Economics.

Phelps Brown, E.H. (1936) *The Framework of The Pricing System*. Oxford: Oxford University Press.

Pigou, A.C. (ed.) (1925) *Memorials of Alfred Marshall*. London; Macmillan.

Robbins, L.C. (1958) *Robert Torrens and the Evolution of Classical Economics*. London; Macmillan.

Robbins, L.C. (1930) On the elasticity of demand for income in terms of effort. *Economica*, 10, pp. 123-129.

Samuelson, P.A. (1952) Special price equilibrium and linear programming. Reprinted in *The Collected Scientific Papers of Paul A. Samuelson, 2* (ed. by J.E. Stiglitz), pp. 925-945. The MIT Press. (1966).

Schumpeter, J.A. (1954) *History of Economic Analysis*. London; Allen and Unwin.

Shapley, L.S. and Shubik, M. (1977) An example of a trading economy with three competitive equilibria. *Journal of Political Economy*, 85, pp. 873-875.

Stigler, G.J. (1965) *Essays in the History of Economics*. Chicago: University of Chicago Press.

Todhunter, I. (1876) *William Whewell. An Account of his Writings, with Selections from his Correspondence*. London; Macmillan.

Van Daal, J. and Jolink, A. (1993) *The Equilibrium Economics of Leon Walras*. London: Routledge.

Vázquez, A. (1995) Marshall and the mathematization of economics. *Journal of The History of Economic Thought*, 17, pp. 247-265.

Vázquez, A. (1997) The awareness of Cournot's *Recherches* among early British economists. *Research in the History of Economic Thouht and Methodology*, 15, pp. 115-137.

Vickrey, W.S. (1964) *Microstatics.* New York: Harcourt Brace.

Viner, J. (1955) *Studies in the Theory of International Trade.* London: Allen and Unwin.

Viner, J. (1958) *The Long View and the Short.* Glencoe; Free Press

Walras, L. (1954) *Elements of Pure Economics* (translated by W. Jaffé). London; George Allen and Unwin.

Weintraub, E.R. (1985) *General Equilibrium Analysis.* Cambridge: Cambridge University Press.

Whewell, W. (1850) Mathematical exposition of some doctrines of political Economy – Second Memoir. Reprinted (1968) in *On the Mathematical Exposition of Some Doctrines of Political Economy.* Gregg International Publishers.

Wicksell, K. (1954) *Value, Capital and Rent* (translated by S. H. Frowein). London: Allen and Unwin.

Wicksell, K. (1934) *Lectures on Political Economy* (translated by E. Classen and edited by L. Robbins). London: Routledge.

Wicksteed, P.H. (1933) *The Common Sense of Political Economy* (ed. by L. Robbins). London: Routledge.

PART IV

A MIXTURE

The Australian Economic Review, vol. 34, no. 1, pp. 116–24

For the Student

Starting Research

John Creedy*
Department of Economics
The University of Melbourne

1. Introduction

This article provides a brief guide for students undertaking their first piece of research.[1] The activity of research itself and the closely related process of writing a research report or thesis are so different from the standard work of students, that it is helpful to set down explicitly some of those things that experienced researchers often take for granted. It might be useful to refer to this article at regular intervals during the production of your research paper.

In writing the research report, paper, or thesis the major objective, which cannot be overstated, is the achievement of clarity. You need to produce a transparent statement of the issues, methods and results. This is in fact much more difficult than is usually realised. There is no substitute for a careful study of the writing styles of exemplary authors. A willingness to respond to constructive criticisms and suggestions is also essential. You need to develop a new style of writing which is entirely different from the one used to write undergraduate essays. This article aims only to provide some brief practical suggestions for organising the writing and giving a research paper the appropriate 'shape' or appearance: it must look like a serious piece of research.[2]

* This guide arose from a number of lectures given over recent years to Honours and Graduate students in Economics at the University of Melbourne. I have benefited from comments by Denis O'Brien and Sheila Cameron on earlier drafts.

The nature of the research process and a brief description of the main properties of a research paper are provided in Section 2. Suggestions for arriving at a research topic and making a start on research are made in Section 3, which stresses the importance of the plan. General features of the research report are described in Section 4. A research paper must satisfy certain fundamental scholarly requirements; these proprieties are explained in Section 4, which also provides some suggestions regarding the basic layout and appearance of the report and some comments regarding literature reviews. Some suggestions regarding the writing process are given in Section 5, with recommendations regarding features to avoid. Section 6 provides some checklists, and a brief summary is in Section 7.

2. The Nature of Research

The major difference between research and coursework is that it is the responsibility of the researcher to identify a question; you must specify the question to be examined and decide on the approach to be used. The need to say something new necessarily involves a movement into unknown territory; there is no easy way to check if the answers are right or if the right method of attack is being used. Research therefore involves not only the continual exercise of judgement, but also a degree of confidence. In addition, there is no way to avoid occasionally following false leads and reaching an impasse, that is, going down 'dead ends'.

These aspects combine to ensure that the work should be more interesting and rewarding than ordinary coursework, while it also gives rise to alternating phases of optimism and pessimism. Additionally, it is necessary to convince others that it has been worthwhile. There are times when all researchers feel overwhelmed by difficulties, and are confused, anxious and not at all sure that they have anything worth reporting. At other times progress can seem unusually rapid, often helped by what can only be described as the substantial role played by serendipity, the faculty of making happy discoveries by accident. However, remember that 'fortune favours the prepared mind'. Experienced researchers simply know that they will go through these phases. For those who are carrying out research for the first time, it is worth anticipating these features and understanding that their experience is not unique.

Perhaps the most important rule of research is the following: there is no simple relationship between inputs of time and outputs of useful results. All research meets difficulties. Overcoming them may take a few minutes or it may take days or weeks. Successful research requires a willingness to do whatever is needed in order to overcome the problem, however unimportant it may seem at the time. Associated with this rule is the recognition that everything takes longer than anticipated.

Research also involves intense concentration over long periods. It is not possible to return to a research project casually at irregular intervals or just when there are no other pressing commitments. It is necessary to allocate regular times to research and always to keep a project moving forward. Indeed, concentration has to be such that it becomes something that is extremely hard to *stop* thinking about.

A simplistic view of research may be described in terms of a linear model in which the first stage involves reading as much as possible on a chosen topic and, after having a brilliant idea of how to proceed, this is followed by the analysis. The process is completed by simply writing up the results. However, progress in research is actually highly non-linear. It involves a complex process described in terms of a re-

peated cycle of writing and returning to further analyses and reading.

Writing is itself a process of discovery, not least of the author's own level of understanding. It reveals gaps in the argument and suggests new avenues of research as well as, importantly, providing an error-trapping process.

Most good research, however narrowly defined it may appear initially, has its own momentum. That is, the process of researching a particular topic leads to further questions and issues. The completion of a research paper is therefore often accompanied by negative feelings that, after all, not much has been achieved. It is worth remembering that this is simply an aspect of the general truth that the more we learn, the more conscious we are of our ignorance. Furthermore. progress is in fact largely achieved by making a series of small steps, rather than taking giant leaps.

2.1   The Research Paper

It is not easy to summarise briefly the characteristics of a good research paper. However, any research paper or thesis must at least satisfy the following requirements.

(i)   Demonstrate a clear perception of the research problem, its relation to the 'bigger picture' and the relevant literature.

(ii)   Provide motivation for the research question and the approach used.

(iii) Demonstrate an ability to formulate a useful approach and show good judgement in selecting techniques and, where relevant, data.

(iv)   Show an appreciation of the value and limitations of the results.

(v)   Indicate the potential for further developments.

3.   Getting Started

Getting started is usually a hard and worrying part of research for newcomers. You can often benefit from discussions with other people. However, the research topic is your choice, so do something that you find interesting. Do not worry about what other students or friends think of your topic, though you will want to take advice from experienced researchers who are familiar with the area and its potential problems. The fact that you set the agenda is an important positive feature of research, but at the same time it presents an unfamiliar challenge.

3.1 Finding a Research Topic

With the first research exercise, your major concern is initially the question of how to settle on a topic. It is important to begin with a well-defined question that is not too broad in scope. Think in terms of taking a number of small steps.

The following suggestions are designed to make your process of arriving at a precise topic reasonably systematic. Remember, however, that this process may take a long time.

(i)   Consider an area of economics that, from previous studies, you find interesting. This may, for example, be labour economics, monetary economics, public finance, or international economics. Identify the types of issue that attract you most.

(ii)   The next stage takes place in a library. Go to the journals section of the library and look through the contents pages of key journals in the chosen area. From there, identify papers to look at. You should also look at the general journals. There is no substitute for getting your hands dirty in this way. At this early stage, do not simply undertake computer searches based on keywords.

(iii) When reading journal articles or other research papers, keep the following points in mind.

- Journal papers are usually terse. They represent work which has matured over several years. Hence, a full understanding of the methods and the significance of the results can only be obtained after detailed and extensive study. This involves re-reading them several times. Investigate whether an earlier version, in the form of a departmental Discussion Paper, is available. This can often provide more details.

- However, a quick initial read will generally be enough to allow you to identify (i) the main question considered by the author, (ii) the methods of analysis used, (iii) the data required and (iv) the nature of the results. These are the four major features that should receive your initial attention.

- After this preliminary look at particular papers, you will judge whether they are of potential interest. You may reject several papers in this way before finding one that stimulates you to look closer. If you continue studying the paper, make notes about other literature cited in it, data used, analytical methods and principal results.

- Even at this early stage, keep orderly notes about the works you consult, including full bibliographical details.

(iv)   There is one fundamental ingredient without which research will never begin. That ingredient is curiosity. If you have this, you will never have a problem finding a research topic. When you read papers, always ask yourself questions, such as:

- Can the approach used in a particular study be applied to other contexts, countries or time periods?

- What assumptions are implicit? Are all the assumptions sensible? To what extent might the results be sensitive to the assumptions? How can they be relaxed? Are there any unnecessary assumptions?

- Is the econometric approach used the appropriate one? Have all relevant statistical tests been carried out?

- Often, precise data relating to the theoretical concepts are not available. Are the constructed variables the most appropriate for the task?

- Are there any implications of the study which have not been fully drawn out by the author? Can these be exploited in your work?

(v) In addition to curiosity, you also need a willingness and the energy to pursue avenues, even if some of these may lead to a dead end. Furthermore, you need the imagination and flexibility to overcome the many inevitable problems along the road. You also require good judgement to select the appropriate techniques of analysis, to decide which aspects can be safely ignored and which assumptions are fundamental for the particular context, and to assess the value of your results at each stage. The best research reports will reflect these qualities.

3.2   The Plan of Attack

Research should not be allowed to drift along in a haphazard way: planning is crucial. You should have a plan for the 'big picture' as well as having daily or weekly lists of things to be done.

(i) At a very early stage, draw up a detailed table of contents. This may take several days, as working out the arrangement of material is often difficult. The table should contain all your chapter, section and subsection titles. This plan allows you to see the sequence at a glance. In writing, you will not necessarily move linearly from the first to the last chapter, and having a clear view of the arrangement will allow you more easily to write in the most convenient order, while keeping the overall shape in mind.

(ii) Attach a time schedule to your plan. Aim to finish with several weeks to spare. This will allow you to leave the paper alone for a while and then give it a final polish after returning to it refreshed. You will be surprised by how many small but significant improvements can be made.

(iii) Start writing immediately. As mentioned above, writing is itself a process of discovery, revealing gaps in the argument (and your own understanding) and suggesting new lines of enquiry.

4.   Basic Features of a Research Paper

Any piece of research, whether a short paper, report or thesis, is expected to have a number of basic features. Some general points, concentrating on introductory material, are described in Subsection 4.1. Subsection 4.2 lists important characteristics which absolutely must be present. The general layout, structure and appearance are discussed in Subsection 4.3, and finally the literature review is examined in Subsection 4.4.

4.1   General Points

(i) It has been mentioned more than once that you must specify the precise questions that drive your research. The reader of your paper has to be made familiar with these questions and the broad structure of your paper or thesis at an early stage. You must provide the motivation for the study and the approach. The following advice to theatrical producers, by W. S. Gilbert, may appear to be rather vague, but is worth repeating in this context: 'Tell 'em what you are going to do; let 'em see you doing it; then tell 'em what you have done'.

(ii) Your introduction needs to let the reader know, as quickly as possible, three important things. It must answer the questions 'what', 'why' and 'how'. Do not digress, but say what is already known and signal what is new about your own work. It is worth returning to your introduction at the last stage in the 'polishing' process. As suggested by Blaise Pascal, 'the last thing one knows in constructing a work is what to put in first'. However, remember that your introduction should be intelligible to someone turning to the topic for the first time.

(iii) You need to give the reader a clear view of where each section or chapter is going. Provide plenty of signposts, which point the way forward. These can most easily be added at a later stage, after the first draft has been completed. Ensure that you have provided appropriate linkages between various sections. These help to clarify the logical structure of your thesis.

(iv) Try to form a clear view of your reader. In particular, you are not writing a textbook, so a certain amount of knowledge can be assumed. However, avoid being too allusive. It is perhaps useful, in getting the level right, to imagine that you are giving a seminar presentation to your peers.

(v) Remember that the first draft is not the final draft: it is simply the start of a long process of revision. It is worth keeping in mind Samuel Johnson's statement that 'what is written without effort is in general read without pleasure'. It is remarkable how small changes to crucial expressions, or minor rearrangements of material, can improve the clarity substantially.

4.2 Some Proprieties

There are many aspects of writing research reports, such as style and arrangement, which involve choices. However, there are some things that *must* be done to satisfy the minimum requirements of scholarship. These are listed here.

(i) Always acknowledge earlier work. Give precise sources of the results, diagrams and equations of other authors.

(ii) State when you are summarising other people's arguments. This also helps you to be explicit about precisely how you have made modifications and original contributions.

(iii) Ensure that quotations are accurate and give exact page references. Do not alter quotations by, for example, adding emphasis (with italics). Avoid the use of ellipses (...), at least if the material omitted is part of the argument in the quoted material, as distinct from an allusion or reference.

(iv) For all data sources, full details must be given, including page numbers. It must be possible for someone to replicate your results with the minimum of effort in obtaining the same data. Keep fully documented data files in case you are asked to make the data available to other researchers.

(v) All bibliographical details in your list of references, arranged alphabetically by author, must be complete and accurate. A consistent style must be used regarding capitalisation, italics, initials, and ordering of material. This will require much more time than you imagine. Several styles are used, and each publisher and journal has its own house style. It is important, having settled on a style, to be consistent. Investigate style requirements imposed by your department or university at an early stage.

4.3 Some Mechanics

It is important to pay attention to the 'mechanics' of producing a research paper. For example, you must be consistent in the use of titles and numbering systems. Make decisions regarding the following aspects at an early stage as it can be very time consuming to make changes later.

(i) You are unlikely to need more than three levels of titles. These are the chapter titles (numbered 1, 2, ...), section titles (numbered 1.1, 1.2, ...), and subsection titles (numbered 1.1.1, 1.1.2, ...). Use a consistent font, capitalisation, spacing and position (either centred or against the margin), so that the reader immediately identifies the status of the title. Keep the titles succinct but meaningful. The first sentence after the title should not rely on that title for its meaning.

(ii)   For tables and figures use a decimal numbering system within chapters (for example, Table 1.1, and so on). Give all tables and figures succinct descriptive titles. Refer to all tables and figures in the text. Produce separate lists of tables and figures after the contents page.

(iii) For equations, use a decimal numbering system within chapters. Number all equations, even if you do not refer to them. The numbers are useful when other researchers wish to make reference to the equations.

(iv)   Use appendices for extensive data descriptions, longer derivations of analytical results, and.for subsidiary analytical or empirical results. Do not use appendices to define notation.

(v)   Use footnotes for groups of references to literature, or qualifications of the main argument. Do not break a sentence with a footnote flag. Depending on the style requirements, endnotes may be used instead of footnotes. Be sparing in the use of footnotes; that is, avoid 'foot-and-note disease'.

(vi)   In reporting others' work, use the past tense (as in, 'economist X found that ...'). In indicating the contents of your later chapters or sections, use the present tense (as in, 'section X reports estimates of ...').

4.4   The Literature Review

The aim of a literature review is to place your own work clearly within the larger picture.

While research involves a focus on a narrow range of questions, it is obviously important to understand how it relates to wider issues. A brief review of the existing literature can help to provide some motivation for your analysis. In addition, it is only possible to establish a claim to have extended the literature by making clear the relevant contributions of others. This can often be achieved relatively quickly, without creating the need for a separate section or chapter.

Sometimes it may be necessary to provide an extensive review of earlier literature in a separate chapter. This presents a difficult challenge as it calls for quite a mature and confident approach. Ideally, the discussion of the literature should be organised along analytical or taxonomic lines. This provides clear criteria for deciding whether, and where, an earlier work needs to be mentioned. Hence:

(i)   Start with a clear statement of the broad problem.

(ii)   Distinguish alternative possible approaches, whose features may be:

   • analytical, involving a range of assumptions and techniques; or

   • statistical or econometric, associated with data constraints and estimation techniques.

(iii) Refer to earlier contributions in the context of these different approaches. Some works may therefore be included only as part of a list while others, judged to be the most important, may require further discussion.

(iv)   Indicate the strengths and weaknesses, in your judgement, of the various approaches and explain precisely where your study fits into the taxonomy.

The main thing to avoid is what might be called the 'card index' method, which consists of a dull and poorly organised sequence along the lines of 'A said this ... B said that ... and C said ...'.

5.   The Writing Process

The writing process is much more difficult than is often recognised, though the production of a clearly written and readable manuscript can be very satisfying. Subsection 5.1 provides some general hints regarding writing and revising research work. Subsection 5.2 makes further suggestions, concentrating on things to avoid.

5.1   Initial Hints

The aim of writing is to achieve clarity. This requires great care and a capacity to read your own work as if it were written by someone else. The economist Jacob Viner referred to two basic types of 'balderdash'. The first, simple balderdash, arises where the author believes that he or she understands, but cannot make it intelligible to the reader. The second, compound balderdash, comes in two varieties. In one variety, neither the author nor the reader can make any sense of the text, and in the second variety, the reader thinks he or she understands but the author knows it is meaningless. Your aim is to avoid such balderdash.

(i)   Recognise that your first draft will not be the last. There is a story of a visitor to an English stately house asking how the splendid lawns are produced; the answer is simply to sow the seed and then weed and roll it for five hundred years. An analogy can be drawn with good, clear writing.

(ii)   Re-read as you go along. In particular, before turning to a new paragraph, read the previous one. Before starting a new writing session, re-read the previous work. This will help to improve continuity. Regularly check the linkages between sections.

(iii) Stop writing while at a convenient point, when it is going well. If your writing is going well, resist the temptation to keep going until you have reached the end of the particular section or chapter, or you have exhausted your current ideas. By stopping before reaching that point, you will find it much easier to pick up the work the next time and start again, knowing how it needs to proceed.

(iv)   Ask a friend to read your draft. Be careful to select someone you know to be sympathetic and constructive, as anyone can find negative things to say, however good the paper. As George Canning, the 19th century British Prime Minister, pleaded, 'save me from the Candid Friend'. However, do not try to defend the indefensible. Do not fall in love with your own writing. Be willing to respond to suggestions.

(v)   When reading through what you have written, try to produce a succinct summary of each paragraph. This will help to determine whether a subtitle is needed, or whether you should change the order of the material, or whether anything needs to be added to improve continuity or clarity. Ask yourself if it is repetitive. If you cannot summarise the paragraph, delete it!

5.2   Further Suggestions

A research paper is not meant to be read aloud or to entertain the reader. It should be written in a calm and clear manner so that the emphasis is always on the issue at hand. Some suggestions, largely of features to avoid, are listed here.

(i)   Avoid colloquial, conversational and highly personalised expressions.

(ii)   Avoid abbreviations (such as &, don't, and etc.).

(iii) Avoid personal pronouns (I, we, you, me).

(iv)   Avoid antiquated, verbose, pedantic and pompous language.

(v)   Do not be allusive.

(vi)   Do not annoy the reader by making gratuitous negative remarks about others' work.

(vii) Avoid an excessive use of adjectives and adverbs. When editing your first draft, look out in particular for 'very', 'extremely' and 'highly', which are usually best deleted. In addition, 'had' can often be deleted.

(viii) Do not use metaphors, which usually add colour at the expense of clarity.

(ix) Be gender neutral. This can easily be achieved without mixing singular and plural or overusing 'he or she'.

6.   Checklists

When you are close to producing a polished draft, it is useful to go through your manuscript several times, paying special attention to the overall structure as well as a number of details of its appearance. Subsection 6.1 provides a list of structural features to check. Subsection 6.2 lists some of the mechanical aspects that require careful attention. It is usually best to go through your manuscript separately for each of the items mentioned in Subsection 6.2, rather than trying to cover several at one reading.

6.1   The Structure of the Analysis

(i)   Is the problem clearly stated?

(ii)   Are hypotheses and assumptions explicit?

(iii) Is the relationship to previous work clear?

(iv)   Are the limitations acknowledged?

(v)   Are the data fully described and their precise sources given?

(vi)   Are the conclusions explicitly stated?

6.2   The Basic Appearance of the Paper

(i)   Format: Check the prelims, title pages and contents pages.

(ii)   Headings: Check the consistency of style, fonts, numbering, and spacing.

(iii) Quotations: Check their accuracy and page references. A large proportion of quotations are inaccurate!

(iv)   Tables: Check titles, abbreviations and details needed for interpretation and cross-references.

(v)   Equations: Check numbering and cross-references.

(vi)   References: Are all cited works included? Do not include those not cited. Are works in alphabetical order? Is the style consistent? Are all details given, such as volume number, page numbers, date and place of publication and publisher?

7.   Summary

There is no easy formula for producing good research papers. You need curiosity, energy, imagination and flexibility to overcome the inevitable problems. You also require good judgement to select the appropriate assumptions and techniques of analysis, and to assess the value of your results. The best research reports will reflect these qualities.

Many challenges must be overcome and even researchers with considerable experience cannot avoid going down dead ends, occasionally writing sentences containing one of the two types of balderdash described above, or even forgetting to mention their key findings and assumptions. All work must be checked as carefully as possible and all drafts must be edited and polished many times, paying close attention to detail as well as the overall shape and flow of the argument.

All this takes longer than envisaged. When planning your work, produce a generous estimate, fully allowing for the fact that everything takes longer—then double the time and add some more for good measure. This is not an exaggeration!

In developing a style of writing research papers, a great deal can be learned by close study of authors who are particularly clear. You may begin by imitating a style that you strongly admire and find attractive, but of course ultimately you need to find your own 'voice'. However, be warned that, as the jazz musician Miles Davis once said, 'sometimes you have to play a long time before you learn to sound like yourself'.

October 2000

Endnotes

1. This is not a scholarly paper, so I have taken the liberty of not following all the instructions given here. In particular, sources of brief remarks by famous people are not given.

2. There are numerous books devoted to thesis writing, and it would be useful to consult some of these. Examples include the books by Anderson and Poole (1994) and Taylor (1989). The short guide to clear writing by Gowers (1948) is still well worth reading today. The AGPS style manual (1995) is a useful publication.

References

Anderson, J. and Poole, M. 1994, *Thesis and Assignment Writing*, J. Wiley, Brisbane.

Gowers, E. 1948, *Plain Words: A Guide to the Use of English*, HMSO, London.

Style Manual for Authors, Editors and Printers 1995, AGPS, Canberra.

Taylor, G. 1989, *The Student's Writing Guide for the Arts and Social Sciences*, Cambridge University Press, Cambridge.

[11]
Adam Smith and All That*

John Creedy

Abstract

This paper tells you everything you need to know in order to impress your friends with your knowledge of the most famous people and the useful past of the subject of economics. However, it is recommended that this paper should not be read in the company of anyone who reads dusty old books, and who therefore has a tendency to sneeze.

1 Introduction

Students of economics no longer study the history of economic thought, for the simple reason that it is much too difficult. It requires a lot of reading of books that do not have convenient introductions and summaries, and so takes up far too much time. As a consequence, most economists are not familiar with the great names of the past and are unable to place modern analyses in historical, or any other, perspective.

This paper is designed to overcome this deficiency in one simple lesson. It collects all the useful past possessed by the

---

*Inspiration for this highly progressive (or degenerate, depending on your point of view) research programme in economics was provided, as an unintended consequence of their timeless text, by W.C. Sellar and R.J. Yeatman. It was not supported by a peer-reviewed competitive research grant. It has not benefited from referees' comments – life is much too short to wait for them. It has not been cut in half by an editor desperate to make the articles unintelligible. It has not been presented at any seminars or international conferences held in exotic locations. None of the errors is mine. All remaining ones are unimportant.

1

subject into one convenient, and therefore easy to plagiarise, source.

This aim is possible because economics is a relatively young subject, though it has attracted the attention of many interesting characters. Many of these people were polymaths, though they did not actually learn their subject parrot-fashion and were often ignorant of maths. Many were frequently highly innovative, and some were totally confused.

It will be seen that economists have always been very keen on building models. Unfortunately they must have used poor glue because their models have a tendency to fall apart as soon as any weight is placed on them. Also, many economists are rather belligerent and jump up and down on each others' models. Furthermore, many of the models involve flows of water, and consequently end up going down the drain. Too often the baby gets thrown out with the bath water.

Importantly, the general public does not like being treated as subjects of models, and has the quite irrational fear that model makers will start to believe that their models are more important than the real world. Hence, as soon as they learn that they are being modelled, ordinary people have developed the clever knack of fighting back by changing their behaviour. This is part of the general phenomenon, understood by producers of television programmes, that if a lens is pointed at people, they immediately behave in peculiar and antisocial ways.

Many economic analyses have been illustrated using hypothetical factories, sometimes making unusual commodities. For

2

example, there is one famous pin factory; these pins were urgently needed to burst lots of South Sea bubbles, as well as to deflate opponents. Although there are also examples of wig makers, this paper is relatively free of wig history. It also positively avoids discussion of abstruse methodological arguments, as most economists have not cared what scientific status their pronouncements may or may not possess. However, in view of the importance of taxes, there is quite a lot of taxonomy. Similarly, the importance of trade and exchange, combined with the fact that some economists were also trained as lawyers, means that tortologies often appear.

Some historians see the history of economics in terms of a series of revolutions. This may have something to do with the observation that many economists have spent their professional lives going round in circles, and some of them were indeed quite revolting.

This paper is accompanied by a number of self-testing questions which are designed to boost the confidence of readers, confirming what they knew all along, that they know more than the writer. The answers can be found on the world wide web, at the address: www\andallwhat\edu.au\. To view these answers, which are supplemented by dramatic reconstructions of debates, by out-of-work actors wearing silly wigs and using strange voices, you may need to download the free easy-to-use text-and-image-handling innovative software, crib.zip. This takes just over three hours to download and install, is not necessarily virus-free, and is quite likely to wreck your hard disk.

3

2 Before Adam Smith

Surprising as it may seem in view of his name, economics did not begin with Adam Smith. Classical scholars wrote about economic issues. However, they did not use the word 'economics' and they wrote in Greek and Latin, so they can safely be ignored here.

Medieval scholars also wrote on economic subjects. They were highly interested in low interest rates on loans. But as they were monks, they can be dismissed as having worked in monasteries in isolation from the real world, unlike modern academic economists.

Later there were the mercantilists, in the 17th century, made up of a group of war-mongering and monopoly-seeking merchants. Their aim was to accumulate more gold than any other county, by cutting imports and increasing exports. But it was later realised that this would lead to an imbalance by changing the centre of gravity of the earth.

In order to finance wars, the mercantilists wanted to assess the taxable capacity of the country, and so began the important task of constructing the first measures of National Income and population. This involved a highly esoteric procedure, which has been copied many times since, of making up the numbers. This was called Political Arithmetic, and has never been out of fashion.

In their obsession with adding up their assets, the mercantilists were strongly influenced by the contemporary flowering of

4

the natural sciences, exemplified by the work of Isaac Newton, which built on years of careful observation of the planets (by other people). Newton was rewarded by being allowed to take over the Royal Mint, where he used his skills to have forgers put to death. As every one knows, Newton was influenced, like Adam and Eve before him, and the Beatles after him, and even the builders of New York, by an apple. It is shown below that a discarded apple later had an important influence on the origins of a fundamental economic theorem.

The earlier scientific work of Galileo did not have a comparable influence on economic analysis. This was because economists believed they had a rather imperfect telescope and anyway they were impatient to get on with other things.

The mercantilist period also saw the passing of the first economic law, and this was by royal decree. King Davenant passed a law saying that when corn crops are lower than normal as a result of crop failures, the price of corn should be raised so high that farmers actually make more money than in normal times. Strangely, later generations of historians have found it hard to identify this king, or his law.

After the mercantilists, the physiocrats began to think about economics, but they were French and had unfortunate connections with the French Revolution. They realised the folly of the mercantilists' idea that a country could endlessly accummulate gold from a trade surplus, and thereby invented the circular flow. This stressed the fact that money goes round and round the economy. It probably also explains why coins were usually

5

round and why misers clipped the edge of their coins to stop them rolling away.

The physiocrats also recognised the important principle that what goes in must come out, but they were not able to invert a matrix, so further development of this insight had to wait another 150 years when it was later reinvented as input-output analysis.

3 Adam Smith and Classical Economics

Adam Smith is the most famous economist ever, as well as being a Good Man (in fact he was so good, he was said by his friends to be overflowing with moral sentiments). He was the leading economist of the British school of classical economists. However they had the good sense to write in English rather than Latin, and not to wear togas.

His most famous book is called *The Wealth of Nations*, of which every literate person has heard. However, no one reads this book any longer: it therefore can be said to have aquired the status of a true classic. One reason it is not read these days is that, like Shakespeare's plays and the King James Bible, modern readers realise immediately that it is made up entirely of famous quotations. It is not quite clear why his contemporaries failed to recognise this obvious point.

Adam Smith was born, educated, taught and lived in Scotland most of his life. However, he travelled on horseback to Balliol College to find out if education in Oxford was really as bad as he had been told – it was. Like many students at that university ever since, he simply spent a few years getting on with his own private studies in the library. The fact that we have all indirectly benefited by Oxford being so appallingly bad eventually led to the important idea of external effects from higher education.

Shortly before his death, Adam Smith had a large number of cheap medallions of himself made. Indeed, there were so many, that they are still given away as consolation prizes to students of economics in British universities who have to become merchant bankers because they cannot find anything useful to do with their degrees.

Smith objected to unproductive labour, so he opened a famous pin factory, mentioned above, to keep the people busy. In doing this, he invented the idea of the division of labour: this states that the poor work while the rich supervise.

He had many skills. He even tried to be the first person to invent the invisible man, but he only got as far as the invisible hand. However, this hand was very powerful, and managed to imbue markets and prices with the ability to coordinate economic activity, even though people could not see the hand signals. Many later governments, by failing to see this hand although it was in front of their faces, have thought they could do better, with disastrous results.

Adam Smith was concerned by the question of the legitimate role of government. He developed a number of maxims for taxation, but this turned out to be a very bad name for them, as it

7

has led to the idea that taxation should be maximised.

Smith managed to confuse later writers by appearing to argue that economic values were determined by the labour content of the goods in the production process. As will be seen below, this was the centre of much controversy and resulted in the expenditure of much labour, to little value.

A contemporary of Smith was a French economist called Say. Instead of adopting a labour theory of value, Say tried to work out a theory of value based on demand. This involved piles of cannon balls, in a complex illustration of the problem of aggregation. This theory had little influence because no one could see what cannon balls had to do with the demand for goods. Many years later, an economist called Samuelson built a canonical classical model, but by then Say was dead so it didn't matter.

Say also found that supplying things was very demanding, so he invented the law that 'supply creates its own demand'. This was quite often misunderstood, probably because it was in French and was hard to translate. He was later heavily criticised by Keynes, who thought it was safe to criticise someone who was both dead and French.

4   T. R. Malthus

Malthus was another important classical economist. He was also a vicar and therefore a Good Man, at least until he became a professor of economics.

Malthus was very worried about population growth. He thought the poor would be crushed under the weight of childbearing, and this led to the subsidence theory of wages. This became a corner stone, or impediment, of the classical theory.

He became worried about over-population after being terrified by the horror story written by the daughter of William Godwin, in which an attempt to create a perfect man resulted in the creation of a perfect monster. Malthus tried to persuade the poor not to have too many children, by drawing diagrams for them; but the ignorant poor thought that they were meant to multiply geometrically. This all added up to a rather dismal story.

Malthus's theory of population eventually evolved into Charles Darwin. To show his gratitude, Darwin had ten children and persuaded one of them, a mathematician, to defend the theories of an economist called Jevons (see below).

Malthus had a very good friend called David Ricardo. They were such good friends that each one disagreed with virtually everything that the other one said.

5   David Ricardo

Ricardo made a fortune from speculating, particularly during the Napoleonic Wars, so he was able to retire to the country at a relatively young age. After he died, a member of the royal family used his house and grounds to go horse riding at weekends; it is not known what she did with Ricardo's collected works, a house-warming present from the Royal Economic Society.

Even though Ricardo had lent the government a large amount of money so that it could beat the French, he was worried by the burden of the National Debt. The Bank of England was built in 1694 to store the initial debt, which had itself been created to finance a war. Ricardo thought the Bank was in danger of bursting at the seams. He thought it was becoming such a huge pile, it got confused with a Sinking Fund.

He also thought that people would be indifferent about borrowing in order to pay their taxes, so long as they could force their children to pay the interest charges, and anyway they would have a long time to think about it: this was called Ricardian Equivocation.

Ricardo had lots of spare time in retirement, so he began to construct a corn model, in which corn was made into corn, except for the bits that he kept eating to keep up his strength. He found it so laborious that he started, under Adam Smith's influence, to work out a labour theory of value, but he only got 97 per cent of the way through it.

Years later, Sraffa gave this effort much higher marks (but a typographical error led this to be printed as Marx, a source of much confusion). After spending many years editing Ricardo's works, Sraffa tried to complete the model. However, he only managed to write the introduction. He was so ashamed that he called it a prologomena instead, so that no one would realise. Other economists have followed this example and have written what they called propaedutic essays, relying on the narrow vocabulary of most of their colleagues.

10

On becoming a landlord, Ricardo worked out an analysis of rent. He devised this theory while reading the works of his friend Malthus, and wrote copious notes in the margins of Malthus's books. This gave rise to the concept of the extensive margin.

Ricardo was a supporter of the Poor Law, which was drafted by a Senior member of a committee. This argued that the poor should be kept poor, and was based on an application of the law that supply creates its own demand; that is, giving too much to the poor would only result in more of them. This problem has still not been solved.

Ricardo was bullied into writing his book, *The Theory of Political Economy and Taxation*, by his friend James Mill, who could not stand to see anyone idle for long. James Mill argued that Ricardo had a comparative advantage in writing economic analysis. This had the double advantage that he could also use the manuscript to keep his son, John Stuart Mill, busy by forcing him to make summaries of it at the breakfast table. He was given small sections at a time, somewhat like a breakfast serial.

His book was considered to be very important, even though it was published before Ricardo got round to writing the sections on taxation. For some years afterwards Ricardo had a very strong grip on the economics profession in Britain. This gave rise to the expression, 'Ricardian vice-like grip'. It was later used to describe the way people cling to models that are in danger of falling down.

11

6 J. S. Mill

John Stuart Mill was, as already mentioned, the son of James Mill. He was a leading figure in the utilitarian movement, which believed that all actions should aim to maximise the total happiness of the greatest number of people. His strenuous work programme from early childhood led to a nervous breakdown, until he realised that you become happy only by not trying to be happy, but by doing something interesting, like economics.

Some people found it hard to accept that one man could have so many original insights over such a wide range of learning, so they started to accuse him of being eclectic. This is the worst insult that can be thrown at an economist, and is even worse than being called scholarly. Both of these sins are far, far worse than being completely wrong, which can actually be an advantage if it is done cleverly enough.

Mill reciprocated by building a model of international trade. This explained relative prices on the grounds that when one hand gives, the other takes. This is a good example of the principle that good ideas often seem platitudinous in retrospect. However, many other economists, misunderstanding this principle, have started from platitudes which they have then attempted to dress in fancy clothes.

He also discussed the wages fund, which was put to one side in order to pay the subsistence wages of workers. Later economists have found it hard to find such a wages fund, and have argued about whether Mill might have decanted it into a large sack.

12

7   W. S. Jevons

William Stanley Jevons was in the middle of a science degree when his father lost all his money. So Jevons went to Sydney, in Australia, where he made a mint. This enabled him to return to England. We have it on good authority that Jevons had little respect for authorities, especially J. S. Mill. He also criticised Ricardo, who he said had gone off the rails.

After hearing a lecture by the Vice Chancellor of Melbourne university, Jevons had a revelation that a utility theory of exchange could provide the basis of a complete model of the economy. This shifted the emphasis from growth, the preoccupation of the classical economists, to exchange as the central problem. Later generations called this the marginal revelation, but this led to much confusion about its nature, especially as the margin had already been invented.

Jevons was worried about coal reserves running out. This attracted the attention of the Prime Minister, Gladstone, who became worried about the effect this might have on the amount of hot air in the House of Commons, so he started a debate about income taxation.

Jevons was interested in, and made original contributions to, many subjects, including the history of economic thought. However, later generations of economists appear to have forgiven him for this latter aberration, and have politely ignored it.

Jevons had a strong influence on Edgeworth, who produced many original papers. However, he was indifferent to success and instead of making his discoveries known, he placed the papers in a box, called the Edgeworth Box, where they remained for many years before their secrets became widely known. Unlike some other economic boxes that had been built to scale, this one was certainly not empty.

It turned out that one of his findings followed in the long tradition established by Newton. Edgeworth found that if a half-eaten apple is left in the sun for long, the core shrinks. Some economists found it hard to appreciated the relevance of this finding for economics, and suggested that he was simply playing games.

8 L. Walras

Walras, a Frenchman, was the son of an economist and the father of general equilibrium theory, according to which everything is connected to everything else. This was a Good Idea, but unfortunately he did not have the equipment needed to get his model working. He was inspired to extend the partial equilibrium model of his countryman Cournot, who owned a mineral water spring and was also a mathematician. Due to failing eyesight, Cournot could not see how to extend his own model, or to correct his own proofs properly.

Walras's attempt to persuade people that mathematics could be useful in economics consisted of filling his huge book, published in 1874, with 'an exuberance of algebraic foliage', consisting of endless symbols and unreadable diagrams. It did not become as well known as Walras hoped, largely because it has to be read with a wet towel over the head, and there simply were not enough towels to go round. Also, his strategy for promoting the book consisted of falling out with all the economists he could find. This method has been widely adopted since, with varying success.

Walras invented a tatonnement process. This enabled him to discover the general principle that if the analysis is mixed with vague foreign words and curious metaphors, other economists will argue for many years about what the author might have had in mind, and end up using the interpretation that fits their own ends. He also tried to auction the unsold copies of his book, but forgot to pay the auctioneer, who ran off with the takings.

The Swedish economist Cassell wrote a simplified version of Walras's general equilibrium model and stated the analytical problems clearly. He had his own version immediately translated into English – always a good idea – but accidentally forgot to mention Walras's name and so for a while became more famous than Walras.

Walras's successor was Pareto, who had earlier been employed by the Italian railways to try to help the trains run on time. This gave rise to the expression, 'Pareto efficiency'. He also thought it was a cardinal sin to compare the utilities of different individuals.

15

9   Alfred Marshall

Alfred Marshall was the father of the Cambridge School. He had a library named after him, and this was the origin of the saying, 'it's all in Marshall'. He was responsible for establishing the economics tripod in Cambridge. Despite having three legs, it had only a partial equilibrium, and kept falling over.

Marshall did not like Jevons's emphasis on the demand side, to the neglect of supply, so he cut up Jevons's book with a pair of scissors.

By a great stretch of the imagination, Marshall invented the concept of elasticity. Like Archimedes, he was in the bath when his discovery was made. He also examined the representative firm in great detail, but the complexity meant that his colleagues were unable to see the wood for the trees.

Marshall's early love was mathematics, and he began economics by translating J. S. Mill's models into maths. But he was so ashamed by the pleasure it gave him, that he translated the maths into diagrams. However, this still gave too much pleasure, so he buried them all. Economists are now encouraged to reverse this process.

Marshall has the distinction of having written the last Treatise in economics. Thus, he treated his readers as serious adults concerned with the fundamental nature of the subject and interested in appreciating the special vision of economics, with its strengths and limitations, which the author has allowed to mature over some years and laboured hard to explain. Modern, and therefore obviously superior, writers instead produce textbooks in which they talk down to readers who are regarded as having the sole aim of being able to tick the right boxes in multiple choice exams. Alternatively, they write introductory papers like the present one.

10 Conclusions

This paper has presented a succinct summary of much of the history of economics in one easy lesson. It is entirely descriptive and therefore fully objective and uncontroversial. It has been seen that economics is a very serious, though far from dismal, subject. It is therefore surprising that a number of famous fiction writers have poked fun at it in the past. However, these writers can easily be dismissed as merely having made swift attempts to display, peacock like, their satirical skills.

This paper has closed with discussion of Alfred Marshall who, like many other important economists, died in the 1920s. A sequel is planned but, since this deals with people who may still be alive, or whose relatives may still be alive, or whose look-alike has been spotted somewhere in the south east of England, a first draft is currently in the hands of a team of solicitors.

11 Some Questions

Here are some questions to test your knowledge of the useful history of economic thought. Some of them are only slightly impossible. While answering these questions, keep the following simple points in mind:

- If you don't know the answers, just make them up, but only if they are outrageous and difficult to check.

- It is alright to cheat flagrantly, but do not on any account repeat yourself. If you are caught doing either of these things, become aggressive and threaten legal action, while claiming that no one told you that stupidity is stupid.

- Your answers may be allusive, but certainly not affected (well, only slightly).

- Above all, remember at all times the economist's motto: don't allow facts to get in the way of a good story.

Attempt as many questions as possible until you fall asleep, indicating the time and place.

1. Was Say closer to Malthus than Ricardo was to Marshall? You may prevaricate noisily, but remain seated at all times.

2. Was Adam Smith as important as is generally thought? Feel no obligation to stick to the subject.

3. Could William Petty have counted on the support of Adam Smith? And if not, how often?

4. How many Irish economists does it take to change Galbraith's mind? You are allowed to scoff knowingly.

18

5. Who invented Pareto optimality? If not, who did? And was it the best he could come up with?

6. Can economic laws be effectively policed? If so, what is the opportunity cost? (Carefully avoid mention of Robert Peel).

7. Why didn't Ricardo invent Political Arithmetic? Was he constructing one of his many numerical examples at the time?

8. Are there any economic subjects you regard as too boring to mention? Yawn loudly, but politely, as you think of them.

9. Is it true that Mirabeau was a handsome but narcissistic Frenchman who kept looking at his own reflection? How does this reflect on the physiocrats?

10. Discuss vaguely, paying special attention to rumours to the contrary, the suggestion that economists don't know any better.

11. Cantillon was baked by his cook after an argument. What has this got to do with economics?

12. Deplore the failure of effective demand. You may place an order for more paper at this point in the exam.

13. Stigmatise Malthus's theory of population growth. How did he conceive it? And who put him up to it?

19

14. Why did J.S. Mill find so many questions unsettling? Did he neglect to revise before his final exams, or did he just have a nervous disposition?

15. Economics is full of stylised facts without theories and theories without facts. Is this a fact or a theory? If so, how would a linguistic philosopher answer this question? (You are only allowed to use 'it all depends on what you mean' 53 times).

16. Who was right, Malthus or Ricardo? If so, does it matter? And what if it did?

17. Expatiate briefly on the idea that the utility of the calculus to utilitarians is decreasing at the margin. What does it all add up to? And what is the greatest number? (Does it exceed x^y?).

18. Can apples give rise to theories that bear fruit? Did Edgeworth say 'cor blimey' when he stumbled across the core of an economy? And did it drive Marshall nuts?

19. Is Ricardo's theory of rent any use to landlords? Restrict your answer to illegible scribble in the right-hand margin of the exam script.

20. Be mercifully brief about the labour theory of value. Do adherents invariably measure prices properly?

21. Comment abrasively on the suggestion that you don't know what you are talking about in your answers to questions

3(b) and 7(c).

22. Complain loudly that economics was ever invented. What should take its place?

23. If all economists were placed end-to-end, would it be an unstable equilibrium? Would there be multiple equilibria?

24. Why are Smith and Marshall generally referred to as Adam Smith and Alfred Marshall, while Jevons and Edgeworth are know merely by their last names? Only deep philosophical and politically correct answers are permitted to this question.

25. What does it mean in the end to say that ends can't be distinguished from means, and would Robbins agree or even care?

26. Did Mill and Cairnes form a noncompeting group, and if so, against whom?

27. Is it realistic to assume that economists don't care about the realism of assumptions? And is this an example?

28. Comment elliptically on the suggestion that if Keynes was a post-Keynesian then Ricardo was a Sraffian and Smith was a general equilibrium theorist, and pigs really can fly.

29. Are economists subject to diminishing returns? Be careful, as this might be a trick question.

Name index